1998

DE HAVILLAND VAMPIRE

THE COMPLETE HISTORY

Vampires were used by the Swiss Air Force for almost 45 years. Illustrated are two Vampire FB.6s (J—1173 and J—1187) during May 1990. Both are fitted with Venom-style noses to improve stability. (Militaerflugdienst Ôubendorf)

DE HAVILLAND VAMPIRE

THE COMPLETE HISTORY

DAVID WATKINS

Foreword by John Wilson
(De Havilland experimental test pilot, 1948–57)

SUTTON PUBLISHING

First published in 1996 by
Sutton Publishing Limited • Phoenix Mill
Thrupp • Stroud • Gloucestershire • GL5 2BU

Paperback edition first published in 1998

British Library Cataloguing in Publication Data
A catalogue record for this book is available from the British Library

ISBN 07509 1984 1

Title page photograph: A Vampire FB.5 of 93 Squadron from Celle, March 1952. (MoD)

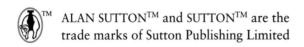 ALAN SUTTON™ and SUTTON™ are the trade marks of Sutton Publishing Limited

Typeset in 10/13 Sabon.
Typesetting and origination by
Sutton Publishing Limited
Printed in Great Britain by
WBC Limited, Bridgend, Mid-Glamorgan.

CONTENTS

This book is dedicated to my wife, Anne. Her courage and determination to overcome a cruel illness is an inspiration to us all.

FOREWORD

BY JOHN WILSON

It gives me great pleasure to write the foreword to this thorough account of the de Havilland Vampire. David Watkins has researched its conception, development and utilization with great diligence and accuracy, and included many pilots' reports and recollections of the aircraft and their operation around the world.

It is astonishing to find that 3,269 Vampires of all types were built in England – 1,311 at English Electric, Preston; 1,858 at DH factories at Hatfield, Chester and Christchurch, and 100 at subcontractors' premises. A further 1,097 were manufactured under licence abroad.

Much of the considerable success of the single-engined Vampire was due to the reliability of the Goblin engine; in the days before ejection seats the prospect of baling out was not attractive, especially from the clamshell canopy of the NF.10 and the early T.11s.

I am glad that the author has been able to use some of my flight test reports from those years, and apologize for the colloquial style – they were written hurriedly after landing from notes scribbled on a small scrolling knee pad.

Having attended the fiftieth anniversary celebrations of the first flight of the Spider

Former experimental test pilot John Wilson with an ex-Swiss AF Vampire T.55 (G–HELV/U1215) belonging to Jet Heritage at Hurn in September 1993. (John Wilson)

Crab at Hurn in September 1993 with former colleagues, John Cunningham, Neville Duke and Ron Clear, it is singularly appropriate that this splendid tribute to the Vampire is now to be published.

John Wilson
1995

John Wilson first flew in a Vampire while he was serving with the Air Fighting Development Squadron at the Central Fighter Establishment, West Raynham, in 1947; after leading the Vampire 'Tropical Trials' in Malaya during 1948, he returned to the CFE for a few months before joining de Havilland at Hatfield, where he served as an experimental test pilot from 1948 to 1957. He was initially occupied with the development of the Vampire FB5/FB9, NF.10 and T.11. In addition to flight testing the Vampire and Venom series, he was involved with the DH 106 (Comet) in 1959 and was responsible for continuing flight development of the DH 110 (Sea Vixen) between 1953 and 1957.

ACKNOWLEDGEMENTS

In writing this book, I have tried to avoid depending on previously published works on the subject as references, preferring instead to consult official documents, memoranda and so on, and to interview personnel directly associated with the aircraft. In this way I believe that I have avoided repeating some of the popular misconceptions that have surrounded the aircraft and arrived at what I hope is an accurate account of the Vampire's development and operational history.

I received an immense amount of first-hand information during the compilation of this book, and only lack of space prevents me from acknowledging everyone who contributed; I hope, therefore, that all those I have not mentioned will accept my sincerest apologies. It is probably quite improper to single out those who deserve a special mention, but I must extend my gratitude to my wife, Anne, for her patience and understanding, and to the 'Edgelers' – Audrey, Su and John – for their support. The following also deserve a special mention: Derek Dempster, journalist, author, publisher and ex-Vampire pilot with 604 Sqn, for his continued encouragement; Gp Capt. Alan Hastings OBE, for tracing ex-Vampire pilots on my behalf; AVM Brian Huxley CB, CBE, for providing an intelligent and critical appraisal of my rough drafts; John Rawlings, for providing the generous and unfailing response to various requests; and Alan Roach, for untangling the Vampire production details. I would also like to thank John Wilson for kindly agreeing to write the Foreword; his first-hand experience and enthusiastic assistance, together with the loan of his log-books and test reports, were instrumental in providing the integrity of much of the information contained within the text.

Of no less importance was the considerable help provided by the following: Flt Lt. R.J. Adams; ACM Sir Michael Armitage KCB, CB; Air Cdre D.A. Arnott DFC, AFC; Wg Cdr R.P. Beamont CBE, DSO, DFC; Sqn Ldr M.J. Biggs; Col. Juan Flores Blanco (Director, Del Museo Aeronautico FAV); Wg Cdr R.J.E. Boulding; Winston Brent; Capt. E.M. Brown CBE, DSC, AFC; Robin Brown; S.N. Burge; Ken Burvill; Sqn Ldr P.W. Carr AFC; D.G. Catt; Capt. A.B.B. Clark; David Clegg; Lt. Alan Clifford; Rick Cluley; Air Marshal C.V. Cole, IAF; AVM C.W. Coulthard CB, AFC; Brian Courtney; Air Cdre R.H. Crompton OBE; Air Marshal Sir Denis Crowley-Milling KCB, CBE, DSO, DFC; Gp Capt. N. Curtis; Noel Davis, Sqn Ldr I. Dick; Pat Dobbs; Flt Lt. J. Donaldson DFC; Alberto Fernandez Donoso; Brian Ellis; Fg Off. Rich Fewtrell; Sgt Santiago A. Flores; Sqn Ldr The Revd R.G. Follis AFC; Flt G. 'Kiwi' Francis DFC; Lt. Cdr R.E. Geale MBE (Curator, Australian Naval Air Museum); Rear Admiral P.D. Gick OBE, DSC; Rear Admiral H.C.N. Goodhart CB; Wg Cdr C.A. Gunaratna (Sri Lanka AF); A.E. 'Ben' Gunn; Cdr D. Hamilton; Wg Cdr O.L. Hardy DFC; Sqn Ldr J.T. Harvey; John Havers; Gp Capt. J.H. Hedger; P.X. Henry; R.E. Hillard; Sqn Ldr H.J.E. Howe; Rear Admiral J.E. Ievers; Lt. Cdr L.A. Jeyes; Sqn Ldr F.A. Johnson; AVM J.E. Johnson CB, CBE, DSO, DFC; Max Kagi (Bundesamt Fuer

Militaerflugplaetze); Wg Cdr E.A. Knighton; Walter Kunzler (FFA Altenrheim); Rear Admiral W.D. Lang; Capt. Dick Law MBE, DSC; Lt. Cdr H.J.M. Lawrence (Fleet Air Arm Officers Association); Admiral Sir Raymond Lygo KCB; AVM M.D. Lyne CB, DFC; Lt.-Col. Samir Maalouly (Lebanese Air Force); Sqn Ldr R. Maclachlan AFC; Gp Capt. Deryk Maddox; Major A.L. 'Paul' Mahmood; Sqn Ldr W.J. Malone; Henry Matthews (Beirut University); AVM C. Maughan; Hugh Merewether/Mrs R.A. Simpson; Paddy Minnis; Sqn Ldr P. Murton; Wg Cdr G. Nelson-Edwards DFC; Sqn Ldr Bob Newall; Dr David Nicolle; Cdr S.G. Orr DSC, AFC; Mrs Joy Oxspring; Lt. Cdr S.G.H. Perkins; Cdr N. Perrett; Brian Pettit; AVM L.W. Phipps CB, AFC; AVM Sir Richard Pierse KCVO, CB; Mrs Pat Plumtree; Lt. Cdr J. Purvis; Gp Capt. A.C. Rawlinson CB, DFC, AFC; Ken Reeve; Sqn Ldr P.H.P. Roberts; R.A. Scholefield; Richard Searle (RAE); Col. A. Al-Shiyab (Dir. Maint. RJAF); Sqn Ldr Bill Shrubsole; Sqn Ldr R.J. Skinner; Colin Sloan; Wg Cdr J. Smith-Carington AFC; John Squier; Geoff Steggall; Peter Strugnell (Curator, RNZAF Museum, Ohakea); Bill Sykens; George Thornton; Sqn Ldr E. Trees; Sqn Ldr Joe Warne; Lt. Col. Doug Warren, RCAF; Lt. Cdr Peter Wheatley; Lt. Cdr Ken Whittaker; ACM Sir Keith Williamson GCB, AFC; Gp Capt. H.J. Wilson CBE, AFC; Flt Lt. W.C. Wood AFC; Air Cdre E.W. Wright CBE, DFC, DFM; Air Marshal Sir Peter Wykeham KCB, DSO, OBE, DFC, AFC; G.P. Young.

Valuable support was also received from various information specialists including the following: Air Britain; AHB (MoD); Air HQ, IAF (Wg Cdr M.M. Singh, Sqn Ldr R.T.S. Chhina); Directorate of History, National Defence HQ, RCAF; Fleet Air Arm Museum; Office of the Air Attaché, Caracas (Capt. R.J. Perrett, Orlando James), Italy (Lt.-Col. A. Tangorra), Portugal (Col. Albano Fernandes), Riyadh (Cdr T. Waddington) and Santiago (Gp Capt. B.R. Hoskins, Sgt J.R. King); RAAF Historical Section, Canberra; PRO Kew; RAE Farnborough and Pyestock; RAF Museum, RAF Quedgeley (Wg Cdr Brook and staff); Stato Maggiore Aeronautica, Rome; the Swiss Federal Aircraft Factory, Emmen; and the Warbirds of Norway (Øyvind Ellingsen).

Finally, I make no apologies for the quality of some of the photographs chosen to accompany the text – for many people, the ubiquitous Box Brownie camera was more a means of providing personal snapshots than a method of recording historical material. Nevertheless the use of these photographs is well justified as they provide an authentic contemporary record of previously unknown aircraft markings and so on. It was also difficult to select appropriate photographs to illustrate this book from the many available. In some instances it has not been possible to trace the origin and owner of the photographs – please accept my sincere apologies if your name has not been justly credited.

David Watkins
1996

INTRODUCTION

It was appropriate that de Havilland's 100th design was the Vampire jet-propelled, single-seat, interceptor fighter which was, coincidentally, almost identical in layout to the DH 2 single-seat pusher Scout of 1915. The success of de Havilland's first jet aeroplane was largely due to the very close collaboration between the aircraft engineers and designers: when first asked whether the aeroplane was designed for the engine or the engine for the aeroplane, Assistant Chief Designer R.M. Clarkson could not say which started first; they both grew together as an inseparable couple.

De Havilland's interest in jet propulsion arose as the natural consequence of the company's desire to remain in the forefront of the production of high-performance aeroplanes, following the success of the Mosquito. Clarkson had been attracted by the speed potential of the jet and had discussed the matter at some length with experts at the Royal Aircraft Establishment (RAE) at Farnborough in 1940. In January 1941 Sir Henry Tizard, the Chairman of the Aeronautical Research Council, summoned engine designer Frank Halford to the Air Ministry to discuss the applicability of Frank Whittle's gas turbine engine, and informed him that either a lot of money was being spent on something that would ultimately end in failure or not nearly enough on a valuable invention.

Following the subsequent invitation to design not only a single-seat jet fighter but also the engine to power it, Halford decided not to copy Whittle's layout but chose instead to incorporate a single-entry centrifugal compressor. The result was the Halford H.1. In January 1943 two of the engines were successfully test flown in the Gloster F.9/40, and had already completed a number of flying hours by the time the DH 100 prototype first flew in the following September.

De Havilland had originally wanted to build a high-speed unarmed jet bomber; however, the overriding national requirement to give the Allies mastery of the air was the best and fastest fighter, and so the DH 100 project was directed towards fighter design. Due to the company's commitment to the production of the Mosquito, progress on the project was slow, but following a demonstration of the Gloster E.28/39 to the Prime Minister in June 1943, Churchill was so impressed that he immediately wanted to know why the RAF was not equipped with squadrons of jet fighters. As a result de Havilland's jet fighter received a higher priority.

The fuselage and undercarriage were designed to meet the characteristics of the Goblin turbo-jet – which many cynics suspected was developed from the vacuum cleaner of the same name – and the aircraft layout was unique. The fuselage was constructed on similar lines to the Mosquito, and comprised an inner and outer skin of birch plywood sandwiching balsa planking, while the unusual twin-boom layout displayed a fresh approach to the problems of keeping both the engine intake ducting and tailpipe length to a minimum in order to avoid undue friction losses.

Like all the other single-seat fighters, the

Vampire began life as an interceptor and it saw service in the immediate post-war period in the UK in that role. It was soon evident that the Meteor's higher rate of climb made it a better aeroplane for the regular home defence squadrons, while the Vampire's relative simplicity, lighter weight and longer endurance on internal fuel offered greater potential for the wider range of duties expected by the overseas squadrons. Thus the Vampire, like the Typhoon and Tempest, spent comparatively little time as an interceptor, instead leaving its mark on history through its service with day fighter/ground attack squadrons. Not only did the Vampire provide the backbone of the 2 TAF from 1948 to 1954, but it was also the first jet fighter to enter service with the squadrons of the Middle East Air Force (MEAF) and Far East Air Force (FEAF).

Non-Vampire pilots gave it the rather dismissive nickname 'Aerial Kiddy Car', which was partly derived from the aircraft's unsophisticated 'first-generation' jet fighter technology. To those who flew it, however, the Vampire was considered delightful: it needed minimal take-off checks, offered a superb view from the cockpit, and was light and sensitive on the controls. Without underwing stores it performed well, but it was underpowered and took time to reach operational altitude. However, the Vampire also had excellent manoeuvrability and gave a good account of itself in the low-level ground attack role. But in contrast to the Meteor, it lacked the power to accelerate away from an undesirable encounter; the

later Venom was more suited to, and more manoeuvrable at high altitudes, and possessed a higher rate of climb. In the day fighter role, most pilots agreed that the Vampire would have been seriously outpaced by the Soviet fighters of the day, and would have suffered heavy losses.

Throughout its long career the Vampire collected many notable 'firsts': it was the first jet fighter to cross the Atlantic Ocean; the first jet to land on an aircraft carrier; the first jet fighter to equip post-war reserve squadrons; the first jet fighter to fly formation aerobatics; the first naval jet fighter; and the first jet trainer on which student pilots actually qualified for their 'wings'. Suitably modified Vampires also set a new world altitude record in April 1948, were used for aerodynamic and engine research, tropical trials, and the development of the Royal Navy's Deck Landing Mirror Sight and the IAM's Air Ventilated Suit.

Between 1944 and 1961 some 4,365 aircraft were built for the RAF, the Royal Navy and the export market (the Vampire was the first jet aircraft in many countries). During its forty-six years of service throughout the world, the Vampire fulfilled a variety of operational roles – as interceptor fighter, ground attack aircraft, night-fighter, advanced trainer and weapons trainer – and although it was developed too late to see service in the Second World War, it was used with effect by the RAF in Aden and Malaya, as well as serving with foreign air forces in Algeria, Burma, the Dominican Republic, Egypt, India, Iraq, Jordan, Lebanon, Rhodesia and Venezuela.

Airframe Development

In 1942 the Air Ministry began to show interest in the application of jet propulsion to either a high-speed bomber without rear defence or an interceptor fighter, and the considerations were set out in detail in a subsequent communication to the major aircraft manufacturers. The case for the bomber application was that a bomber could choose the most suitable altitude for reaching the target, and could therefore make effective use of jet propulsion by flying near its service ceiling. The fighter on the other hand had not the same choice, having to engage the enemy at whatever height he flew at; at that time most of the fighting took place at high altitudes. The fact that a jet-propelled aircraft showed its greatest speed superiority at low altitudes (though for a relatively short duration) also had to be taken into account.

It was decided to proceed with the fighter application on the grounds that it was more important as 'insurance' against the probability that the enemy might soon be able to operate jet-propelled fighters. It was also realized that, in view of the limited resources available, the design and manufacture of a fighter would be a quicker way of reaching a practical trial of jet propulsion.

'Ministry of Aircraft Production Specification E.6/41', which was finalized on 8 December 1942, covered the design and construction of a high-altitude jet-propelled fighter with a service ceiling of not less than 48,000 ft and which would therefore require a pressure cabin. Its construction should be as simple as possible and the aeroplane was to be kept as small as practicable. Other requirements of the specification called for the installation of Frank Halford's jet engine, four fixed 20 mm Hispano cannon and adequate pilot protection against armour-piercing .303 ammunition, including a bullet-proof windscreen. A maximum speed of not less than 490 mph at 35,000 ft was stipulated, as well as permanent tankage for 250 gallons of fuel. The military load specified for the E.6/41's flight trials, not including fuel, was 1,295.5 lb.

By the time this specification was issued, the de Havilland Aircraft Company had

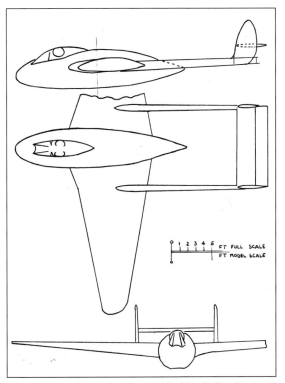

Original drawing of the wind tunnel model of the de Havilland E.6/41. (De Havilland)

1

Wind tunnel model of the E.6/41. (De Havilland via Sqn Ldr M. Biggs)

already examined the application of Halford's jet propulsion unit. Following discussions between their aircraft and engine design teams in early 1941, they arrived at the conclusion that the time had come for them to enter the field of jet-propelled aircraft development. Discussions led to the decision that an engine thrust rating of 3,000 lb at sea-level would be necessary to give a performance sufficiently in advance of the latest Spitfire and Typhoon types to justify the introduction of a new fighter at this phase of the air war. This was some three times the thrust that had been achieved by any engine then in existence, and greater than any engine then projected.

In April 1941 negotiations were initiated between Sir Henry Tizard, the Air Member for Development and Production, and de Havilland's with regard to Project 227, an airframe that would accommodate Frank Halford's 2,700–3,000 lb thrust jet propulsion unit. An original order to proceed with the E.6/41 airframe development had been frustrated when Sir Sydney Camm,

Chief Designer at Hawker Aircraft, was brought into the negotiations. On 29 May 1941 Mr N.E. Rowe CBE, DIC, the Ministry of Aircraft Production's (MAP) Director of Technical Development, wrote to Sir Henry Tizard to voice his doubts over de Havilland's suitability to design the new fighter:

REFERENCE: DE HAVILLAND HALFORD AEROPLANE

It is suggested that the design of the E.6/41 should be put in the hands of Camm of Hawkers, one of our most experienced designers of fighter types. Although there is a business connection between de Havilland and Halford, it would be unwise to press this to the extent of a construction of aircraft building which might fall down because of the lack of experience of one of the aircraft partners on the specialised design techniques associated with this type. This class of design calls for the best design capability we have on both the engine and the airframe. Hence, the right thing to do is to ask Camm of Hawkers to take it on, shelving his fighter/bomber project for it.

Camm was heavily involved in a scheme to install Whittle's experimental Power Jet engines in the Hawker P.1005 twin-engined, high-speed bomber design and was unable, in the foreseeable future, to divert his attentions to the E.6/41. At a subsequent meeting held at the Air Ministry, Rowe decided to proceed with the de Havilland/Halford design partnership, and asked for details of the fighter's weight and performance estimates to be sent to his department as soon as possible.

The required specifications were conveyed to Rowe on 7 June 1941, and were quite explicit:

Single-engined, mid-wing, all-metal tail-boom monoplane
Halford Power Jet engine of 2,900 lb static thrust (s.t.)
Crew: One
Nose wheel undercarriage
Wing span: 40 ft; length: 31 ft; height: 8 ft
Wing area: 260 sq. ft; all-up weight (AUW): 7,970 lb
Max. speed at sea-level: 445 mph
Max. speed at 45,000 ft: 469 mph
Rate of climb: 4,950 ft/min
178 gallons of fuel in fuselage; 2 × 26 gallons in wings

The design and performance specifications sent to the MAP referred to the aircraft as the DH 99 and stated that although the fighter carried an armament of four cannon, provision was also made for two extra cannon to be mounted in the wing roots.

The design team for the DH 100 jet fighter was headed by Sir Geoffrey de Havilland, the company's Chairman, and included R.E. Bishop, the firm's Chief Designer, who had been largely responsible for work on the Mosquito, the Chief Aerodynamicist and

Assistant Chief Designer, R.M. Clarkson, and C.C. Walker, Chief Engineer of de Havilland (Engines). It was decided that the minimum size of a nacelle to house the pilot, fuel and guns would permit an engine diameter of 50 in. It was appreciated that intakes large enough to handle 100 tons of air per hour would be a major design problem, and that the penalty would be paid for every excess foot of exhaust system in lost thrust and increased drag.

Although not a popular design in the past, the team decided to opt for a twin-boom tail for their fighter. This arrangement possessed several advantages, such as simplifying engine changes, and it also minimized air intake ducting and tailpipe lengths, which would therefore avoid undue friction losses. The disadvantages usually associated with this layout – increased weight, decreased tail stiffness and increased wetted areas – were minimized by careful design.

The Halford H.1 engine was to be fitted at the rear of a short central nacelle, which would allow easy access and draw air from wing-root intakes, the design of which allowed some 90–95 per cent of available ram effect to be utilized. The pilot's cockpit would be positioned forward of the wing and afford a better view than that from a piston-engined fighter during take-off and landing because of the absence of a large expanse of engine cowling ahead of the windscreen.

The absence of a propeller made a tricycle undercarriage a practical proposition. This assisted in improving the forward view from the cockpit, and could not only be shortened to lower the aircraft nearer to the ground, but would also be substantially lighter and take up less space, making retraction easier. The low weight of the jet engine also affected the aircraft's layout, enabling the four 20 mm cannon to be mounted in the fuselage, well forward of the centre of gravity.

De Havilland's tender for Specification E.6/41 was accepted, and on 11 April 1942 the

MAP placed an order for two prototype aircraft to be built at Hatfield at a cost of £40,000. Contract No. SB/24539/C.23(a) covered the construction of the two prototypes, LZ548 and LZ551, and was amended on 14 April to include a third prototype, MP838. The first two prototypes would be used to develop the airframe and airframe/engine combination, while the third aircraft was to be built to operational standards, carrying four belly-mounted 20 mm cannon.

Permission had been given to build the DH 100 fighter at Hatfield, providing that the work did not hinder de Havilland's heavy commitment to Mosquito production or the development of their projected DH 102 piston-engined night bomber. The MAP also hinted that development of the DH 100 might well be dropped because of the possibility of the construction of a twin-jet bomber centred on production lines away from Hatfield. However, by September 1942 progress on the mock-up of the DH 100 was well advanced; the twin-boom tailplane arrangement had been mounted on a test rig with the Halford H.1 engine installed to confirm that the jet efflux clearance was satisfactory.

Work on the DH 102 Mosquito Replacement Project took priority, so design work on the new fighter was slow. In November 1942, after some discussion with the Vice-Chief of Air Staff Sir Wilfred Freeman, whose responsibility lay in coordinating research with production, de Havilland's decided to abandon the night bomber project in favour of the DH 103 Hornet and give priority to the jet fighter. This decision not only secured the future of the DH 100 but also that of the Halford engine, for which there was no other project at that time. Under conditions of the greatest secrecy, construction of the three prototype E.6/41s was begun immediately at Hatfield's experimental department. The airframe was a composite construction, having both wooden and metal components in its structure. The wooden

section comprised that part of the fuselage extending from bulkhead no. 1 to bulkhead no. 4 at the rear, with the remainder of the aircraft being of metal construction. This form of composite construction not only served to reduce weight and improve performance, but also, coincidentally, conserved cockpit warmth; it had been developed by the company in 1937 for the four-engined DH 91 Albatross airliner and was later successfully employed in the Mosquito and Hornet fighters.

The oval cross-sectioned fuselage was built in two halves, with each half of the fuselage shell shaped to the interior profile in a pre-formed wooden or cement mould. The inner birch ply skin was fitted over the structural members, and was built up from conveniently sized panels. Broad flexible steel bands, which were tensioned and anchored by turnbuckles, were employed to cramp the skin to the mould profile. Once the complete bond had been formed the bands were removed and spruce insert members were attached, these being glued to the inner skin. Balsa or Quipo wood was used as a filling and as a stabilizing medium for the relatively thin plywood skin, and was applied in the form of battens to the outside of the inner skin to fill in all the positions not occupied by spruce stress members. The timber was then glued into position and the clamping bands reapplied.

Once the bands were removed and the whole surface smoothed to a flush surface outer contour, the fuselage half-shells were removed from the moulds and mounted on cradles for the installation of the internal components. The joining of the fuselage halves was performed with a special alignment rig, the two halves being offered up to each other and clamped in position to maintain the correct contour and then bonded together along the top and bottom centre-lines with a synthetic resin. Fuselage-length filler strips of birch ply were then glued and screwed inside. The outer surface of the fuselage was then covered with Madapollam fabric as part of the external plywood protective treatment; this not only afforded a degree of weathering resistance, but also provided an excellent key for subsequent dope applications.

In this carapace unit there were three primary bulkheads: the rear bulkhead (no. 3) was fireproofed and consisted of a tubular engine mounting on the two crucial transverse members which took the main wing attachment bolts; through this bulkhead passed the intake ducts from the wing roots. The T.R. 1464 four-channel radio equipment, gun breeches and ammunition containers were housed in the space between no. 2 bulkhead and the rear armour plate, and were reached through access doors on each side. The IFF set, glycol tank for windscreen de-icing and ciné camera were carried forward of the instrument panel and no. 1 armoured bulkhead.

A rearward-sliding two-piece perspex canopy was fitted, together with a bullet-proof windscreen; pressurizing air was obtained from a Marshall cabin supercharger,

an expanding rubber seal providing an effective means of sealing the canopy.

The wings, booms and tail were all of flush-riveted aluminium construction; to reduce the large number of rivets required, skins were bonded to stringers and doublers with Redux, an extremely powerful metal glue devised by Aero Research at Duxford, hence its name. The glue allowed the use of thinner aluminium plate and was used extensively for pressure cabins.

The mainplane was built as two wings, each wing being sharply tapered in both plan and thickness to give the least possible drag at high speeds, coupled with good low-speed characteristics. The wings were also made with a single 'I' section main spar joined by Alclad ribs and a stringer-stiffened Alclad skin covering to a false rear spar. The wings, attached to the fuselage by three bolts, were fitted with split flaps, dive brakes and round-nose ailerons; all controls were cable-operated through a system of pulleys. For its class, the aircraft's wing loading of 32 lb/sq. ft at normal operational weight was very low indeed (some 10–12 lb less than that of the Mosquito or Hornet), which in turn offered excellent manoeuvrability in conjunction with a good power/weight ratio.

Cockpit of the prototype E.6/41, LZ548. (via George Jenks)

The mainplane is fitted to the fuselage of the first prototype E.6/41, LZ548, in Hatfield's experimental department. (via George Jenks)

The front portions of the two oval-section tail-booms, of semi-monocoque design with heavy gauge skin, were an integral part of the wing structure, and the wing/tail-boom joint was a straightforward bolted flange. One feature of the prototypes was the taller, Mosquito-style metal fins and rudders which were attached to the rear of the tail-booms; the tailplane was positioned high up on the fin to clear the jet efflux, with the elevator extending the width of the tailplane. The hydraulically operated undercarriage consisted of two main wheels, retracting outboard into the wings and a self-centring nosewheel which retracted rearwards into the fuselage. The main wheels were fitted with pneumatically operated brakes, with a differential valve controlled by the rudder pedals to assist ground steering. The combined weight of the three undercarriage legs accounted for only 3½ per cent of the aircraft's total weight.

The engine was attached to the nacelle by four bolts and was fed by fuel carried in three internal tanks, one in the fuselage nacelle between nos 1 and 2 bulkheads, and one in each wing; subsequent marks were fitted with additional tanks outboard of the undercarriage wells. Two jettisonable wing tanks with a capacity of either 50 or 100 gallons could also be carried; if necessary, both tanks could be dropped from an electrically fired release-slip. Access to the engine was by two detachable cowlings, one above and one below the unit, and four hinged doors.

On 21 August 1943, in a 'Most Secret' memo, the Director of Technical Development Mr N.E. Rowe at last named de Havilland's jet fighter project, which he said was suggested by the odd appearance of the aircraft by the twin-boom tail layout. He concluded: '. . . PS 5(b) have given the code word "Spider Crab" which will be used henceforth with work referring to the E.6/41'.

Three days later, on 24 August, the first prototype Spider Crab, LZ548/G ('G' for

Guard) was ready for taxiing trials at Hatfield. Piloted by Geoffrey de Havilland junior, chief test pilot and son of the company's founder, the aircraft made five runs, leaving the ground for approximately 100 yd during each run. During one run, the tail unit accidentally touched the ground and it was deemed necessary to increase the aircraft's tail clearance by altering its ground angle in relation to the longitudinal datum.

On 20 September 1943 Geoffrey de Havilland Jnr lifted LZ548/G into the air from Hatfield's grass airfield on its maiden flight. It was powered by a Halford H.1 engine, rated at 2,700 lb thrust. Those watching this historic flight included Messrs J.P. Herriot and E.A. Lombard of Rolls-Royce, D.N. Walker and Gp Capt. Whittle of Power Jets, and E.S. Moult and C.C. Walker of de Havilland (Engines). A few minor criticisms arose from its satisfactory half-hour flight: the ailerons were overbalanced at speeds exceeding 400 mph indicated air speed (IAS), and the aircraft was out of trim, left wing down. Directional instability was also noticed when the aircraft was yawed by rudder movement.

By 1944 the two other Spider Crab prototypes, LZ551/G and MP838/G had joined the test and development programmes. LZ551/G first flew on 17 March 1944; it was later fitted with an arrestor hook and flown to Farnborough in September 1945 as the prototype of a navalized version of the Vampire, known as the Sea Vampire F.10. Unfortunately the first prototype LZ548/G was lost on 23 July 1945: due to a fuel pump failure it crashed soon after take-off at Hatfield. The pilot, Geoffrey Pike, was unhurt. The third prototype, MP838/G, with a Halford H.1A engine and four 20 mm cannon first flew on 21 January 1944; in early March this aircraft was transferred to Farnborough for evaluation by the RAE's Tactical Flight. This Flight was commanded by Gp Capt. (then

The first prototype Spider Crab, LZ548/G, undergoing engine runs at Hatfield in August 1943, prior to its first flight. The serial has yet to be applied. (Darryl Cott)

LZ548/G before its first flight at Hatfield in September 1943. (De Havilland)

Wg Cdr) H.J. 'Willie' Wilson AFC, who was later to establish a new air speed record for Britain of 606.262 mph whilst flying a Gloster Meteor in November 1945:

In 1943 I was given the job of supervising and speeding up jet aircraft research and development, as Glosters were dragging their heels and the Messerschmitt 262 was becoming an established menace.

Having flown the Gloster and American jet products, it was a great day when Geoffrey de Havilland Jnr delivered the Spider Crab to my 'T' Flight at Farnborough. Part of the plan was to de-bunk the mysticism of jet flying, so I arranged for the propeller-oriented 'aces', such as John Cunningham, 'Sailor' Malan and Atcherley to fly their first jet. I chose the Spider Crab for them.

I had first flown the Spider Crab (LZ548/G) on 12 December 1943, and found it an extremely pleasant and easy aircraft to fly. The directional hunting needed correcting, and I suggested that the lack of any stall warning – which usually

The third prototype Spider Crab, MP838/G, was used for armament trials at the RAE and A&AEE. It was written off following an accident at Hatfield during August 1948. (Ray Sturtivant)

occurred at 86 mph with the flaps down and 95 mph with them up – was disconcerting, even though there were aircraft already in service with similar qualities. I also suggested that it would probably be wiser to make the elevator heavier to correct the overbalance at high speeds.

Wg Cdr Wilson was also tasked with compiling the official notes for the Spider Crab's tactical trials, which were conducted with MP838/G at Farnborough in the spring of 1944. These trials were divided into four phases:

Phase one: Tactical trials of operational aircraft
Phase two: Operational pilots' opinions of strategical use of jet-propelled aircraft
Phase three: Test pilots' opinions of E.6/41.
Phase four: Future designs

Phase one was requested by the Controller of Research and Design, who insisted that information should be gathered about the tactical handling of jet-propelled aircraft as soon as possible, in order to advise the Commands concerned of their operational use, and also to obtain vital information for laying down specifications for future designs. Much to everyone's satisfaction, the results of this phase showed that from a tactical aspect there was little difference between the handling qualities of a jet aircraft and that of a standard fighter.

For the second phase, Wg Cdr Wilson enlisted the specialist help of four pilots: Air Cdre J.N. Boothman AFC; Gp Capt. A.G. Malan DSO, DFC; Gp Capt. J. Cunningham DSO, DFC; and Sqn Ldr T.S. Wade DFC. Air Cdre Boothman flew MP838/G during March 1944 and considered the aircraft ideal for photo-reconnaissance work. Later in the month, on 23 March 1944, 'Sailor' Malan flew the aircraft to establish the general handling characteristics and its fighting qualities compared to that of a Spitfire (in this instance, a Mark Vb, W3248, flown by Sqn Ldr Nelson). Malan concluded that there was a definite requirement for dive brakes to be fitted and that the endurance and rear view from the cockpit needed to be improved.

On the same day, 23 March, John Cunningham assessed MP838/G as a night-fighter during a 35-minute flight. His report found the aeroplane's controls light and positive, its stability good, and its forward visibility exceptional. However, for a successful night-fighter, some form of radar apparatus was essential, as was a second crew member to operate it.

The final operational pilot to assess the aircraft during its tactical trials was 'Wimpey' Wade, whose main criticism concerned the all-round view from the cockpit, especially to the rear, which was obstructed by the armour plate of the pilot's seat.

Wg Cdr Wilson flew the aircraft twice at the conclusion of the tactical trials, and his first report stated:

The stall characteristics of the aircraft are now considered completely satisfactory. The directional stability characteristics are considered acceptable, but not ideal. The view from the cockpit and the freedom from noise and vibration inspires the pilot with great confidence and, personally, I have never flown a nicer aircraft.

In April 1944 MP838/G was transferred to Boscombe Down to allow the A&AEE to assess its general handling and performance characteristics. A preliminary report concluded that the flying qualities of the aircraft compared very favourably with present-day fighter aircraft. The most positive aspects of the report commended the excellent aileron control, the ease of manoeuvrability in the looping plane, and the comfortable and well laid out cockpit. The chief criticisms arising from the brief tests were the poor vision from the cockpit due to the thickness of the canopy framework, the limited endurance, low rate of climb, and poor acceleration in level flight compared with current fighters.

Flights of the prototype LZ548/G had suggested that excessive vertical tail surface caused the severe yawing oscillation which could seriously affect the aeroplane as a gun platform. It was concluded that directional damping was too great and this was confirmed by installing a 8.65 sq. ft fin on to the front of the fuselage, mounted vertically ahead of the pilot's windscreen. By placing this fin area forward, the relative effectiveness of the tail fins and rudders was reduced.

Wind tunnel tests were able to establish that, after the removal of the nose fin and cutting down the area of the fins and rudders from 11.42 to 9.10 sq. ft, the 'snaking' was reduced to acceptable proportions. This modification was confirmed to the MAP in a memo from de Havilland's soon after the tests were completed. 'The height of the fin and rudders of MP838/G has been reduced to improve the unpleasant "snaking" by rendering the damping less violent.' The two other prototypes, LZ551/G and MP838/G, were quickly modified with the 'flat top' fin and rudders, which were recommended for further production models during a meeting at Hatfield later in the year, under the construction specification: 'Type Two – Raised Boom'.

Another problem which occurred during the early flight trials was the oversensitive ailerons, which were also considered too light. This was cured by replacing the original convex ailerons with flat-sided ones with blunt trailing edges. The absence of any stall warning (which had been noted by 'Willie' Wilson during his early test flight) had also been remedied by fitting a sharper lip to the air intakes.

After these problems had been corrected, it was decided to proceed with production of the aircraft, which had been officially called Vampire in April 1944, as soon as possible. It was felt that other minor irritations could be rectified before the aircraft entered service with the RAF. Specification Vampire F.Mk.1/P.1 had been issued to cover the design of the aircraft at Hatfield. However, as Hatfield was already heavily committed to work on the Mosquito, production was sub-contracted to the English Electric Company at Preston under a further specification, Vampire F.Mk.1/P.2. This company was chosen on the basis of its performance in the production of Hampden and Halifax bombers during the war.

A destabilizing fin was fitted to the nose of LZ548/G during January 1944 to assess the effects of directional stability. (de Havilland via Sqn Ldr M. Biggs)

Moreover, the abandonment of work on the Folland 117A, single-seat, cannon-armed fighter had left the company with resources available for Vampire construction.

On 13 May 1944 Contract No. 6/ACFT/4182/C.4(b) was issued for 120 Vampire F.Mk.1s, serialled TG274–TG315, TG328–TG355, TG370–389 and TG419–TG448. Work started on 24 May 1944 at the Strand Road factory, Preston, with final assembly at Samlesbury. To speed up production, it was decided that the first fifty aircraft would not be fitted with a pressure cabin, and that the required cabin heating would be obtained by tapping air from a heater muff on the jet pipe, by the way of the gun heating system. After the fiftieth aircraft (TG336), a cabin pressurization system was installed, which supplied cabin air through a

cooler from a Marshall Type 6 blower, with the Dunlop canopy seal being pressurized from the engine impeller.

It was also decided that the first forty production aircraft would be fitted with Goblin I engines, but from TG314 onwards, these would be replaced by 3,100 lb s.t. Goblin 2s, and the aircraft would have an increased internal fuel capacity in the wings. As a result of earlier canopy failures, some with fatal consequences, a single-piece 'teardrop' canopy was introduced on the production lines from the eighty-seventh aircraft, TG386, replacing the original three-piece, double-skin, dry air sandwich type. This new canopy also improved visibility and eventually removed the height restrictions imposed on the Vampire; it was retro-fitted to many of the earlier aircraft.

The height limitation of 20,000 ft was

Vampire F.1s in the final assembly shop at Preston in October 1945. The aircraft in the foreground, TG/292, was delivered to the ECFS at Hullavington the following month. (English Electric Co.)

partly a result of the canopy seal, which was inflated by the pressure side of the Pesco pump (the instrument vacuum pump) and produced about 2 lb psi. Consequently, when the cabin pressure reached this figure, the seal collapsed and let the pressure out. This problem was only resolved on the Vampire F.3s, when the canopy seal was inflated from the engine compressor. (The Vampire F.3 was in turn limited to 35,000 ft for a while owing to contraction of the perspex canopy caused by the low temperature at high altitude.)

The first production Vampire, TG274, flew from Samlesbury on 20 April 1945, and was transferred to Hatfield three days later for manufacturer's trials. A month later TG274 was delivered to the A&AEE at Boscombe Down for an engineering assessment and general handling trials to enable the type to be cleared for Service use. The results of these trials showed it to be very pleasant for general flying, but the stick force per 'g' to

manoeuvre in the looping plane was unacceptably low, and considered to be much lighter than was desirable for a modern fighter. Aileron overbalance at high Mach numbers (which had also been present on the prototype Spider Crab, MP838), was more marked on this aircraft. The trials also restated an earlier test criticism of the prototype, which reported that the rudder effectiveness was poor, especially at low speeds, and the tendency to oscillate directionally was such that the aircraft would probably make a poor gunnery platform.

Although the A&AEE report stated that the cockpit layout was considered satisfactory, the view was still poor, especially to the side and rear, and, although differently shaped, the flap and undercarriage selector levers could not be easily distinguished because of their close proximity. Finally, the results of the Vampire level speed trials, which were conducted at the same time,

TG386 was delivered to Hatfield during July 1946 and became the first Vampire to feature the new, one-piece perspex canopy. It was used exclusively as a trials aircraft and struck off charge in September 1953. (De Havilland via Mike Stroud)

showed that, using combat engine conditions of 10,000 rpm and at a weight of 8,180 lb, the maximum level speed attainable was 526 mph true air speed (TAS) at 25,500 ft.

On 3 December 1945 the A&AEE trials were cut short when Sqn Ldr Jan Zurakowski stalled TG274 whilst demonstrating the Vampire's low-speed handling qualities at Boscombe Down, and it hit the ground. The aircraft was declared a write-off.

A short time after TG274 had made its first flight, a second order for 120 F.Mk.1s, serialled VF265–VF283, VF300–VF348, VF362–VF392 and VF330–VF350, was placed with English Electric on 7 May 1945. With the end of the war in sight, the order was subsequently cut back to thirty-four aircraft, with VF265–VF314 emerging as Vampire F.Mk.1s, and the remainder of the order completed as F.Mk.3s. A later batch of sixty F.Mk.1s ordered in August 1945 was cancelled the following month, and the final Vampire F.Mk.1, VF314 rolled off the production line at Preston in December 1946.

The second production aircraft, TG275, was converted to the prototype Vampire F.Mk.3 in June 1945, and TG276 was

diverted off the production line as the prototype F.Mk.II; trials continued with TG277, which was retained by de Havilland (Engines) for Goblin engine development work. As a consequence of Air Cdre Boothman's suggestion during the Spider Crab's tactical trials in March 1944 that the aircraft would be ideal for photo-reconnaissance work, the fifth production Vampire, TG278, was delivered to Hatfield in August 1945 to be fitted with cameras and became the prototype for a proposed PR version. Although these trials were abandoned in October 1945, the aircraft was retained at Hatfield as a flying test bed for an improved development Goblin engine, the 4,500 lb s.t. de Havilland Ghost 2; the company considered the aircraft to be ideal for thrust and consumption measurement at speeds and altitudes out of reach of the Avro Lancastrian–Ghost test bed already in use.

By May 1947 TG278 was further modified for high altitude and pressure cabin development flying with de Havilland (Engines). A centre-section rib on each side had been modified to allow for the extra 3 in diameter of the Ghost. The cockpit was

Vampire F.1 TG278, photographed from an Albemarle prior to delivery during August 1945. (Chas. E. Brown)

pressurized from the main engine compressor to supply a differential pressure of 2½ lb sq. in; this gave the pilot an equivalent height of 37,000 ft at 60,000 ft – which was well above the maximum design altitude of the Vampire. The cockpit was also fitted with a heater, ten emergency compressed-air bottles, a special pressure canopy with a metal hood and 'porthole' windows, and a 4 ft extension to each wingtip. To provide higher jet pipe temperatures and engine speeds while operating at altitude, a slightly enlarged

engine exhaust pipe was fitted and, although retaining the standard wing-root intakes, four small scoops around the Ghost engine supplied engine cooling. The aircraft was also stripped of its paint, which saved 25 lb in weight and was worth 50 ft of altitude.

Following modification, TG278 was used by the Engine Division of de Havilland's for the high altitude development of the Ghost engine. Encouraged by the results obtained by the aircraft in early 1948, the company planned an attempt at the Aeroplane Height Record,

The fifth production Vampire F.1, TG278, at Samlesbury. It was later delivered to Hatfield in June 1947 for Ghost 2 engine trials, and established the new world height record the following year, flown by John Cunningham. It ended its days as an instructional airframe at Halton. (BAe)

which was at the time held by Italy – in 1938 a Caproni biplane had reached 56,046 ft. On 23 March 1948 John Cunningham flew TG278 to the test flying area between Cambridge and Lakenheath, and during the 45 minute flight he was able to attain a world high altitude record of 59,446 ft. This record was held for five years until an Olympus-powered Canberra achieved 63,668 ft in May 1953.

TG278 continued to provide a useful contribution to the Ghost engine development programme until October 1950, when it was badly damaged following an engine fire, and its fuselage ended its days as a training airframe at RAF Halton.

In 1945 it was felt necessary to conduct comparison trials between the Vampire and the Meteor. On 27 November 1945 the DFT Ops published their report which favoured the Meteor, stating that the aircraft was a steadier gun platform and possessed a better role of climb and higher Mach number than the Vampire. Although the Vampire was more manoeuvrable and was capable of a greater range, the Meteor enjoyed better development potential, mainly because of its twin-engined layout, which also offered a higher safety factor. This report was to have a far-reaching effect on the future of the Vampire development programme.

The following year, Vampire tactical trials were undertaken by the Central Fighter Establishment at West Raynham. During these trials the CFE also took the opportunity to compare the Vampire against a Meteor F.Mk.3 and a Spitfire XIV. Two of the four Vampires used in the trials (TG295 and TG305) were fitted with Goblin I engines, while the other two (TG332 and TG346) were fitted with Goblin 2 engines.

Their report criticized the rearward vision of the bubble hood, preferring instead the excellent view of the 'teardrop' canopy. It continues:

As an interceptor fighter the Vampire appears capable of intercepting aircraft of the Mosquito class. However, the rate of climb and maximum speed are not good enough to make it suitable for the interception of jet-propelled bombers. The Vampire is superior in all tactical combat manoeuvres to the Meteor F.Mk.3, and fitted with either Goblin I or Goblin 2 engines has proven itself entirely suitable as a short-range, low-altitude fighter.

During company engine and pressure cabin development trials at Hatfield, TG278 established a new world height record on 23 March 1948. It was suitably modified for the attempt with extended wingtips and a metal hood. (De Havilland)

Vampire F.1 TG346 was one of four aircraft issued to the CFE at West Raynham during 1946 for tactical trials. It later served with 605 Squadron and No. 208 AFS. (Author collection)

Gunnery trials were carried out at the A&AEE in early 1946 after TG284 was delivered from Hatfield on 2 February. The object of the trials was to assess the suitability of the four 20 mm Hispano Mk.5 cannon and, although briefly interrupted when the aircraft's nose panels were damaged by gun blast, the trials were completed on 8 July 1946. In all a total of 14,138 rounds had been fired during the gunnery trials. The result was that the installation was considered satisfactory up to heights of 20,000 ft and at speeds up to 448 knots, providing certain recommendations were incorporated. It was also considered that the Vampire was an unsatisfactory gun platform because of the tendency to 'snake' and the restricted search view.

Three Vampire F.Mk.1 airframes, TG276, TG280 and TX807, were experimentally fitted with 4,500 lb s.t. Rolls-Royce Nene engines to Specification F.11/45, and designated F.Mk.2s in February 1945. Instantly recognizable by two 'elephant's ears' auxiliary intakes on top of the nacelle which fed air to the engine's double-sided impeller, production of the type, modified to later standards with a low-set tailplane, was proposed as the F.Mk.IV.

A further two Vampire fuselages, TG283 and TG306, were taken from the Preston production lines in late 1945 for conversion to the DH 108 swept-wing, tailless research aircraft at Hatfield. On 3 December 1945 the third prototype, LZ551/G, made the first-ever deck landing by a jet aircraft when Lt. Cdr E.M. Brown landed on HMS *Ocean*. Some of the naval development Vampires were modified by de Havilland's with an arrestor hook and enlarged flaps for rubber deck landing experiments at Farnborough in 1946.

In 1947 the MEAF was seeking to re-equip its fighter squadrons with jets and this, coupled with the fact that de Havilland's were looking at the lucrative Middle Eastern export market (the Gloster Meteor had already undergone its tropical trials), meant that performance tests were required to assess the suitability of the Vampire for operation in tropical conditions. Not only was particular reference to be paid to the effect of heat and sand on the functioning of all services, but information was also required on the failure of components, irrespective of whether or not the failure was directly attributable to the climatic conditions. The final Vampire F.Mk.1 airframe to be produced, VF314, was selected for the trials and dispatched to Hatfield in April 1947, arriving at the Tropical Experimental Unit at Khartoum in late October 1947.

Tests began in January 1948 and were

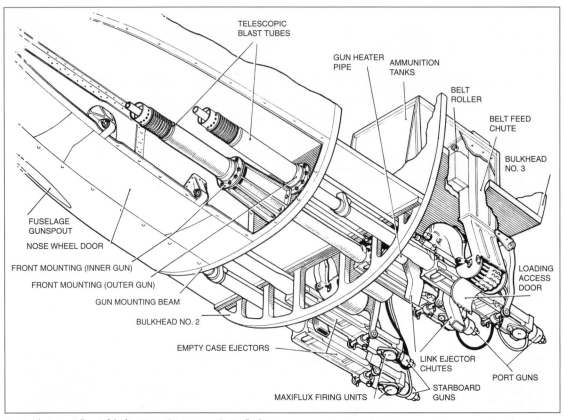

TELESCOPIC
BLAST TUBES

GUN HEATER
PIPE

AMMUNITION
TANKS

BELT
ROLLER

BELT FEED
CHUTE

BULKHEAD
NO. 3

FUSELAGE
GUNSPOUT

NOSE WHEEL DOOR

FRONT MOUNTING (INNER GUN)

FRONT MOUNTING (OUTER GUN)

GUN MOUNTING BEAM

BULKHEAD NO. 2

EMPTY CASE EJECTORS

MAXIFLUX FIRING UNITS

STARBOARD
GUNS

LINK EJECTOR
CHUTES

PORT GUNS

LOADING
ACCESS
DOOR

Diagram showing installation of the four Hispano-Suiza cannon. (De Havilland)

Vampires were first issued to 247 Squadron at Chilbolton in March 1946; TG/301 is depicted two months later flown by the Squadron's CO, Sqn Ldr
C. Scott-Vos. It was lost in a flying accident the following year. (Sqn Ldr P.G. Murton)

TG296 of 247 Squadron getting airborne from Chilbolton in June 1946. This aircraft was later sold to the French Air Force. (Sqn Ldr P.G. Murton)

Air and groundcrews of 247 Squadron at Odiham, July 1946. (Sqn Ldr P.G. Murton)

completed the following June, by which time the three RAF test pilots from Boscombe Down had completed over 100 hours of intensive flying in 124 sorties. High altitude flying above 30,000 ft was restricted at first because of troubles with cracked canopies, and problems with the original engine necessitated a replacement being installed after eighty-four flying hours. However, the aircraft behaved satisfactorily in dry, hot conditions at Khartoum, where the average maximum temperature was recorded at 36° Centigrade; the major problems encountered were difficulty

with engine starting, failure of the internal accumulators to maintain a charge, and shrinkage of the wooden structure, all of which were attributed to the heat and low humidity.

Deliveries of the Vampire F.Mk.1 to the RAF began with 247 Squadron at Chilbolton in March 1946. Commanded by Sqn Ldr Clifford Scott Vos DFC, the squadron completed a trouble-free conversion from Tempests by May and became the centre of inevitable publicity attention, attracting innumerable visits by curious representatives of the government, press and foreign air forces. Many displays and

Vampire F.1s of 247 Squadron over Ilford, Essex, during the Victory fly-past on 8 June 1946. (Sqn Ldr P.G. Murton)

The third squadron to receive Vampires was 130 Squadron; their VF306 is seen at Odiham in 1947. It was later used by Martin Baker for ejection seat installation trials. (John Rawlings)

The first auxiliary unit to receive Vampires was 605 (County of Warwick) Squadron. Normally based at Honiley, TG348 is seen at Horsham St Faith on 16 March 1950. (MoD)

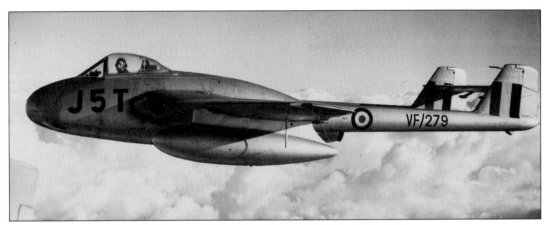

High above Germany, VF279 of 3 Squadron flown by Fg Off. Phineas Rigg on 15 January 1949. (via OC 3 Squadron)

fly-pasts were laid on by the squadron before it moved to Odiham in June 1946, including both the Victory fly-past over Central London and the US Armed Forces Day celebrations. The Odiham Vampire Wing also comprised 54 and 130 Squadrons (the latter being renumbered as 72 Squadron in February 1947), and flew F.Mk.1s until they were replaced by F.3s in 1948.

With the release of Vampire F.Mk.1s from the Regular squadrons, they became the first jet aircraft to enter service with the Royal Auxiliary Air Force when they began to replace the Mosquitos of 605 (County of Warwick) Squadron, normally based at Honiley. Between July 1948 and June 1951 five auxiliary squadrons eventually flew the F.Mk.1.

With new jet aircraft coming off the production lines, priority was given to strengthen and modernize the BAFO fighter squadrons, and on 10 April 1948 the first Vampire F.Mk.1s were delivered to 3 Squadron at Wunstorf. Soon moving to Gutersloh, the squadron was tasked with the operational evaluation of jet fighters in Germany, and became the focus of

At rest between sorties at Bentwaters, VF310 of 247 Squadron and VF329 of Odiham Station Flight during exercise 'Foil', June 1949. (Wg Cdr O.L. Hardy)

TG292 is seen at Odiham soon after 130 Squadron was renumbered 72 Squadron. (Robin Brown)

Between November 1946 and October 1949, Vampire F.1 TG372 underwent extensive cold weather trials at WEE, Edmonton, Canada. It was later preserved at the Canadian Aeronautical Collection at Rockcliffe, Ottawa. It is shown here with Lancaster FM148 at Namao during 1946. (via Pat Dobbs)

international media attention and a great deal of diplomatic activity in August 1948, when PII Pete Jordan force-landed his Vampire (VF272) in the Russian Zone.

The Vampire was now readily available for export; Sweden bought seventy F.Mk.1s, under the designation J 28A, with deliveries commencing in June 1946. Switzerland also bought four F.Mk.1s for evaluation, the first being delivered to Geneva in July 1946. Canadian interest in purchasing the Vampire, and an evaluation of the extreme Arctic weather conditions of Northern Canada in which the aircraft might have to operate, resulted in a F.Mk.1, TG372 being shipped from Liverpool on 4 October 1946. The

aircraft was officially taken on charge by the Winterisation Experimental Establishment at Edmonton, Alberta in November 1946 for extensive trials at Edmonton and at Watson Lake in the Yukon.

In 1948 France signed an agreement with de Havilland's to produce the Vampire under licence. As the French were anxious to rebuild their post-war air force as quickly as possible, thirty F.Mk.1s were transferred to the Armée de l'Air between 1948 and 1950 for pilot training, pending the delivery of their licence-built Vampire Mk.5s and Mistrals.

Further F.Mk.1s, purchased from surplus Swedish stocks, were also operated by Austria and the Dominican Republic.

GOBLIN ENGINE DEVELOPMENT

As far back as the early years of the twentieth century, American and French engineers had been investigating the principle of the gas turbine engine. This made use of a compressor to supply high pressure air to a combustion chamber into which fuel was continuously injected. As the resultant fuel/air mixture was burned, it produced high-energy gases for expansion through a turbine connected to the compressor. Rotation of the turbine turned the compressor, but as early component efficiencies were so low, there could be no net power output from the engine.

Doctor A.A. Griffith of the RAE at Farnborough had examined the use of such a powerplant in aircraft and had outlined the basic principles in a report entitled *An Aerodynamic Theory of Turbine Design*. Griffith's design, however, was based upon a gas turbine engine driving a propeller and little interest was shown in his report which he submitted in 1926.

Two years later, during his fourth term at the Royal Air Force College, Cranwell, Flight Cadet Frank Whittle wrote a thesis, *Future Developments in Aircraft Design*, in which he discussed the possibility of using a gas turbine to drive a propeller. Whittle was unaware of Griffith's work on gas turbines, and when he was given the opportunity to present his proposals to the Air Ministry in 1929, Griffiths wrote a critical review of Whittle's theories and they were officially turned down as impractical.

Frank Whittle had joined the RAF in 1923 as an Aircraft Apprentice at No. 4 Apprentices Wing RAF Cranwell, and after a three year apprenticeship and a further two years as a

Flight Cadet, also at Cranwell, he was posted to Hornchurch in August 1928 to fly Armstrong-Whitworth Siskin fighters with 111 Squadron.

At the end of 1929, while attached to the Central Flying School at Wittering with No. 30 Flying Instructors Course, he further developed his thoughts on gas turbine jet propulsion for a very high altitude, high-speed aeroplane.

Following the rejection of his designs and calculations by the Air Ministry, Whittle qualified as a Flying Instructor and was posted to No. 2 FTS at Digby where he continued to work on his ideas on turbo-jet design. Towards the end of 1930 he approached the British Thomson-Houston (BT-H) steam turbine factory in Rugby where he was told that the development cost of his proposed engine would be £60,000. As the design was only applicable to aircraft, the firm told Whittle that they could not contemplate an expenditure of that magnitude and it was not in their interests to develop it.

In 1934 Whittle was specially selected by the Air Ministry and sent to Cambridge University (Peterhouse) to study for a Mechanical Sciences Tripos; there he was able to obtain some financial support through Messrs R. Dudley Williams and J.C.B. Tinling to continue his work on the gas turbine engine, for which he had taken out a patent in January 1930.

In the autumn of 1935 Whittle approached BT-H again, and with the advantage of some financial backing, he persuaded the company to take a cost-plus contract, and he duly formed his own company Power Jets Limited in March 1936, to build an experimental engine. Construction began four months later and in 1937 they rented part of BT-H's disused foundry at Lutterworth for further test work. By the end of 1938 the Whittle Unit had successfully run for 30 minutes at 16,500 rpm.

At the same time as Whittle was working on the centrifugal compressor turbo-jet, a German post-graduate student at the University of Gottingen, Hans-Joachim Pabst von Ohain, offered his design for a pure jet engine to the aircraft designer Ernst Heinkel and by mid-1939 the HeS 3A turbo-jet had been test flown beneath a Heinkel He 118 V2 experimental dive-bomber. The Heinkel He 178 was built to accommodate the uprated 838 lb thrust HeS 3B engine, and on 27 August 1939 it made its maiden flight, lasting ten minutes, from Heinkel's Marienhe airfield with Flugkapitan Erich Warsitz at the controls; it thereby became the world's first turbo-jet aircraft to fly. The He 178 continued to fly on experimental work and was demonstrated to the German Air Ministry in November 1939. It was eventually placed in the Berlin Air Museum where it was destroyed during an Allied bombing raid in 1943.

During a visit to the Gloster Aircraft works at Brockworth Whittle had discussions with their Chief Designer George W. Carter, and the two men decided to collaborate to design an aircraft powered by the new engine. In August 1939 the Air Ministry was finally persuaded to commission an aeroplane to flight test Whittle's W.1 turbo-jet, and the Gloster Aircraft Company was awarded Contract SB.3229 on 3 February 1940 for two aircraft to be built to Specification E.28/39. Both Gloster Whittle E.28/39s, W4041/G and W4046/G, were built at Gloster's Experimental Department at Hucclecote in the greatest secrecy, and the first of them, W4041/G, was ready for its initial taxiing trials in April 1941. By 12 May 1941 the aircraft was moved by road to Cranwell in readiness for its first flight. Cranwell had been chosen because of its long runway and clear approach and because it was easier there to preserve the strict security precautions surrounding the flight. During the evening of 15 May 1941 W4041/G was able to get airborne with Gloster's chief test pilot Gerry Sayer at the controls. The first flight lasted for seventeen minutes. Later, during subsequent test flights at Edge Hill in Warwickshire, the E.28/39 was able to achieve a top speed of 370 mph in level flight at 25,000 ft and eventually, following completion of its test career, it was put on display in the Science Museum at South Kensington in April 1946. The second prototype, W4046/G, was destroyed in July 1943. During a high altitude test flight from Farnborough, the ailerons jammed; unable to control the resulting spin the pilot, the CO of the E.28/39 Flight Sqn Ldr Douglas Davie, baled out, leaving the aircraft to crash into the garden of Lea Farm Cottage at Bramley near Guildford.

On the evening of 21 May 1941, three of the many visitors invited to Cranwell to watch an impressive demonstration flight of the E.28/39 were Capt. Geoffrey de Havilland, his Chief Engineer C.C. Walker, and the engine designer Maj. Frank Halford. Geoffrey de Havilland was unaware of Whittle's work but was impressed by his concept and was consequently allowed access to his reports and design calculations. Frank Halford had already had some association with Whittle's project as he was an adviser to Vauxhall Motors Ltd, who were originally to produce the W.2B engines to Power Jet's design, before they dropped out in early 1941 because of other commitments.

In January 1941 the Chairman of the Aeronautical Research Council Sir Henry Tizard invited de Havilland's to design a single-seat jet fighter and also the engine to power it. The Air Ministry did not specify what form or size the engine should take, but following due consultation with the aircraft design team it

Gloster E.28/39 W4041/G was used to flight test Whittle's W.1 turbojet. It first flew on 15 May 1941, and is now on display at the Science Museum at South Kensington. (RAF Cranwell via Peter Green)

was decided that an engine diameter of 50 in would be desirable because of the minimum size of the fighter's pressure cabin.

The company had previously designed air-cooled piston engines, and after further consultation the engine design team decided that for simplicity and ease of production, a single engine was the optimum to power the proposed fighter. A thrust rating of about 3,000 lb would be required at sea-level to give a sufficient performance to compete with the Spitfire and Typhoon fighters currently in RAF service.

Whittle had used a double-entry centrifugal compressor, but for the purposes of clean wing design Frank Halford decided on a single-sided compressor. This design simplified installation in the fuselage, with the air intake easily blended into the wing; there would also be no difficulty in positioning the intake ducts to avoid the wing spar. Finally, the single-sided compressor created fewer engine bearing problems than the double-sided system. A feature of the new engine would be the use of sixteen straight-

through combustion chambers connecting the diffuser exit to the turbine entry.

The de Havilland/Halford engine was supplied with air at the rate of 100 tons per hour via the wing root intakes. The compressor/impeller, rotating at a maximum speed of more than 10,000 rpm, accelerated the airflow so that after diffusion it was delivered to the combustion chambers at a pressure of 40 lb/sq. in. Fuel injectors sprayed atomized fuel into the flame tubes where combustion took place. The resulting high-energy gases were fed through the turbine which, at full speed, developed 6,000–8,000 hp to drive the impeller. The gases were then accelerated in the jet pipe propelling nozzle to a speed of 1,000–1,100 mph. The combined effect of the high rate of air mass flow and the high exhaust velocity gave the Halford H.1 a take-off thrust of 3,000 lb. The corresponding fuel consumption was 7½ gallons of kerosene per minute.

The Halford H.1 engine, originally code-named 'Supercharger', was on paper by April 1941 and the drawings were sent to the workshops of the Car Mart factory at Hendon, where the first engine (and all subsequent prototype Goblin engines) was built on 8 August. The engine first ran on its special test bed at Hatfield on 13 April 1942, 248 days after the production of the first drawings. A half-hour acceptance test at half-speed was undertaken two days later and, following a satisfactory inspection strip, the rebuilt engine was accepted by the Air Ministry and began its programme of development running.

On 5 May 1942 the engine test bed intakes were sucked flat by the compressor during a test run, causing the engine to stall when the air supply was cut off. The engine was completely stripped down but revealed little damage; following repair and reassembly, the test programme was resumed. Further problems with engine starting and the collapse of the tailpipe inner cone were overcome, and the engine was eventually run at full speed on 13 June. By the end of the year, this and the other completed engine on test had been run for over 156 hours. Plans for the manufacture of the engine had been submitted during September 1942, when the company had completed the twenty-five hour test run necessary for flight approval.

Such was the rapidity with which Halford had reached this stage of airworthiness with the H.1 engine that no airframe actually existed for it, and as de Havilland's were heavily committed to the production of the Mosquito it was clear that the completion of the first DH 100 would be delayed. To gain flight experience, in January 1943 two H.1 engines were installed in the fifth Gloster Meteor prototype (DG206/G), which was redesignated the F.9/40H and flown from Cranwell on 5 March 1943 by chief test pilot Michael Daunt.

In August 1943 a DH 100 airframe finally became available. The H.1 engine was installed and the aircraft was ready for taxiing trials by the end of the month. The first flight of the DH 100 Spider Crab (LZ548/G) was made at Hatfield on 20 September 1943 with Geoffrey de Havilland Jnr at the controls. The thrust of the H.1 engine had been de-rated to 2,300 lb for the initial thirty minute flight, but this still enabled the prototype DH 100 to take off with ease from Hatfield's grass runway.

By the time the prototype Spider Crab had taken to the air, a development of the Halford H.1 engine, the H.1A, had been submitted to the RAE's Engine Department for an examination of the design and performance calculations. The differences lay in the H.1A's redesigned turbine disc and blading in order to lower the stresses, and its enlarged combustion chambers which reduced the pressure losses and improved the combustion efficiency.

The RAE at Farnborough had developed a combustion chamber with a full-entry swirler, which when tested at Car Mart looked like an incandescent torch as 2 lb of air per second left the chamber. The bias of air caused by the twin compressor ducts was overcome by matching the burner fuel flows to suit the six chambers affected. The RAE also suggested that the two major limitations to future development of the engine were choking at the impeller entry and the high stresses in the turbine disc, and that improvement in engine performance could only be obtained by redesigning the impeller and decreasing the disc diameter. The RAE also confirmed de Havilland's suggested engine rating of 2,700 lb s.t. at 10,000 (maximum) rpm with a specific fuel consumption of 1.27 lb/hr. In late 1943 Halford's engine was given the name Goblin.

Interest in America for a jet-propelled fighter powered by a Goblin engine resulted in the design and construction of the Lockheed XP-80. An engine was flown out to California on 30 October 1943 but was severely damaged when, despite warnings from the manufacturers, the intake ducts collapsed at 8,000 rpm during early ground tests. A replacement engine (which in fact had been destined for the second

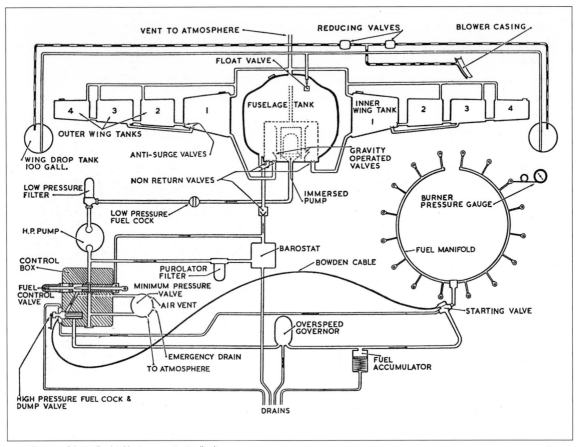

Fuel system of de Havilland Goblin 2 engine. (De Havilland)

prototype DH 100) was sent out on 23 December 1943. The prototype XP–80 Shooting Star (44–83020) was first flown at Muroc Lake on 8 January 1944 by Milo Burcham. The results of the early test flights of the XP-80 encouraged interest from the US Navy in a long-range naval fighter employing both a piston engine in the nose, driving a propeller, and a Goblin engine mounted in the body of the aircraft. Although some of the Goblin engines were built under licence by the Allis-Chalmers Company and flown, the projected Curtiss Wright XF-15C fighter was abandoned after the end of the war with Japan.

Back in England, problems with compressor failures were resolved as was an in-flight fire (achieved by removing the fuel-soaked asbestos lagging around the jet pipe). The next objective was to clear the engine for 3,000 lb thrust, which was achieved by the development of 'flower pot' flame tubes which replaced the original stub-type design. The new flame tubes not only gave better reliability but so improved performance that a thrust of 3,100 lb was achieved at a maximum speed of 10,200 rpm and a fuel consumption of 478 gallons per hour. This engine was type tested during July 1945 and eventually became known as the Goblin 2.

Initial test flying of the Goblin 2 engine was undertaken by the de Havilland Engine Company in October 1945, utilizing Vampire

F.Mk.1 TG282. When Vampire F.Mk.1s (from TG314 onwards), fitted with Goblin 2 engines began to roll off the production lines in May 1946, an intensive test flying programme of the engine was conducted at the A&AEE by three RAF pilots. A standard aircraft (TG381) was sent to Boscombe Down in June 1946, but on 11 July, after only fourteen hours test flying, the engine suffered an impeller blade failure in flight and the pilot was forced to land at Holmsley South. A replacement Vampire (TG447) was received at Boscombe Down at the end of July but suffered a similar misfortune to TG381 on 23 December 1946, when an impeller blade failed during a ground run and the engine caught fire. However, sufficient information had already been gathered so it was decided that the tests should be terminated.

Modifications were made by de Havilland's to prevent further impeller blade failures. Cropping the leading edge of the impeller vanes eliminated the dangerous vane vibration. Further work was also carried out to prevent overheating and subsequent fracturing of the flame tubes. Generally speaking, the Goblin 2 engine performed well during the trials and was considered adequate for Service use once the modifications to the impeller and combustion equipment had been incorporated.

On 2 February 1945 the Goblin I became the first gas turbine engine to pass a Government Type Test Certificate, at 2,700 lb thrust. Later versions of the engine (Goblin 3/35) would achieve 3,500 lb thrust at 10,700 rpm, which was accomplished by slightly reducing the propelling nozzle diameter and fitting hollow static air-cooled blades to the turbine. The effect was to raise the gas velocity through the nozzle and so increase the exhaust momentum which also gave a slight rise of turbine temperature. Vampire F.Mk.1 TG285 was allocated as a flying test bed for Goblin 3 development at de Havilland's in February 1947.

Goblin 2 engine, rated at 3,000 lb thrust. Over three thousand engines were built for the Vampire F.3, FB.5, FB.9, FB.52A and Sea Vampire F.20. (de Havilland Engine Co.)

Between 8 July and 5 August 1948 the Goblin was subjected to the most severe tests ever attempted with an engine when, at the request of the Controller of Supplies (Air), a production Goblin 2 engine underwent a rigorous schedule to simulate the worst wartime operating conditions for fighters with little or no attention between flights. The programme provided the equivalent of 234 combat flights, each of sixty-five minutes duration with ten minute intervals, during which the Goblin received no maintenance; it retained its performance to the end. The success of the tests underlined the reliability of the engine and the capability of the Goblin to satisfy the most stringent demands of the military market.

The Goblin 4 engine was similar to the Goblin 3, with the exception of the blade

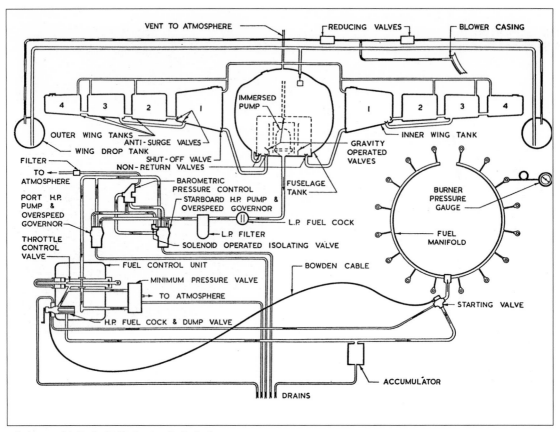

Fuel system of de Havilland Goblin 3 engine. (De Havilland)

material specification which allowed an increased thrust of 3,750 lb; it was developed for the third swept-wing tailless DH 108 research prototype VW120. High-altitude testing of the engine's fuel system was conducted at Hatfield between July 1946 and August 1947 by Vampire I TG443, followed by development testing at Boscombe Down by Vampire F.3 VV190. A Goblin 4 engine was installed into VW120 and run for the first time on 21 July 1947; three days later the DH 108 made its maiden flight at Hatfield. Between that date and its demise in February 1950, the aircraft raised the international speed record to over 605 mph and exceeded (albeit inadvertently) the speed of sound for the first time in Britain.

Production of Goblin engines was controlled by the newly formed de Havilland (Engine) Company at Stone Grove in Edgware with Frank Halford as Chairman and Technical Director and Eric Moult as Chief Engineer. In 1946 all engine production was transferred to Leavesden near Watford; Stag Lane remained as the centre for engine design and development. From 1943 until September 1945, fifty Goblin I engines were produced by the de Havilland (Engine) Company. They were followed on the production lines by the Goblin 2 which was first delivered in October 1945; between this date and March 1953 and a total of 3,606 Goblin 2 engines were built for the Vampire F.3, FB.5, FB.9 and FB.52A and the Sea Vampire F.20. The final production Goblin

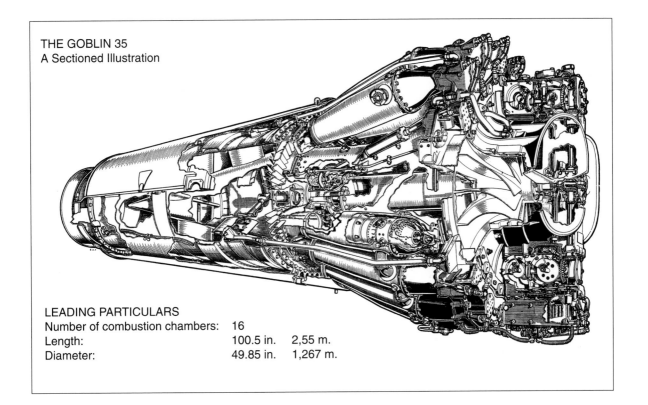

THE GOBLIN 35
A Sectioned Illustration

LEADING PARTICULARS
Number of combustion chambers: 16
Length: 100.5 in.   2,55 m.
Diameter: 49.85 in.   1,267 m.

engines, the Goblin 3 for the Vampire FB.6, NF.10, T.11, FB.50 and FB.52, and the Goblin 35 for the Vampire NF.54 and T.55, were built from October 1948. When production ceased in 1955 a total of 2,688 Goblin 3/35 engines had been built.

The Goblin was also licence-built by Societa per Anzioni Fiat of Turin, Italy and Svenska Flygmotor at Trollhatten in Sweden; the Goblin 2 engines produced for the Swedish J28A Vampires were designated as RM 1s, whereas the later J28Bs and J28Cs had Swedish-built RM 1As (Goblin 3s). The Swedish-built engines were adapted with roller bearings in the engine in place of the standard ball bearings fitted by de Havilland's.

ROLLS-ROYCE NENE

Although de Havilland's proposed in early 1945 to produce a variant of their Vampire design powered by a Nene engine, production was dependent upon a number of factors, primarily its acceptance from aspects of performance and handling. The Rolls-Royce Nene, with its single-stage, double-entry centrifugal compressor with a double-sided impeller, had been developed from the Derwent engine in response to a Ministry of Production Specification issued in 1944 for a jet engine developing a minimum thrust of 4,000 lb. Work had begun on the Nene in May 1944 and it was ready for testing by 27 October 1944; during these early tests the Nene exceeded design expectations in achieving a thrust rating of 5,000 lb.

In January 1947 the Ministry of Supply suggested using the Nene engine, rated at 4,500 lb thrust, instead of the Goblin 3 in de Havilland's proposed ground attack version of the Vampire. The Department of Operational Requirements was quick to point out, in a written reply, that 'the Nene is 300 lb heavier than the Goblin, thus putting the aircraft's centre of gravity further aft, which means more nose ballast and poorer stability.'

The Directorate of Aircraft Research and Development (DARD) had been keen to recommend the Nene–Vampire F.Mk.IV for Service use and estimated that take-off and climb performance would be superior to that of the Goblin-engined variant, and that deliveries could commence in July 1947. In their technical appreciation published in January 1946, the DARD states:

In level flight and with the Goblin engine

(2,700 lb thrust) the Vampire will meet the compressibility limitation at approximately 520 mph true air speed at 25,000 ft; at sea-level the safety margin is 90 mph. With the Goblin 2 (3,000 lb thrust) the corresponding figures are 530 mph at 18,000 ft and the margin is 50 mph. When the Nene, which we expect to be cleared for the RAF at 4,500 lb thrust, is installed in the Vampire Mk.II, the aeroplane should be capable of level flight speeds of 10–20 mph in excess of the compressibility limit if it were possible to ignore the pitching oscillation. This means of course, that in level flight the Nene Vampire will have to be flown throttled, and the full benefit of the extra thrust given by the Nene will show up in an improved rate of climb. At sea-level the rate of climb should be above 7,000 ft/min., whereas the maximum rate of climb with the Goblin 2 is below 5,000 ft/min. In view of the Air Staff's insistence on very high rates of climb for interceptor fighters this is a very clear advantage which the Nene–Vampire enjoys.

It is noteworthy that the Vampire, as all other aircraft, had two speed limitations: an IAS (structural) limit of 455 knots (clean) and a Mach limit of M.76 defined by pitch-up; the cross-over altitude where an IAS of 455 knots equates to M.76 is around 15,000 ft. Thus, below 15,000 ft the thrust of the Nene could be safely used up to the IAS limit for improved acceleration and turning performance. Vampires were regularly test flown to 480 knots at 15,000 ft.

The installation of a Nene engine without major structural alterations to the airframe was constrained by the Vampire's intakes which were not suitable for the double-sided compressor entry. Indeed, later tests made at Rolls-Royce confirmed that the wing-root air intakes as used for the Goblin engine, modified to suit the Nene installation, were unable to supply the increased air flow required: insufficient air circulating to the rear section of the compressor resulted in a reduction in engine performance.

Rolls-Royce developed additional scoop intakes, known as 'elephant ears', fitted to the top of the engine nacelle to admit air direct into the engine bay. Although the scoops increased the intake efficiency by 50 per cent these intakes were to cause handling problems that plagued the Nene–Vampire throughout its trials, giving poor compressibility characteristics at high Mach numbers and elevator buffeting (the term 'limiting Mach number' was later popularized by the post-war press as the 'sound barrier').

To investigate the suitability of a larger and more powerful engine in the Vampire, and for commonality with the Meteor, Rolls-Royce agreed in February 1945 to fit three Vampire F.Mk.IIs with Nene RB.41 engines for trials purposes, the second of which would be fully pressurized. In April 1945 the third and seventh Vampire F.Mk.I production airframes, TG276 and TG280, were selected for conversion to the F.Mk.2 to Specification F.11/45, and allocated to Hucknall for the fitment of the Rolls-Royce Nene RB.41 engine.

On 27 June 1945 the first F.Mk.2, TG276, was delivered to Rolls-Royce to have its engine installed. Preliminary flight tests showed the ram efficiency of the intake to be considerably below estimate due to boundary layer thickening ahead of the intake. The trials were briefly interrupted in October 1946 when the canopy became detached shortly after the aircraft became airborne on a test flight and damaged the tailplane. In December 1946, following repairs, TG276 was transferred to Boscombe Down for brief handling trials at the A&AEE. The resultant report emphasized the need for an improvement in air intake

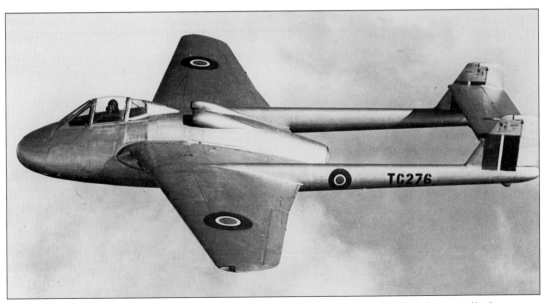

The first prototype Vampire F.11, TG276, was employed for Nene engine and air intake development work until April 1950, when it was sold to France as a testbed for the SNCASE Vampire Mk. 51. (Rolls-Royce)

efficiency and concluded that although there was an increase in the maximum level speed of between 16 and 20 knots TAS at medium height, these figures were reduced to between 6 and 12 knots at altitude in the presence of compressibility effects. Although the additional air intakes made no significant change to the range of the aircraft, they did provide a 15–45° Centigrade decrease in engine jet pipe temperature, depending on the engine rpm.

During the earlier trials at Rolls-Royce the original intakes had been slightly modified in shape at the opening into the plenum chamber, and initial flight tests at Hucknall in March 1946 showed that performance in level flight was seriously down on estimate; the measured ram efficiency of the intake was also below estimate (19 per cent instead of 60 per cent)

and that speed at 12,000 rpm in level flight was some 50 mph TAS below estimate.

The RAE was asked to investigate the problem by wind tunnel tests which confirmed the presence of a forward speed effect, but the magnitude of this effect was less on the wind tunnel model than the full scale aircraft. At the same time it was agreed that various modifications to the intakes should be made in the form of inner wall boundary layer by-pass lips and bell mouths to make the direction of air flow at entry correspond more closely to actual flight conditions. Other modifications to the aircraft intakes made no appreciable difference to intake efficiency and the only improvement of any magnitude was obtained by the fitting of the auxiliary external intakes (elephant's ears) on top of the engine cowling which reduced the flow required through the

Close-up of the auxiliary air intakes, or 'elephant's ears', fitted to Vampire F.11 TG276 at RAE Farnborough. (RAE)

wing intakes. These intakes improved the efficiency of the engine but also increased the aircraft drag – the net result was a small gain in performance under normal flight conditions.

The trials at Boscombe Down had not been without their problems: failure of the jet pipe aluminium jacket (caused by distortion from excessive jacket temperatures) on three separate occasions was solved by the removal of the sealing ring in the Vampire's tail fairing; engine failures and in-flight fires presented further difficulties.

TG276 was returned to Hucknall in February 1948 for further air intake development tests before being sent to Boulton Paul at Wolverhampton for the fitment of larger, redesigned wing-root intakes and the removal of the 'elephant's ear' scoop intakes. The Hawker N7/46 Sea Hawk-type wing-root intakes designed by J.D. North and Dr Renshaw of Boulton Paul, involved the splitting of the main wing spar, with ducting turning through 90° to enter the plenum chamber. Considerable alteration to the wing-root structure was necessary and increased the all-up weight of the aircraft by almost 1,000 lb.

At a meeting at Rolls-Royce in October 1948 following preliminary flight tests, it was agreed that the development work should proceed and that the new Hawker air intake ducts should be fitted to TG276 as soon as possible; wind tunnel tests conducted in April 1949 on a ⅔ scale model showed that the new ducts improved the intake efficiency by 75 per cent compared to the original Nene–Vampire ducts. The Boulton Paul intakes were first flown in TG276 by the company's chief test pilot A.E. 'Ben' Gunn on 5 January 1950. He was impressed by the aircraft's performance and reported that above 15,000 ft he was able to reach the critical Mach number straight and level at full throttle.

Boulton Paul also fitted the aircraft with a standard tailplane and returned it to the A&AEE for handling trials, which were conducted between March and April 1950; it was considered an improvement over the 'elephant ears' version. A 12 in strip of dural fitted to the trailing edge of the elevator, projecting approximately ¼ in above and below the surface, improved the pitching characteristics encountered in flight at the critical Mach number. Pilots were warned of the suddenness of the nose-up change of trim which occurred at M.80.

With the completion of the trials TG276 was delivered to France in April 1950 as a test bed for the SNCASE Vampire Mk.51, until it was sold for scrap in December 1953.

In September 1945 the second prototype Mk.2 TG280 was delivered from Preston to Rolls-Royce at Hucknall for installation and development of the Nene engine. The following July it was transferred to Hatfield for further flight tests which were cut short when the aircraft was badly damaged in a ground accident in October 1946. Following repairs at Hucknall, TG280 was flown to the A&AEE in December 1946 for flight testing at high Mach number.

To improve the efficiency of the air intakes, TG280 was returned to Hucknall in April 1947 for modifications which were flight tested at Boscombe Down in June. In April 1948 the aircraft was flown back to the English Electric Company to have a low-set tailplane fitted, and it was first flown in this form at Samlesbury on 15 June 1948 by the company test pilot, John Squier.

Further development work was undertaken by TG280 at Hucknall and the RAE until June 1951, when the aircraft was dispatched to RAF Cranwell as an instructional airframe. It was eventually struck off charge in May 1954.

A production order had been placed with English Electric for sixty Vampire F.Mk.IIs in February 1945. This order (Contract 6/Acft/4182/C.4(b)) was later reduced to forty Mk.IIs and then amended to two Mk.IIs and thirty-eight Mk.IVs. The contract for the Mk.IVs was subsequently cancelled in September 1945, allowing the two Vampire IIs (TX807 and TX808) to emerge as the survivors of the original order. To add to the confusion, the fuselage of TX808 was used in the repair of the second Nene–Vampire prototype, TG280, which had been extensively damaged in a ground accident at Hatfield, leaving TX807 as the sole out-of-sequence F.Mk.II. A further order for Vampire Mk.IVs to be built in France and designated Mk.51s was also cancelled.

Neville Duke was the chief test pilot at Hawker Aircraft between 1951 and 1956, and flew the Nene-powered Vampire II on several occasions while with the A&AEE:

The first time I flew the Vampire Mk.II (TG276) was on 14 May 1947 on performance work involving partial climbs between 14–16,000 ft. In my log-book I added 'Fire in the air', and I presume I operated the fire extinguisher in response to the action of the fire warning light which was probably set off by the high jacket temperatures being experienced at that time. There was no question of landing on fire or anything so dramatic, but I also presume post-flight examination revealed evidence of local burning of the heat shield.

I did not fly this aircraft again until 8 August 1947 and again on performance work – we obviously used TG276 for performance evaluation and TG280 for handling. I flew the latter twice in August before delivering it back to Hucknall on 8 September 1947. My last flight with the Vampire Mk.II was for handling trials with TX807 on 6 May 1948.

We encountered very poor and unacceptable high Mach number characteristics with the Vampire II's 'elephant's ears', resulting in a sudden and

TX807 was the sole survivor of a cancelled order for sixty Vampire F.IIs. Following Nene engine development trials at Rolls-Royce and the A&AEE, it was transferred to Australia as the first prototype Vampire F.30 and reserialled A78–2. (de Havilland)

very marked and uncontrollable tuck-under. I think that we were very appreciative of the performance of the Nene–Vampire, but the Mach number handling was a major problem.

The development of Modification No. 75, 'Introduction of the Nene Engine', had cost £40,405 and despite its increased performance, orders for the Nene-powered Vampire from the RAF under the designation F.Mk.IV failed to materialize. However, the Royal Navy did show an interest in the Rolls-Royce Nene, and the engine was later selected to power the Supermarine Attacker and Hawker Sea Hawk shipboard fighters.

Australia opted to proceed with the Nene 2–VH version, rated at 5,000 lb s.t., for their Vampires, and consequently 114 engines were built under licence by the Commonwealth Aircraft Corporation Pty Ltd at Fishermans Bend, Melbourne, between December 1948 and July 1954.

On 27 August 1948 the third F.Mk.2, TX807, was received by the RAAF as the first prototype Vampire F.Mk.30 and re-serialled A78-2. Throughout 1949 this aircraft was flown extensively to assess the potential of the Australian-built, Nene-powered F.Mk.30s against the Goblin-powered Vampires A78-1 and A78-3. The Australian Vampires were originally built with the 'elephant ears' on top of the rear fuselage. After losing a number of aircraft and pilots during 'Mach runs' it was determined that the position of the intakes seriously affected the elevator control during recovery: as the aircraft neared the critical Mach number (0.76), the nose dropped irrespective of elevator movement, and recovery had to be positively effected (air brakes became ineffective above Mach 0.78). Repositioning the 'elephant's ears' intakes on the underside of the fuselage caused the Vampire to 'pitch up' more strongly than the standard aircraft as the critical Mach number was reached; this presented the

Australian pilots with more acceptable high Mach characteristics, even if the belly intakes did introduce further problems by sucking up debris from the ground!

Between January and September 1949 Vampire F.Mk.30 prototype A78-2 was flown by pilots of the Aircraft Research and Development Unit and No. 78(F) Wing at Laverton; it was then dispatched to de Havilland (Australia) for the fitment of modified mainplanes and air intakes. The aircraft ended its flying career with the ARDU in August 1956 and after conversion for use as an instructional airframe with the RAAF School of Technical Training at Wagga Wagga, it was finally burnt in 1963.

France also decided to adopt the Nene 104 B engines for their SNCASE Vampire Mk.51s, and built Nenes under licence with the work being sub-contracted to Hispano-Suiza SA at Guadalajara in Spain.

A standard Vampire FB.5, VV568, was taken from the Preston production lines and sent to de Havilland's at Hatfield in February 1949 where it was modified to take a Nene engine as a pattern aircraft to meet the requirements of the French Government. On 13 October 1949 John Wilson airtested VV568 at Hatfield to investigate the poor compressibility characteristics at high Mach numbers due to the 'elephant's ears' (which had been taken from TG280). His report shows that he was less than impressed:

Rapidly increasing pull force is required with the increase of Mach, a force of 20 lb being required after level trim at M.70 has been increased to M.76 at 29,000 ft. With the engine throttled down considerable elevator buffet is evident, increasing with 'g' – at low level and moderate speeds this gives a feeling of sponginess and being near the stall, at speeds and 'g' which are far from the normal Vampire stall. Engine response at low rpm is very slow, accompanied by

The auxiliary air intakes are shown to advantage on this Vampire F.1 of the RAAF during September 1950. Following a series of accidents the intakes were removed to the underside of the aircraft. (The *Herald and Weekly Times*)

rapid rise of jet pipe temperature [JPT] as the throttle is opened.

Following brief handling trials at Farnborough in January 1950, the A&AEE reiterated John Wilson's report and warned that development work should be undertaken to reduce the nose-down change of trim that occurred when throttling back at high Mach numbers and altitude. It was also stressed that attention should be paid to the high stick forces needed to recover from dives at limiting Mach number.

VV568 was eventually shipped to France on 21 January 1950 as the prototype Vampire Mk.51 and flown extensively by the CEV at Bretigny and Marignane. It was eventually written off following an accident at Marignane in December 1952. Another FB.5, VV731, was dispatched to France in June 1949 and converted to the second prototype Vampire Mk.51. It was known to have been flown by the CEV on Boulton Paul air intake development trials in March 1953, but its subsequent history is uncertain.

John Wilson later flew a French Mistral with

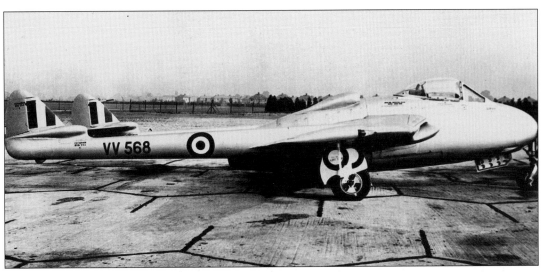

Vampire FB.5 VV568 was fitted with a Nene engine and shipped to France as the prototype Mk.51 in January 1950. (Rolls-Royce)

the Boulton Paul intakes at Marignane on 9 January 1953 and his report shows it to be a much better aircraft than the Vampire Mk.51:

> It is a pleasant aircraft to fly. There was considerable duct noise at normal cruising RPM and engine response at low RPM was poor. The aircraft had a very bad stall, with resultant wing drop, from which spin entry was automatic if corrective action was not taken.

It is certain that the Nene-powered Vampire enjoyed an increased performance when compared to its Goblin-equipped contemporary; during exercises in the Middle East, RAF pilots serving with Vampire squadrons from the Deversoir Wing frequently testified to being outflown by French Air Force Mistrals operating from bases in North Africa.

As a final note, there is an interesting and ironic twist to the story: although the RAF decided not to proceed with the Nene engine, some twenty-five were sold to Russia in 1946 for their MiG-15s; thus for some years RAF Fighter Command was denied the air superiority it was desperate to maintain against a succession of Russian fighters powered with improved versions of the original Nene engine.

DH 108

It was during the development of the Vampire in 1943 that de Havilland's design team at Hatfield began to examine seriously the feasibility of an advanced civilian airliner fitted with four Goblin turbine engines. By the latter half of the year, the design of the proposed airliner had changed to that of a twenty-passenger aircraft, of Vampire layout, with Goblin engines grouped in the tail. However, by August 1944 its design had changed again to that of a three-Ghost engined 'Vampire Mail Carrier', and a scale model was tested in the RAE's wind tunnel at Farnborough.

In October 1945 the de Havilland design team was considering a swept-wing tail-less aircraft of 75,000 lb all-up-weight, carrying twenty-four passengers and powered by four Ghost engines. A forty-degree sweepback of the wings was proposed in order to reduce the weight of the wing structure and cruise drag, whilst the four engines were to be mounted beneath the wings near the trailing edge. By March 1946 the project (which had been designated the DH 106 in October 1944) incorporated a tail, and in this form the radical aircraft design evolved into the world's first commercial jet airliner, the de Havilland Comet.

Practical experience of the behaviour of swept-wing design was strongly recommended, together with flying half-scale models of the proposed DH 106 configuration. In January 1946, to meet Air Staff Requirement OR. 207, Specification E.18/45 was issued to cover the design and construction of two tail-less, single-engined, jet-propelled aircraft prototypes developed from the Vampire F.Mk.1. under the company designation DH 108. The

specification had three objectives: to conduct full-scale experiments into the possibilities of high speed flight using swept-back wings; to obtain quantitative measurements of aerodynamic and structural phenomena under such conditions; and to act as an approximate half-scale version of a projected multi-engined, jet-propelled aircraft.

Originally, two prototype DH 108 aircraft (unofficially referred to as the 'Swallow' by the MoS) were to be built by de Havilland's at Hatfield under Contract SB.66562, dated 13 December 1945, and serialled VN856 and VN860. However, the urgency of the programme and the desire to keep costs to a minimum forced a decision to transfer two Vampire F.1 fuselages, TG283 and TG306, from the English Electric production line at Preston to Hatfield for completion as DH 108s. The serials VN856 and VN860 were accordingly cancelled in February 1946.

The first prototype, TG283, was designed as a low-speed, swept-wing research aircraft incorporating a 3,000 lb thrust Goblin 2 engine. The redesigned and lengthened light alloy fuselage was fitted with forty-degree swept-back wings, complete with Handley Page wing leading edge slats fixed in the open position. To eliminate the need for horizontal tail surfaces, elevons (combined ailerons and elevators) were installed. A swept fin and rudder was mounted on the rear of the nacelle. The absence of an ejection seat was dictated by the lengthy design and modification programme to the basic Vampire fuselage which would have necessitated further delays. Following an RAE warning that during wind tunnel tests the swept-wing design had indicated a tendency to 'dutch roll' [severe rolling and yawing oscillation with a possible loss of control at low speeds], the aircraft was fitted with anti-spin parachutes in cylindrical containers at each wing tip. The first prototype was rolled out on 28 April, seven months after construction had started.

On 5 May 1946 the prototype was taken by road to Woodbridge in Suffolk for its first flight, to take advantage of that airfield's extremely long runway. Six days later Geoffrey de Havilland Jnr achieved a short hop in the aircraft before the wheel brakes overheated, delaying its maiden flight until Wednesday 15 May. Following the flight Geoffrey de Havilland was pleased with the aircraft's handling qualities, especially at low speeds, where he found nothing to confirm the RAE's fears of the DH 108 developing a 'dutch roll'.

The first prototype DH 108, TG283, at Hatfield on 30 May 1946. The swept wings incorporating the fixed, leading edge slats are shown to advantage. (de Havilland)

Between December 1948 and June 1949 the aircraft underwent low-speed trials with the RAE's Aerodynamics Flight. The Flight's commanding officer, Captain Eric 'Winkle' Brown, was critical of the DH 108's approach-to-land qualities, and contradicted Geoffrey de Havilland's earlier report that at speeds below 105 mph the aircraft *would* oscillate and 'dutch roll'.

On 23 August 1946 the second prototype, TG306, was flown for the first time at Hatfield, and made its public debut at the SBAC Display at Radlett in September with an impressive display by Geoffrey de Havilland. The second prototype was designed to assess the high-speed characteristics of the swept-wing and was therefore fitted with Handley Page automatic wing slats which could be locked by the pilot, powered flying controls of a type similar to those of the DH 106, and a wing sweep-back increased to forty-five degrees. A 3,300 lb Goblin 3 engine was installed and the aircraft was soon flying at speeds of up to 650 mph during development testing.

It was at this time that the economics of the tail-less layout and sweep-back wing design for the proposed DH 106 was brought into doubt: the use of elevons limited flap effectiveness and the greater structural weight of a highly swept wing reduced the Atlantic payload of the proposed transport aircraft from 9,200 lb to 5,000 lb. However, the DH 108 was considered an important test bed for high-speed flight research, and in the light of the high Mach numbers obtained during early testing (Mach 0.89 during its fourth flight), it was decided to make an attempt on the World Speed Record, which was currently held by a Gloster Meteor flown by Gp Capt. 'Teddy' Donaldson at 616 mph.

Several preliminary practice runs were made by Geoffrey de Havilland Jnr over the official course at Tangmere. At 17.30 hrs on Friday 27 September 1946, he took off from Hatfield in TG306 for a forty-five minute test flight over

The second prototype DH 108, TG306, being readied for the World Speed Record at Hatfield on 25 September 1946. Two days later it crashed into the Thames estuary, killing Geoffrey de Havilland Jnr. (de Havilland)

the Thames Estuary. It was intended to test the DH 108 by diving from 10,000 ft at a high Mach number to evaluate the aircraft's behaviour: this was to be followed by a high-powered level flight in simulated record attempt conditions. This was to be Geoffrey de Havilland's last scheduled flight before going to Tangmere the following day for a run over the course in a Vampire. He expected to remain at Tangmere until the following Wednesday, when the DH 108 would receive its final polishing at the works in readiness for the attempt on the record.

Half an hour later, reports came through of a jet plane breaking in two after exploding, and falling into the Thames Estuary: both wings had come off and there had been no sign of a parachute. An immediate search was mounted by the police, a life-boat and Air Ministry officials for the wreckage of the DH 108, which was eventually sighted by a Mosquito in shallow water at Egypt Bay, near All-Hallows-on-Sea on the Isle of Grain.

Following the crash of TG306 an investigation was launched to discover the cause of the accident, which had to be based on wind-tunnel results and structural evidence from the wreckage. The engine was cleared of responsibility, and it was established that the aircraft's structure had failed after being subjected to loads far greater than it had been designed or built to withstand. It was determined that as the aircraft approached Mach 0.9 the air had built up in front of it and the normal air flow over the swept-back wings had broken down. The nose of the aircraft was then pitched down in a shock stall and it was believed that the wings folded backwards as the main spar cracked at the roots. Geoffrey de Havilland had died from a violent blow in the back; he was buried next to his brother John, who had been killed whilst flying a Mosquito in August 1943.

Later flight testing with the third prototype by John Derry revealed that pitch damping of the tail-less DH 108 became neutral at Mach 0.870 at high indicated speeds (below 10,000 ft), and was negative at Mach 0.875 – a tiny margin that could disappear in light turbulence. From the data obtained by de Havilland in TG306 during his first seven high-speed flights, it was apparent that on his final flight he reached a speed of 660 mph (Mach 0.88) which resulted in a divergent (undamped) pitch oscillation so severe that structural wing failure occurred in seconds.

In November 1946 Sir Geoffrey de Havilland announced that the company would continue its research work with the DH 108 and the chief test pilot of de Havilland (Engines), John Cunningham, would succeed his son, Geoffrey.

Continued flight trials with a more streamlined and reinforced canopy on Vampire F.1 TG281, together with high-altitude engine tests and the fitment of an elongated and pointed nose on Vampire TG443 between late 1946 and early 1947, had shown that an improved performance could be obtained from the DH 108. Other proposed modifications were the fitment of an elevator power boost, a redesigned cockpit incorporating a lowered pilot's ejection seat, and a 3,750 lb Goblin 4 engine.

It was therefore concluded that a replacement for TG306 should be ordered as soon as possible and on 10 July 1947 Contract 6/ACFT/1067/Cb.7(a) was issued for a third DH 108. Allocated the serial number VW120, the aircraft was built at Hatfield utilizing a Vampire 5 airframe, and first flew on 24 July 1947 with John Cunningham at the controls.

By April 1948, encouraged by the results gained from the third prototype's high-speed research test flying, de Havilland's decided to attempt to raise the FAI Class C.1/1 100 km International Closed-Circuit Speed Record of 564.88 mph, then held by a Supermarine Attacker flown by Mike Lithgow. On the evening of 12 April 1948, de Havilland's experimental test pilot John Derry flew VW120 on the special pentagonal course from Bell Bar near Hatfield, via Puckeridge, Arlesey, Sundon and Redbourne, and set a new record of 605.23 mph.

On 6 September 1948 John Derry became the first pilot in Britain to exceed Mach 1.0,

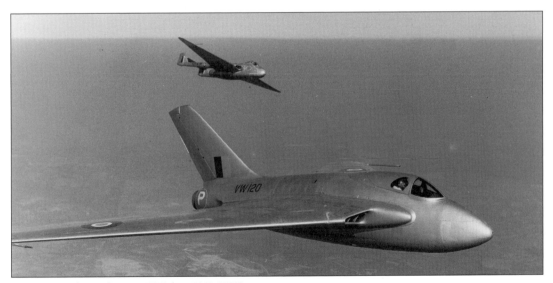

DH 108 VW120 airborne with Vampire TG278 during 1948. (RAFM)

Geoffrey de Havilland Jnr and John Cunningham at Hatfield, 27 July 1946. Behind them is the first Vampire to be exported to Switzerland. (de Havilland)

whilst flying VW120; he repeated this achievement on 1 March 1949 flying the same aircraft. On both flights control was lost during a steep dive from 40,000 ft and recovery accomplished by selecting the wing trailing edge trim flaps. The DH 108 had performed part of an inverted bunt and it was later established that VW120 had decelerated to subsonic speed at around 26,000 ft due to the increased drag at lower altitudes.

With the completion of the swept-wing research trials, the first prototype, TG283, was transferred to the RAE at Farnborough in October 1948 for further test flying. During February and March 1950 TG283 was used to assess low-speed, high-angle-of-attack landings, and was fitted with a long-stroke Sea Vampire undercarriage to avoid damaging the aircraft's jet pipe. Speeds as low as 95 knots were achieved during the tests, although the undercarriage was required to be permanently locked in the down position because the bays had not been modified to accommodate it. On 1 May 1950 TG283 was destroyed when it failed to recover from a spin during stalling tests and crashed close to the village of Hartley Wintney, near Winchfield, Hants, killing the pilot, Sqn Ldr G.E.C. 'Jumbo' Genders AFC DFM, commanding officer of the RAE's Aerodynamics Flight.

The third prototype, VW120, continued with the company trials until 28 June 1949, when it was issued to the RAE to investigate high-speed longitudinal stability. This aircraft was lost in a flying accident on 15 February 1950 when the pilot, Sqn Ldr J.S.R. Muller-Rowland DSO DFC, was presumed to have suffered an oxygen failure and the aircraft dived into the ground at Little Brickhill, near Fenny Stratford, Bucks.

VAMPIRE F.MK.3

The major disadvantages of the early jets undoubtedly lay in their limited range and combat endurance. The Vampire was no exception: the F.Mk.1's three main fuel tanks, with their total fuel capacity of 202 gallons, restricted the aircraft's maximum endurance (assuming a climb to a medium altitude of 25,000 ft) to a mere forty-five minutes. When fitted with two 100 gallon Mosquito-type slipper tanks, the Vampire's maximum endurance was increased to about two hours, again assuming a climb to 20–30,000 ft. The total usable fuel of the Vampire's system (with drop tanks) was 395 gallons, and the figures given above are all based on a 30 gallon reserve; if operating at sea-level, the combat endurance of the aircraft would be reduced to less than half of these figures. To increase this limited endurance the first major production version of the Vampire was developed – the F.Mk.3.

The origins of the Vampire F.Mk.3 go back to June 1945 when an F.Mk.1, TG275, was delivered to Hatfield for installation trials of Mod. No. 15, a long-range wing which effectively increased the aircraft's internal fuel tank capacity to 330 gallons. The fuselage tank capacity of 96 gallons and inner wing tankage of 106 gallons were supplemented by the addition of outer wing tanks, with a total capacity of 128 gallons, divided between three tanks in each wing. At the same time the metal centre-section tanks were changed to Marston bag-tanks and the three wing tanks were similarly constructed. All the tanks were interconnected, feeding into the main fuselage tank by gravity, and were filled through a common fuelling point. A further modification included sinking the drop-tank release gear into the under-surface of the mainplane and the release being manually operated.

Experiments with various types of drop tanks mounted under the wings of TG275 led de Havilland's to opt for two cylindrical, pylon-mounted 100 gallon or 200 gallon tanks; trials showed clearly that regardless of their size or position, the drop tanks adversely affected the longitudinal stability of the aircraft. To overcome this problem de Havilland's radically altered the tail structure by increasing the tailplane chord by 4½ in to 46½ in, reduced the chord of the elevator by 1½ in to 15½ in, and fitted 'acorns' to the fin and tail junction. Further tests showed that the vertical position of the tailplane did not affect the aircraft's compressibility characteristics, so to simplify production the tailplane was lowered by 13 in to a position where it was still clear of the jet efflux. For structural and aerodynamic reasons, the vertical tail surfaces were also changed to the more familiar rounded de Havilland shape, typical of so many of the Vampire's predecessors, particularly Moths, Rapides and Mosquitos.

Lateral buffeting from the tank was experienced in flight as well, and to strengthen the tank supports de Havilland's lengthened the attachment fairings. The company also originally tapped a pressure-line from the engine to force the drop-tank fuel into the main fuel system. The pressure, however, started to bulge the wing-tank doors, deforming the wing section, and so a system was developed to feed the drop-tank fuel into the main tank through a fuel transfer valve.

De Havilland's also decided to install a 3,100 lb thrust Goblin 2 in their new variant,

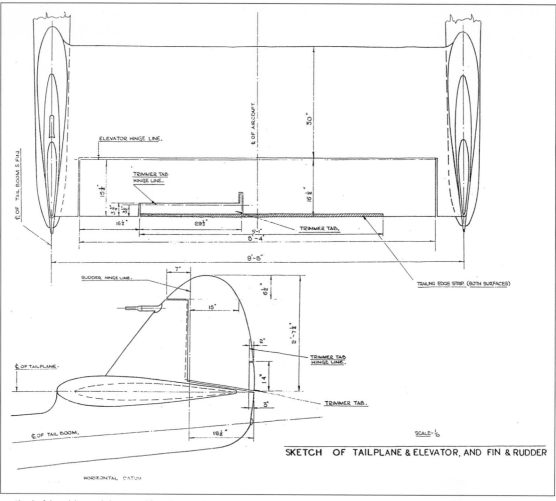

Sketch of the tailplane and elevator, and fin and rudder of the Vampire F.3 showing the 'acorns' fitted to the fin and tail junction. (A&AEE)

and in this form the gross weight of the aircraft was increased from the 8,578 lb of the Mk.1 to 12,170 lb. On 9 March 1946 the version was allocated the new mark number, Vampire F.Mk.3.

TG275 was first flown at Hatfield on 4 November 1946 as the prototype F.Mk.3 and was sent to the A&AEE for handling trials in April 1947 to clear the type for Service use and to cover the aircraft's range at various cruising heights, both with and without the 100 gallon drop tanks. (As the prototype was not pressurized, a production aircraft, VF343,

fitted with a pressure cabin, was later sent to Boscombe Down for testing at higher altitudes.) The trials were conducted between August 1947 and February 1948, and concluded that without drop tanks, the F.Mk.3 had marginal longitudinal stability at altitude together with a general lack of control crispness, and was longitudinally unstable at high indicated airspeeds. The report was unimpressed with the general flying qualities of the aircraft with the 100 gallon drop tanks fitted and considered that it did not reach a standard acceptable for Service use.

Altitude (ft)	Sea-level	10,000	20,000	30,000	35,000
Range clean (n.mls)	275	335	430	570	610
Airborne time (hrs/mins)	1.13	1.19	1.35	2.00	2.00
Range with drop tanks (n.mls)	480	550	680	930	1,000
Airborne time (hrs/mins)	2.06	2.09	2.30	3.16	3.20

Patrol endurance – time at altitude. 170 kts IAS:

Clean (hrs/mins)	1.13	1.34	1.32	1.40	1.30
Drop tanks (hrs/mins)	2.37	2.30	2.32	2.50	2.40

Note: these were all no-wind figures, with best climb and descent techniques, and the optimum IAS varied from 225 knots at sea-level to 175 knots at 30–35,000 ft, giving a TAS of 225–350 knots.

Performance figures gathered during the trials soon showed that the Vampire F.Mk.3's extra fuel capacity greatly increased the aircraft's range (see table above).

One solution to the Vampire's fore-and-aft stability shortcomings was to install extra nose ballast, and in June 1948 tests to increase SF/g were made with VF343 at the A&AEE with a heavier inertia weight fitted to the end of the tranverse bar forward of the control column mounting tube near the floor of the cockpit. This weight gave some artificial 'feel' when pulling positive 'g' – the harder one pulled, the greater the forward force exerted on the control column by the weight, thereby having the effect of increasing the stick force per 'g'. At the conclusion of these tests it was determined that an inertia weight which resulted in a moment of +20 lb/ft at the elevator hinge resolved one of the aircraft's handling problems.

The A&AEE's criticism of the aircraft's poor flying qualities at altitude was that control 'touchiness' made it difficult to fly accurately and would make range flying very tiring. With a tendency to spin off the stall when the flaps and undercarriage were down, the type was also considered potentially dangerous to fly in cloud or at night where an inexperienced pilot might lose control.

However, the F.Mk.3 was recommended to the RAF with the proviso that pilots be warned of these features and that the modifications to improve longitudinal stability be incorporated as soon as possible.

The RAF was keen to make use of the Vampire F.Mk.3's increased range and endurance as soon as possible, so the second contract for 120 F.Mk.1s with English Electric at Preston (6/ACFT/5421/C.20(a)) was modified to allow the fifty-fifth aircraft on the production line, VF315, to be built as the first F.Mk.3. On 22 April 1947 deliveries commenced when VF317 was dispatched to de Havilland's as a trials aircraft, investigating vibration at altitude. Further deliveries continued on 1 May 1947, when VF315 and VF321 were flown to Hatfield, the latter being converted as the prototype of the Sea Vampire F.Mk.20. The first 'true' RAF examples were released on 9 May 1947. Further orders were received between May 1945 and April 1947 for 138 aircraft to be built at Preston, and this was supplemented in May 1946 by an order from the Canadian Government for eighty-five F.Mk.3s for the RCAF.

The Odiham Wing began exchanging its Vampire F.Mk.1s for the F.Mk.3 in April 1948 when 54 Squadron received its first two

Photographed soon after delivery to the RAF Handling Squadron at Manby in March 1948 for the compilation of the Pilot's Notes. Vampire F.3 VT855 was written off the following year during 73 Squadron's goodwill tour of Italy. (RAF)

aircraft (followed by 72 Squadron in June and 247 Squadron in November 1948).

At the same time as the Odiham Wing began to convert to Vampire F.3s, rumours began to circulate that the USAF was planning the first crossing of the Atlantic by jet aircraft. The Air Ministry, eager to show off the long-range capabilities of the new Vampire, decided to try to beat the Americans in their attempt, and 54 Squadron was selected to represent the RAF for the crossing.

Primarily devised as a good-will mission, the long-distance flight by six of the squadron's aircraft, together with their support aircraft and crews, was the product of meticulous planning and dedicated training. With a total fuel capacity of 530 gallons (including the two 100 gallon wing tanks), early trials showed that the Vampire F.Mk.3's maximum still-air range would not permit a direct crossing from Stornoway to Goose Bay (a distance of over two thousand miles). However, staging via Iceland and Greenland was feasible provided that a maximum headwind of 50 knots was not met. (Note: the Vampires' range was less

than normal because of the need to carry out a compromise climb to suit the lower climb performance of the escorting Mosquitos. As the Vampires were not fitted with Machmeters, accurate cruise climbing could not be adopted: the aircraft climbed to 25,000 ft and then resumed the climb to 30,000 ft after the drop tanks had emptied.) Staging via Iceland and Greenland meant that the longest leg was between Bluie West 1 and Goose Bay – a distance of about 780 miles; accurate navigation, weather forecasting and reliable communications were essential, and all three were provided by three Mosquitos which accompanied the crossing.

Leaving Odiham on 1 July 1948 the six Vampires, led by Sqn Ldr R.W. Oxspring DFC, were delayed at Stornoway because of strong headwinds, but finally arrived at Goose Bay on 14 July. Following a display of formation aerobatics by three of the aircraft at Trenton (Ontario), Montreal and Toronto, the squadron moved on to Andrews Field, Washington, on 25 July for further demonstrations. From Washington they flew

Vampire F.3 VF/335 at Hatfield soon after delivery, June 1947. It later served with 54, 604 and 602 Squadrons, before being relegated to instructional airframe status in September 1953. (Derek Dempster)

Vampire F.3s of 54 Squadron departing from Odiham on 1 July 1948 for the first ever jet crossing of the Atlantic. (via Mike Hooks)

to the headquarters of the US 9th Tactical Air Force at Greenville, Carolina, for formation displays and tactical exercises, and then on to Langley Field, Norfolk, Virginia. The Vampires finally flew to Mitchell Field, New York, on 30 July to participate in the International Air Exposition at Idlewild Airport. Returning to Trenton on 10 August, they arrived back at Odiham on 26 August.

The trans-Atlantic flight and the tour of Canada and the USA by 54 Squadron proved to be of significant importance in confirming that jet aircraft, in spite of their limited endurance, were no longer restricted in their Fighter Command duties. Thus it was established that a self-contained unit, comprising relatively short-range jet aircraft, could move over long distances at short notice. Valuable information about high-altitude Atlantic weather conditions was also of extreme importance to military and civilian aircraft designers in their plans for regular trans-Atlantic flights.

Members of the Trans-Atlantic Force, Odiham, June 1948. Left to right: Flt Lt 'Jeep' Heale, Flt Lt 'Ricky' Wright, Flt Lt Frank Woolley, Sqn Ldr 'Buck' Courtney, Sqn Ldr Bobby Oxspring, Wg Cdr Macdonald (Force Commander), Sqn Ldr Mickey Martin (Mosquito Leader), Pl Bill Wood, Pl 'Taff' Evans, Pll Roy Skinner. (Sqn Ldr Roy Skinner)

Before the arrival of 54 Squadron a series of unfortunate accidents to the Vampires of the Canadian auxiliary squadrons had seriously undermined the Service and civilian faith in the aircraft; the squadron's visit did much to restore the Canadians' confidence and establish the Vampire as a safe and reliable fighter aircraft. Besides the demonstration flights and ground attack exercises, the squadron's Vampires had also flown practice interception sorties against American F-51 and F-80 fighters; one American F-80 pilot, after flying a Vampire, reported the aircraft to be 'The best God-damn piece of machinery I have ever flown!'

The squadron had also managed to beat the Americans in crossing the Atlantic: on 21 July 1948 sixteen F-80A Shooting Stars from the 56th Fighter Group, led by Lt. Col. David Schilling, became the first US jet aircraft to make the crossing from west to east when they arrived at Odiham from Selfridge AFB, Michigan.

Five auxiliary squadrons were also equipped with F.Mk.3s as an interim step in their transition from Spitfires to Vampire FB.Mk.5s or Meteors. First to receive F.Mk.3s were 601 (County of London) Squadron and 604 (County of Middlesex) Squadron at North Weald in November 1949. They were followed by 608 (North Riding) Squadron at Thornaby in December 1949, 614 (County of Glamorgan) Squadron at Llandow in July 1950, and 602 (City of Glasgow) Squadron at Abbotsinch in August 1953.

In late 1947 a joint RAF and de Havilland working party was set up to examine the feasibility of operating jet fighters in the tropics and to assess the effects of extreme temperatures on the Vampire's wooden airframe and cockpit ventilation. The unit responsible for these trials, the Vampire Trials Unit, was also

Chief of the Air Defence Command Lt Gen George E. Stratemayer welcomes the pilots of 54 Squadron at Mitchell Field, New York, on 31 July 1948. The squadron put on an aerobatic display as part of the opening ceremony of NY International Airport (Idlewild). (Air Comm. E.W. Wright)

A flight of Vampire F.3s from 604 (County of Middlesex) Squadron, North Weald, during November 1950. They are VV194 (Tommy Turnbull), VF329 (Derek Dempster) and VT823 (Ian Ponsford). (Derek Dempster)

tasked with evaluating the aircraft's armament. The tactical trials would also include the Vampire's general suitability for use in the Far East on fighter/ground attack duties. The Unit's advance party arrived in Tengah, Singapore, on 15 December 1947 and were followed by two

Vampire F.3s, VG702 and VG703, which arrived aboard SS *Tantalus* on 16 January 1948. Both aircraft were reassembled and VG702 was air tested in preparation for storage at Seletar, where it was to remain as a static weathering airframe for twelve months under the supervision of personnel from No. 390 MU. On 17 February VG703 was also air tested and flown to Tengah, where the tropical trials were to be carried out.

Commanding the Vampire Trials Unit at Tengah was Flt Lt. John Wilson, who arrived in February 1948 to carry out the tactical trials phase before handing over to Flt Lt. George 'Kiwi' Francis, who would not only be responsible for the tropical trials, but also would verify route staging and act as a 'flying guinea-pig' for the RAE's Aeromedical Branch. The Unit's support team comprised six SNCOs and the de Havilland Field Service Engineer, Mr Lance Westlake.

Demonstration flights were organized for the benefit of the civilian and military residents of Singapore, many of whom had

never seen a jet aircraft before. A local newspaper, *The Free Press*, was impressed with the Vampire's displays and it headlined one of its editions with 'Display Of Bloodsucking Devil Plane'.

On 28 April 1948, accompanied by a Dakota from 52 Squadron carrying the ground crew and essential spares, John Wilson and 'Kiwi' Francis departed for the Malay States with VG703 on the first of several planned demonstration tours. The primary reason for the tour was to gather experience of operating from airfields of varying size and surfaces, and to assess the effect of local conditions on take-off performance and serviceability. The great interest the jets generated and the excitement of the crowds at Taiping, Ipoh, Kuala Lumpur and Butterworth were an added bonus for the RAF

Personnel of the Vampire Trials Unit, Singapore, June 1948. Back row, left to right: Sgts Smith (Engines), Willson (Electrics), Crabbe and Tucker; front row: FSgt Harris (I/c ASDP), Mr L. Westlake (de Havilland rep.), Flt Lt John Wilson, Flt Lt 'Kiwi' Francis, FSgt Ratcliffe (Armament). (John Wilson)

One of the Vampire Trials Unit's two F.3s, VG703 is seen at Singapore in May 1948 during the demonstration tour of the Malay States. ('Kiwi' Francis)

and Great Britain. The Malayan tour finished at George Town on 10 May and the unit returned to Butterworth, having completed a trouble-free tour. John Wilson returned to the UK in June 1948, leaving 'Kiwi' Francis to continue with trials which involved humidity and cockpit temperature testing (at both high and low altitudes), air firing and night flying.

A four week tour of French Indo-China got under way on 21 October when 'Kiwi' Francis and his attendant Dakota left for Saigon. A month later (on 9 December) the team left Singapore for Bangkok for further demonstrations to representatives of the Thai Government and air force.

The Hong Kong and Pacific Tour commenced on 11 January 1949 – a trip that would cause 'Kiwi' Francis more than a little concern. An incorrect weather report that promised clear conditions for the flight to Hong Kong left the Vampire desperately short of fuel when 'Kiwi' was unable to land at Hong Kong, which was covered in thick cloud. He climbed the Vampire away from the airfield, but after a few minutes flying the engine ran down as the fuel tanks emptied. Letting down through the cloud layer, 'Kiwi' was surprised to

see a small sandy beach in front of him. After a quick decision that a forced landing might be possible, he glided the Vampire down for a successful 'dead-stick' landing.

The forced landing had been made on a strip of sand on Bias Bay in the South China Sea, a traditional haunt of Chinese pirates, and in particular that of the infamous Madam Wong, alias Chung Lo-Yu. Bias Bay was clearly an unhealthy spot in which to forceland a potentially valuable prize. However, Hong Kong ATC was quick to inform a patrolling Sunderland flying-boat from 88 Squadron which located the stranded Vampire, whose position was passed to the cruiser HMS Belfast. As the cruiser proceeded at full speed to the area, the Sunderland alighted in Bias Bay and moored offshore to provide protection against the Chinese pirates who were already gathering in some strength.

It was decided that it would be impossible to refuel in situ, and too risky to attempt a take-off from the soft sandy beach. The only alternative was to hoist the aircraft aboard HMS Belfast from a ramp landing craft supplied by the RASC; this was achieved with some difficulty the following day. Arriving back at Hong Kong,

SINGAPORE
MALAYA
SIAM
FRENCH-INDO CHINA
HONG-KONG
MANILA
BORNEO
BURMA
INDIA
PAKISTAN
BALUCHISTAN

SAUDI ARABIA
ADEN
KAMARAN
SUDAN
EGYPT
CYPRUS
TRIPOLITANIA
MALTA
FRANCE
U.K.

FLt Lt 'Kiwi' Francis handing over VG703 to de Havilland's Chief Engineer, Dave Evans, at the completion of tropical trials, Hatfield, October 1949. ('Kiwi' Francis)

the Vampire was overhauled and within forty-eight hours was flying again – a tribute to the teamwork and cooperation from all the Services involved in the rescue.

The Pacific demonstration tour resumed on 25 February with the 650 mile leg to the USAF base at Clark Field in the Philippines. During the following days, the Vampire was put through its paces at Clark Field, Lipa and Florida Blanca before departing to Borneo on 2 March for the second part of the tour. Jesselton, the Seria oilfields and Labuan were the last engagements before 'Kiwi' moved on to the Middle East.

Francis flew the Vampire to the Tropical Experimental Establishment at Khartoum on 13 March, the 6,100 mile trip being one of the longest staging flights made by a jet aircraft. The twelve day journey covered the following route: Rangoon, Calcutta, Delhi, Karachi, Jiwani, Sallalah, Aden, Kamoran Island and Khartoum, at an average ground speed of 325 mph.

On 7 October 'Kiwi' Francis flew VG703 back to the UK. The return trip lasted eight days and included en route stops at El Adem, Malta, Sardinia, Istres and Manston, before the Vampire was officially handed over to de Havilland's Chief Service Engineer, Dave Evans, at Hatfield on 14 October.

The work of the Vampire Trials Unit was considered immensely valuable, not only to the RAF but also to other air forces who were later to operate Vampires in all latitudes from the Equator to the Arctic Circle. Although many minor recommendations were made by the pilots following the trials, the general conclusion was that the Vampire F.Mk.3 should prove very suitable for operations in the Far East as a fighter/ground attack aircraft, with alternative roles as a fighter-reconnaissance or interceptor fighter. The trials also resulted in many changes in operational procedures and equipment, including development of a new lightweight suit, sun goggles and visors, and revised maps for aircrew, together with

Vampire F.3 VV196 of 32 Squadron off the Cyprus coast near Kyrenia. (Colin Sloan)

improved methods of cockpit cooling.

At the conclusion of the trials, both Vampires VG702 and VG703 were subjected to rigorous tests and examinations: VG702 was later cut up into sections to determine whether the plywood skin of the fuselage had parted from the balsa core and whether the wooden joints had deteriorated in the humidity or extremes of temperature. No serious problems were found and the aircraft were cleared for use in the Middle and Far East theatres of operations. Both aircraft were eventually struck off charge in June 1950.

In July 1948 32 Squadron at Nicosia and 73 Squadron at Ta Kali both received the F.Mk.3 to replace their Spitfires and thereby became the first operational jet fighter squadrons outside Europe. Soon after becoming operational, Sqn Ldr Bobby Oxspring assumed command of 73 Squadron and in September 1949 had the dubious honour of leading a squadron demonstration visit to Italy, when an entire formation of Vampires was lost near Milan. The squadron had been invited as guests of the Italian Air Force and Milan Aero

Club to appear in a series of air shows as part of a good-will tour, aimed at promoting the Vampire. Five pilots were selected to participate in the tour: Sqn Ldr Bobby Oxspring, Flt Lt. Frank Sumner, Fg Off. Derrick Grubb, PII Pete Carr and PII Geoff Parker. Parker was also to be the team's solo aerobatic pilot.

On 22 September the formation set off for Rome/Ciampino. After an overnight stay, the team prepared to fly on to Malpensa, 20 miles to the west of Milan, which they were to use as a base because of the airfield's extended runway. Flt Lt. Geoff Parker (retd) takes up the story:

The morning of the 23rd September dawned bright and clear. Bobby Oxspring's briefing informed us that we were to fly on to Malpensa at 25,000 feet, and he assured us that the weather forecast would be fine all the way, with the possibility of scattered cloud near the Alps. He also said that, if we had plenty of fuel in reserve, we would make a detour and fly over Milan to let them know we had arrived.

VF345 was loaned to de Havilland's in 1948 for demonstration flights to representatives of the Australian and Argentine governments. Badly damaged during 73 Squadron's disastrous goodwill tour of Italy in September 1949, it was later issued to the Italian Air Force as MM6022. (De Havilland)

We took off from Rome at 10.00 hours and set course, with Bobby Oxspring leading. Shortly afterwards, Bobby's radio failed – which proved to be the decisive factor in the disaster which was soon to follow.

About 40 miles from Milan, Bobby signalled us in to close formation; our course and timing was absolutely precise. However, after flying over Milan the problems rapidly began to increase; the sky was then half covered in cloud, with visibility down to about a mile because of the haze. Bobby turned and headed for Malpensa, but couldn't find it. He was map reading and had obviously got the wrong course. So we turned back for Milan.

Three further attempts to find the airfield failed, and we finally headed eastwards in search of the Italian bomber base at Brescia. We had been airborne for just over two hours and our fuel was now very low – which meant five minutes flying time – added to which the last 35 gallons in a

Vampire may be unobtainable, but we still managed to keep together in formation.

Attempts to contact Milan airport on the emergency frequency proved ineffectual, and with no airfield in sight, their position had become perilous. Suddenly, the rest of the formation noticed that Bobby Oxspring was making an approach to a small field. Geoff Parker continues the story:

We were at 1,000 feet, when Bobby (in VF345) pulled out of formation and went down into this little field some 400 yards long, underneath some power cables which were about 50 feet high. Each aircraft took it in turn to repeat his incredible landing, and as Bobby was climbing out of his cockpit, so the second Vampire (VT809), flown by Frank Sumner, struck some trees at the end of his landing run. Derrick Grubb (in VT855) went in next, and we suddenly saw him slew to the left after hitting an unseen ditch along the centre of the field.

Now it was my turn. There were three aircraft in the field and there wasn't room for me, so I went off to find one of my own. The first one I saw was a long narrow one, about 600 yards long with some poplar trees at one end. I planned to side-slip them, but then saw that it wouldn't be possible. I hit the throttle and lifted my Vampire (VT813) at a crazy angle over the roof of a bungalow, and then saw another field. Keeping my undercarriage retracted, I motored in very gingerly and dropped it in just over the hedge. The Vampire started sliding to the right, throwing up clods of earth, before eventually stopping with one wingtip in a hedge. It was impossible to cut the engine because the heavy landing had buckled the HP cock linkage.

This only left Pete Carr (in VV204), and his landing proved to be the most dramatic of all. Having watched with great interest the other four aircraft come to rest in various states of disrepair, the odds on his own survival appeared to be shortening rapidly and it seemed prudent to attempt a landing alongside the first three aircraft so that help might be at hand if needed. Pete Carr continues:

I approached slowly with my wheels up for the shortest possible landing, but just before the roundout I noticed to my dismay that two or three people were running from the hedge on the left across my intended landing path. Full power was immediately applied for the overshoot, but by then the aircraft was too low and actually slid on its belly some distance before climbing away. When I tried to throttle back, however, I found that it had jammed in the fully open position, caused apparently by the fuel mechanism on the underside of the engine being damaged when the aircraft hit the ground.

It was difficult to give calm consideration

to finding a larger and more suitable field for an engine-off landing whilst rushing around at low level, with full power and a dangerously low fuel state. A reasonable field some 600 yards long did appear, however, but despite my shutting down the engine at what appeared to be the appropriate moment on the approach, plus use of speed brakes, flaps and undercarriage, I was obviously too conscious of the danger of overshooting with a dead engine because I crossed the threshold too fast, touching down some 300 yards past the intended touchdown point.

From then onwards the ride was very fast and completely uncontrolled through the hedge at the far end, then a small forest and finally a garden, before coming to rest in a stream alongside a lone farmhouse.

Apart from the dents from several tree trunks on the leading edges of the wings, the Vampire was in one piece. Amazingly, Pete Carr was uninjured and was able to walk away with only damaged pride, and as soon as the pilots had rested at a local farmhouse they were transported to a hotel. With a prodigious display of flying skill and some good fortune, all five pilots had achieved miraculous escapes from the jaws of disaster. The aircraft fared less well: both VT809 and VV204 were damaged beyond repair after striking trees at the end of their landing run; VT855 lost its undercarriage when it struck a furrow as it careered across the field, and VT813 was seriously damaged during its belly landing.

Bobby Oxspring's Vampire had landed with relatively little damage, and was considered worth repairing by a team from No. 137 MU at Safi. On 17 October Fg Off. Derek Hampton was sent from Malta to bring the Vampire back, but he crashed during take-off at Bergamo, extensively damaging it; the Italians thought differently, for after repair by the AMI it

Pete Carr's Vampire VV204 after crashlanding during 73 Squadron's goodwill tour of Italy, September 1949. He was fortunate to escape uninjured. (Sqn Ldr Pete Carr)

was issued to No. 1 RTA at Brenso as MM6022.

The AOC, Malta, AVM Charles Steele, decided to continue with the planned demonstration tour by the squadron, and ordered four more Vampires to be flown to Rome on 24 September. As one of the aircraft (VT807) touched down at Ciampino, it started to drift to port in a strong cross-wind and collided with a pedestal-type runway light. The pilot, Fg Off. Graham Moreau, was unhurt, but the accident only added to the squadron's misfortunes. The planned show at the Turin Air Fair on 24 September had now been abandoned, but the following day the squadron flew on to Malpensa to demonstrate before 80,000 spectators at the Milan Show. The team returned to Ta Kali on 29 September.

Despite all the misadventures encountered by the squadron's Vampires during the tour, the Italian Government and air force officials appeared impressed with the structural qualities of the aircraft and the nature of the pilots' escape from disaster. It was enough to persuade them to proceed with the contract,

and in October 1949 the Italian Government placed an initial contract for eighty aircraft to be built by FIAT.

For the next nine months, 73 Squadron continued to fly Vampire F.Mk.3s on a variety of exercises, including fighter affiliation against the Bearcats from the US aircraft carriers visiting the Mediterranean. By June 1950 both 32 and 73 Squadrons had been re-equipped with Vampire FB.5s.

Between April 1948 and March 1954, seven regular, six auxiliary, and four second-line RAF units flew the Vampire F.Mk.3. A total of 224 aircraft were produced by English Electric, including 86 for Canada, 10 for Norway, 6 for the Royal Navy, 3 for India and 1 for Sweden. The last F.Mk.3, VV214, was delivered to the RAF in May 1949.

One example of the F.Mk.3, VT812, is preserved at the RAF Museum, Hendon, in the markings of 601 (County of London) Squadron, Royal Auxiliary Air Force, then based at North Weald. Built at Preston, the aircraft joined 32 Squadron in December 1948 and was used as the 'personal' aircraft

A Vampire F.3 of 54 Squadron is joined by aircraft of 601 and 604 Squadrons RAuxAF during the 1950 RAF Display at Farnborough. Together with a formation of Spitfires, the twelve Vampires effectively demonstrated air drill to a large crowd. (de Havilland via Daryl Cott)

Vampire F.3 VT812 is currently preserved in its former markings of 601 (County of London) Squadron at the RAF Museum, Hendon. It is depicted here with the RAF Review, Abingdon, in June 1968 while on the strength of the Colerne Collection. (via P.R. Keating)

of Fg Off. Henry Litherland until it was returned to the UK in July 1950. Following service with 614, 601 and 602 Squadrons of the RAuxAF, the aircraft was retired to No. 48 MU at Hawarden and transferred to non-effective stock on 25 October 1954. In May 1955 VT812 became an instructional airframe and was allocated the maintenance serial 7200M. From June 1964 until August 1975 the aircraft was held by the now-defunct Colerne Collection, and after temporary storage at Shawbury and Cosford, it was presented to the RAF Museum as a permanent exhibit in October 1978.

VAMPIRE FB.5

Following the RAF's decision to adopt the Gloster Meteor as its standard interceptor fighter, de Havilland's realized that, because of the Vampire's excellent performance and load-carrying capabilities, the aircraft could easily be adapted for service as a low-level ground attack fighter. The Vampire had been conceived during the war as a high-altitude fighter and low wing loading had been chosen to ensure manoeuvrability at altitudes above 30,000 ft. A ground attack fighter version of the Vampire would modify this parameter so that the aircraft could be used more effectively at low altitudes, a factor which was seen as important during the closing stages of the war.

Official interest in a ground attack version was first shown in December 1946 when the Air Ministry issued a report in response to a de Havilland proposal for such a type. The report concluded: 'Although it [the Vampire] may not meet all our requirements as Ground Attack type, it is a useful step in the transition to the use of jet aircraft in the role.' Based on this report, the Air Ministry simultaneously issued Air Staff Requirement No. OR/237, which called for a ground attack version of the Vampire F.Mk.IV to replace the RAF's Hawker Tempest single-seat fighter/bomber. The requirement stated that the ground attack Vampire should be suitable for operations in all parts of the world, with the minimum of ground facilities and from hastily prepared runways, using cannon and/or rocket projectiles (RPs) in the dive and low-level bombing roles.

When carrying a full operational load, the cruising speed and range at 5,000 ft was to be not less than 250 knots and 300 nautical miles respectively. An operating altitude of between sea-level and 20,000 ft was called for, while the service ceiling was to be not less than 40,000 ft. The aircraft must also be a steady gun platform, and should be capable – after releasing its bombs or rockets – of fighting on equal terms with enemy fighters.

The Vampire's standard installation of four 150 rpg 20 mm cannon with fifteen seconds of fire was considered to be satisfactory, but the aircraft would also be required to carry two wing-mounted 1,000 lb bombs, or two 500 lb bombs plus eight 60 lb RPs. Although pilot and ammunition protection was considered adequate, additional armour plate would be required for the engine for protection from ground fire. The fitment of an ejector seat was also necessary.

By January 1947 the MoS was considering the use of a 5,000 lb s.t. Rolls-Royce Nene engine to power the ground attack Vampire, instead of the Goblin 3 which was still under development. However, the Director of Operational Requirements (DOR) pointed out that the Nene engine was some 300 lb heavier than the Goblin, which would result in the aircraft's centre of gravity being further aft; to locate the centre of gravity at its original position more nose ballast would be required to ensure lower pitch stability. In the end the 3,000 lb s.t. Goblin 2 engine was eventually chosen for the ground attack Vampire in view of the protracted development of the Nene.

At the same time the Director of Operational Research and Development suggested modifications to the basic Vampire airframe to make it more suitable for ground attack and low-level roles and to accord with Sea Vampire requirements; these modifications included additional protection for the engine against small shell splinters from beneath.

The main design modifications to the ground attack version of the Vampire concerned the wing structure. Each wing would be strengthened by the doubling of certain stringers, a thicker top-wing skin and rewiring to provide the fitment of removable rocket rails, bomb gear and fairings; each wing tip would be reduced by 1 ft to give a squared-off appearance and improve low-altitude manoeuvrability. A strengthened longer-stroke main undercarriage would be required to cope with the increased all-up weight of the aircraft. Other modifications included extra supports for the main fuel tank and a Class 1 protective treatment consisting of anodized aluminium castings; the Alclad sheet used in the airframe was to be pickled; internal surfaces were to be painted; stainless steel bolts were to be used through wood; magnesium parts were to be isolated from wood by zinc shims; steel fittings were to be cadmium-plated and painted and all zinc-plated parts were to be 'passivated'.

The Director of Aircraft Research and Design was eager to recommend the Vampire IV (fitted with the Nene engine) for Service use, and estimated that deliveries to the RAF would commence in July 1947; considerable interest for such a variant was received from the RCAF, who envisaged the conversion of a number of Vampire 1 airframes at their Toronto plant. The project was subsequently dropped when the cost of the structural alterations (i.e., new wings, tail-booms, flying controls, and so on) was presented to the Canadian Government.

The Vampire F.Mk.IV ground attack fighter was dogged by development problems: an initial batch of thirty-eight aircraft to be built at Preston was cancelled, and in early 1947, due to lack of interest on the part of the RAF and that of the French, who were to build the version under the designation Mk.51, the project was abandoned. But even though the F.Mk.IV project had been dropped, the RAF's requirement for a ground attack fighter to replace its Hawker Tempests still existed. As much of the design and development work had already been carried out, both the DARD and RAF concluded that the existing Vampire F.3 airframe could be adapted for ground attack duties, and in April 1947, following positive discussions with de Havilland's, the DOR issued Specification F.3/47, 'A Ground Attack Version of the Vampire Mk.III'.

The specification required the inclusion of many of the modifications which had been incorporated into the longer-range Vampire F.3: Mod. No. 15 – increased built-in fuel tankage; Mod. No. 184 – provision for two 100 gallon drop tanks; Mod. No. 276 – new tailplane; and Mod. No. 362 – larger elevator trim tabs. The specification also called for the aircraft to be capable of dive and low-level bombing with cannon and/or rocket projectiles, and insisted upon the embodiment of a system of pilot ejection. Perhaps surprisingly, it still required the aircraft to be powered by the Goblin 3 engine.

In May 1947 the MoS was approached by de Havilland's for a new mark number for the proposed ground attack (GA) Vampire. As the designation for the Nene-powered Vampire IV variant had already been allocated, the MoS suggested the logical follow-on of Vampire GA.Mk.V – this was subsequently changed to FB.Mk.5 because of the aircraft's intended dual role as a ground attack/interceptor fighter.

The requirement for an ejector seat was soon to cause many problems for the design team at de Havilland's. A preliminary examination into the fitting of either a Martin Baker or Malcolm seat had been undertaken by de Havilland's in August 1946, but as the cockpit was only 22 in wide an ejector seat could not be installed without considerable alterations to the cockpit and airframe structure. Between April and October 1947 a mock-up of a redesigned metal fuselage was

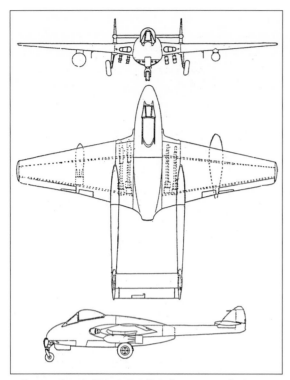

Three-view drawing of Vampire FB.5/FB.6, showing position of underwing stores options. (de Havilland)

assessed on a standard Vampire Mk.1, TG338, at Hatfield. A memo from de Havilland's to the Air Ministry in April 1947 suggested that if the aircraft was eventually fitted with an ejector seat, pilots would have to be trained to keep their elbows in!

The requirement to fit ejector seats in the Vampire FB.5 was subsequently abandoned. However, the design experience was not wasted and in January 1950 the fuselage of Vampire Mk.1 VF306 was sent to Martin Baker's at Denham for the trial fitting of their ejector seat. In September of the same year, VF306 was transferred to Hatfield as a design mock-up and joined FB.5 VZ835 which had been allocated to confirm that the cockpit arrangements were operationally suitable for the de Havilland Venom fighter/bomber. Martin Baker ejection seats were later installed in RAF Venoms in 1954 and in Vampire FB.6s

of the Swiss Air Force during a modification programme in 1960, which also included the fitting of new single-skin canopies.

In July 1947 all design work on the Vampire FB.5 at de Havilland's was suspended for six months because of other commitments and delays due to Geoffrey de Havilland's tragic death in the DH 108, and was not started again until January 1948 when work recommenced on converting a F.Mk.3 airframe, VT818, to the FB.5 prototype. VT818 had been delivered to Hatfield on 22 December 1947 for conversion to the prototype Vampire FB.5 (at a cost estimated at £14,000). The aircraft made its first flight on 23 June 1948, and was retained by the manufacturers for the next three months for bomb installation and handling trials.

Between September and December 1948 VT818 was loaned to the A&AEE for investigation into the behaviour of the aircraft in incipient spins at varying heights between 15–30,000 ft. Although the spin characteristics were considered satisfactory and the normal recovery action was effective from a half to three turns, pilots were warned that, as in all fighter aircraft, practice spins should not be made. Following the completion of company trials in March 1949, VT818 was restored to its original F.Mk.3 configuration.

Production of the Vampire FB.5 started when Contract No. 6/ACFT/1053/CB.7(a), which originally covered forty-six F.Mk.3s at Preston, was amended to allow the last eighteen aircraft (VV215–VV232) to emerge as FB.5s. On 24 May 1948 FB.5 VV215 made its first flight, lasting ten minutes, and was delivered to 787 Squadron at West Raynham on brief loan the same day. The second production aircraft, VV216, which was ready for collection on 24 June 1948, was sent to the A&AEE (via Hatfield) five days later for the bomb handling trials, arriving on 23 July. Here it joined VV215 which had arrived at Boscombe Down on 22 July for handling and

Cockpit instrument panel of Vampire FB.5. (de Havilland)

stability trials which included the Vampire's long-range configuration with 100 gallon underwing drop tanks.

These trials were conducted at Boscombe Down throughout August 1948 and at their conclusion the A&AEE issued the following statement:

The flying qualities of the Vampire FB.5 are of a standard acceptable for general Service use, both 'clean' and with drop tanks; though when carrying drop tanks a full ammunition load or ballast in lieu must also be carried. At low or medium altitudes the stick force per 'g' is a little heavy for fighter

aircraft, but at high altitudes the value is just satisfactory. Windscreen misting and icing are an embarrassment at altitude and when descending.

The A&AEE report also advised pilots that the maximum Machmeter reading recommended for Service use was 0.78 and that porpoising would occur without warning at this speed.

Between August 1948 and November 1952, the A&AEE was responsible for the Vampire FB.5 bomb and RP handling trials, and for the installation of modifications found necessary during these trials. The weapons handling trials were conducted

By May 1949 Vampire FB.5 VV454 was fitted with a non-standard high tailplane and Goblin engine fitted with experimental reheat in an extended rear fuselage. Trials were conducted during late 1949, and the aircraft is seen here at RAE Farnborough in September 1949. (Hawker Siddeley via Philip Birtles)

using three aircraft, VV216, VV220 and VZ324, and commenced with handling tests (on VV216 and VV220) with a variety of underwing ordnance loads. A long-standing problem encountered when firing rocket projectiles lay in the vulnerability of the aircraft's tail to damage from the sealing discs and leads of the rocket motor during its release from the standard Mk.8 Type 14 Rocket Projector guide rail. The installation consisted of two stations per wing, each station having one front and one rear post fitted to the under-surface of the wing between the fuselage and tail-boom. During the acceptance trials of the Mk.8 RP installation on VV216, tested between September and October 1949, severe damage to the Vampire's wing leading edge and the underside surface of the tailplane was caused by rocket motor debris. The A&AEE, however, considered the Mk.8 installation

satisfactory for Service use providing the guide rails were modified as soon as possible.

By shortening the front post of the assembly, the rocket was inclined at minus 1° to the wing chord which pointed the axis of the rocket away from the tailplane and projected the lead and disc downwards and below the tail. A total of 103 sorties were flown in early 1951 using VV216 as the trials aircraft, and 3 in RPs were fired in pairs, ripple and salvo, using 60 lb concrete heads with the shortened front post installation. Although slight damage still occurred to the tailplane, the Mark 8 Type 14 RP installation was considered to be within acceptable limits and was approved for Service use on FB.5 aircraft.

The standard RP consisted of a 3 in diameter light alloy tube filled with cordite, and lit by an igniter connected to the aircraft's electrical system; to provide stability in free flight, four fins were fitted at the end

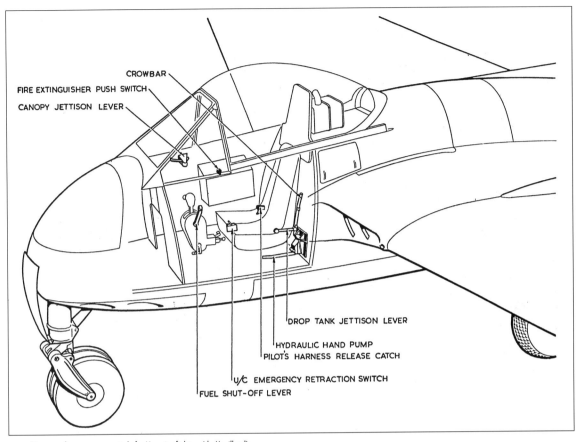

Diagram of emergency controls for Vampire fighter. (de Havilland)

Emergency Equipment

(i) A crowbar is stowed in spring clips on the left-hand side of the bulkhead behind the pilot's seat.

(ii) Desert equipment is stowed as follows:

Waterbottle — Reached from outside by opening the port ammunition access door.

Ordinary rations
Verey pistol
Compass
Heliograph
Cartridges — Reached from outside by opening the starboard ammunition access door.

A.P. 3031
Signalling strips
Tool kit
Water bottle carrier
Flying rations — On floor of cockpit to right and left-hand of pilot's seat.

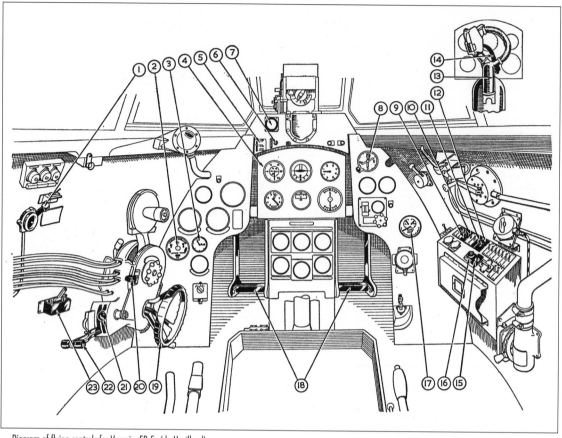

Diagram of flying controls for Vampire FB.5. (de Havilland)

KEY TO FLYING CONTROLS

1. Electrical services master switch
2. Undercarriage position indicator
3. Flaps position indicator
4. Instrument flying panel
5. Elevator trim tab position indicator
6. Undercarriage warning lamp
7. Accelerometer
8. R.I. compass
9. Pitot head heater switch
10. R.I. compass switch
11. Navigation lights switch
12. Identification lights selector switch
13. Control column
14. Wheel brake lever
15. Landing lamp switch
16. Identification light morsing push switch
17. Brake pressure gauge
18. Rudder pedals
19. Elevator trim tab control wheel
20. Dive brake selector lever
21. Flaps selector lever
22. Undercarriage selector lever
23. Undercarriage emergency retraction switch

of the tube. The 6 ft long rocket was attached by two saddles to a rail fitted on the underside of the wing. The warhead was screwed onto the front of the tube and consisted of either 25 lb armour-piercing, 60 lb incendiary, 60 lb semi-armour-piercing, or 60 lb high-explosive heads. For training purposes a 60 lb concrete head was fitted.

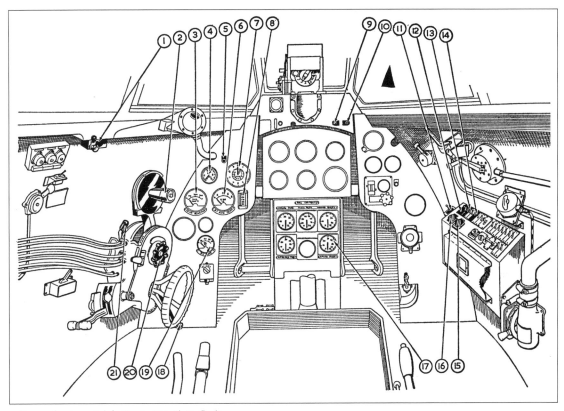

Diagram of engine controls for Vampire FB.5. (de Havilland)

KEY TO ENGINE CONTROLS

1. Booster coils test push switch
2. Throttle lever
3. Rear bearing temperature gauge
4. Burner pressure warning light
5. Fuel pressure warning light
6. Jet pipe temperature gauge
7. Engine speed indicator
8. Oil pressure gauge
9. Fire warning light
10. Generator warning light
11. Auxiliary starting light
12. Starter master switch
13. Boost pump switch
14. Fuel pump emergency switch
15. Fire extinguisher push switch
16. Engine starting push switch
17. Fuel tank contents gauge
18. Low pressure fuel cock lever
19. Oil temperature gauge
20. Throttle lever friction control
21. High pressure fuel cock lever

Pilots were later to come to consider the Vampire a stable platform for rocketry and thought it capable of sustaining a fair amount of damage from debris thrown up during rocket attacks, and from bird strikes during low-level flying. The 3 in rocket, or 3 in 'drain' as it was more commonly known, was a heavy and relatively slow mover, and this led to a large gravity drop after firing. As a consequence, the aiming of the rocket was not straightforward and needed a fair amount of practice to obtain accurate results.

Another hazard encountered during rocket

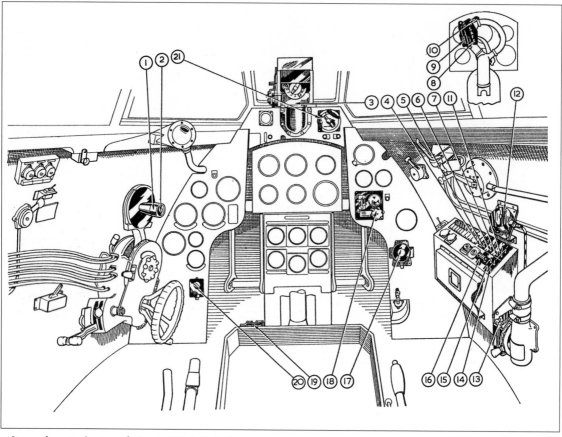

Diagram of operational equipment for Vampire FB.5. (de Havilland)

KEY TO OPERATIONAL EQUIPMENT

1. Gunsight range control
2. R.P. and bomb firing switch
3. Gunsight
4. Cine-camera switch
5. Gunsight switch
6. R.P. pairs-salvo switch
7. Port selector switch (bombs)
8. Selective gun firing switch
9. Camera independent operating switch
10. Press-to-speak switch
11. Starboard bomb selector switch
12. R.P. guns, selector switch
13. R.P. auto-selector switch
14. Bomb tail fusing switch
15. Bomb nose fusing switch
16. R.P. bombs selector switch
17. Camera footage indicator
18. Oxygen regulator
19. Mic-tel socket
20. S.T.R. 9 controller
21. Gunsight selector dimmer control

firing was 'weather-cocking', as Sqn Ldr Bill Shrubsole commented:

Regarding 'weather-cocking', it is true that at times the rockets appeared to have a mind of their own and occasionally performed quite amazing manoeuvres. In the majority of cases, however, weather-cocking was confined to jinking of the tail end of the rocket. Whether gentle jinking

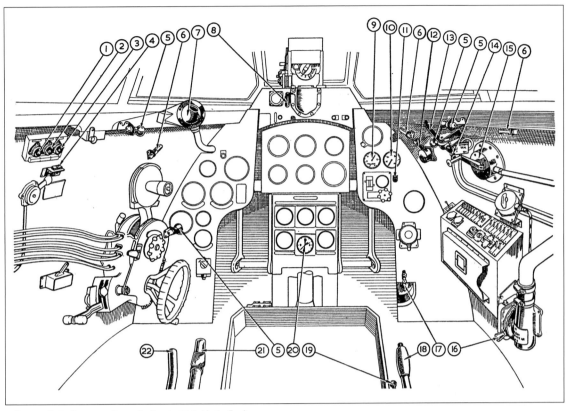

Diagram of miscellaneous equipment for Vampire FB.5. (de Havilland)

KEY TO MISCELLANEOUS EQUIPMENT

1. Ultra-violet lamps dimmer switch
2. Instrument panel floodlights dimmer switch
3. Floodlight dimmer switch (electrical panel)
4. Emergency light switch
5. Ultra-violet lamps
6. Red floodlights
7. Cold air ventilator
8. Emergency light
9. Cabin air pressure gauge
10. Cabin altimeter
11. Cabin air pressure warning light
12. Cabin supercharger lever
13. Canopy jettison lever
14. Canopy seal cock
15. Canopy winding handle
16. Cabin heat control lever
17. De-icing hand pump and regulator
18. Seat adjusting lever
19. Harness release lever
20. Clock
21. Drop tank and bomb gear jettison lever
22. Handle for hydraulic hand pump

or manic manoeuvres there was always a reason for the weather-cocking. Often, but not always, it was caused by a tail fin or fins being bent, loosely fitted or coming off – all the products of human mishandling. If weather-cocking was of a reasonably gentle nature the accuracy of the rocket did not appear to be noticeably degraded.

As I recall the rockets came in DIY form – motor, tail fins and a choice of heads. Provided they were securely assembled and were not damaged through mishandling, the rockets would go where they were intended

The 'Hatfield Workhorse', Vampire FB.5 VV217, flown by de Havilland test pilot John Wilson on 9 March 1949. The aircraft was employed on a variety of company trials from July 1948 until March 1956, and is currently preserved with the North Eastern Aircraft Museum at Sunderland. (Hawker Siddeley via Mike Stroud)

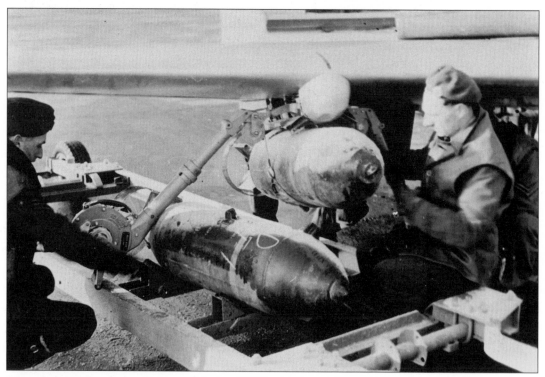

Armourers loading 500 lb m.c. bombs onto a 26 Squadron Vampire at Gutersloh, 1949. (Sqn Ldr M.C. Biggs)

VV221 was delivered to the Handling Squadron at Hullavington in August 1948 for the compilation of the official Pilot's Notes. After service in the Middle East and Germany, it was eventually struck off charge in March 1957. (MoD)

Between 1948 and 1952 VV216 was used by the A&AEE for armament trials. It is seen here at Boscombe Down during 1950. (via John Rawlings)

to go at the precise moment of leaving the rocket rails. A number of factors influenced accuracy at the crucial moment and it depended upon the skill of the pilot to recognize and, if necessary, overcome them.

A proposed 'thin-wing' production version of the Vampire, powered by a Ghost engine and designed to Specification F.15/49, was conceived in March 1948. The following

October the project was given the name Vampire FB.8 and de Havilland was awarded a £180,000 contract for two prototypes: Vampire FB.5 airframes VV612 and VV613 were transferred from Preston to Hatfield in January 1949 for conversion. The conversion incorporated an extensive redesign of the wing to take advantage of the increased power from the Ghost engine; namely a 17° leading edge sweep-back and a reduction of the

Vampire FB.5 WA319 of 93 Squadron firing practice rockets on the Fassberg range, 14 March 1952. (MoD)

thickness/chord ratio from 14 to 10 per cent. The wings were also stressed to carry 75 gallon jettisonable fuel tanks at each tip, and underwing weapons loads and drop tanks grossing 2,000 lb under full combat conditions.

It soon became apparent that the work being undertaken to redesign and convert the Vampire airframe would result in a completely new aircraft type. Performance estimates were promising, and following a high-level meeting at the DARD in the spring of 1949, it was decided to proceed with the type (designated DH 112) as a replacement for the Vampire fighter/bomber, with the suggested name Valkyrie. In August 1949 the aircraft was named the Venom, and the first prototype, VV612, was flown at Hatfield on 2 September 1949 by John Derry.

On 16 November the Central Fighter Establishment at West Raynham began to receive its first examples of the FB.5 when VV443, VV449 and VV454 were collected from Shawbury for the Air Fighting Development Squadron. The AFDS began to evaluate the variant in a series of trials, including fuel consumption, deceleration, combat climb, and salvo rocket firing. Flt Lt. John Wilson served with the CFE between October 1947 and December 1948, where he investigated high-altitude head-on attacks against B.29 bombers:

An interesting assessment I carried out whilst with the AFDS involved the head-on interceptions of B.29s at 35,000 feet over East Anglia. Between July and August 1948, I flew Vampire F.3s VT824 and VT829, culminating with Exercise 'Dagger' in September 1948. Further assessments were made in December 1948 using Vampire FB.5s VV443, VV449 and VV454. The camera gun records of the attacks were analysed to determine minimum head-on range to see whether 20 mm guns would be effective used in this way to reduce the intrusion distance that Soviet bombers would achieve if jets were radar-vectored to attack from the side or rear quarters. The B.29 pilots were extremely concerned at the small fin clearance that occurred with the very latest moment of pull-up.

Originally designated the Vampire FB.8, the prototype Venom, V V612, gets airborne during the RAF display at Farnborough, 8 July 1950. (de Havilland)

Vampire FB.5 V V475 was retained for armament trials, and is shown here with two 100 lb bombs on underwing pylons during November 1948. (Hawker Siddeley via Philip Birtles)

By this time production of the FB.5 was well under way, and deliveries to the RAF's operational squadrons commenced in December 1948 when 16 Squadron at Gutersloh received the first of its ground attack Vampires. The squadron converted from the Tempest F.Mk.2 and quickly worked up to a state of operational readiness; on 15 June 1949 the squadron carried out rocket firing for the first time with their Vampires on the Nordhorn range.

Following a brief hiatus, deliveries of FB.5s to fighter squadrons in BAFO started again in the spring of 1949, commencing with the Gutersloh Wing (3 and 26 Squadrons). With the rapid expansion of the RAF in Germany during the early 1950s, occasioned by the international tension of the Korean War, nineteen squadrons were eventually equipped with Vampire FB.5s; they included 3, 4, 5, 11, 14, 16, 20, 26, 67, 71, 93, 94, 98, 112, 118, 130, 145, 234 and 266

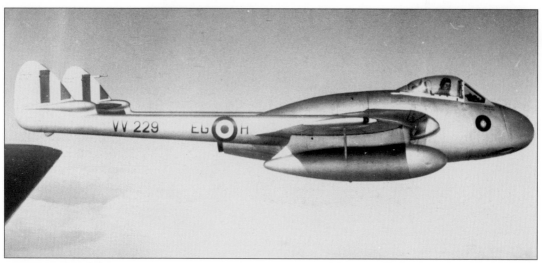

One of the many Vampire squadrons operating from Germany, 16 Squadron was the first to equip with the ground attack FB.5 at Gutersloh in December 1948. VV229 is seen in 1949, soon after delivery. (Sqn Ldr M. Biggs)

Squadrons. As with their contemporaries in the other RAF overseas commands, the Vampire squadrons in Germany were highly mobile and could, if necessary, pack up and rapidly deploy to another base, taking all their operational equipment with them.

Despite its limitations, the Vampire proved an effective ground attack and high-altitude fighter and provided the backbone of the RAF's tactical squadrons in Germany for four years. However, the appearance of the mass-produced MiG-15 jet fighter in the Eastern Bloc air forces, which totally outclassed the Vampire (and the Meteor) in both speed and performance, required the squadrons to re-equip with F-86 Sabres and Venoms. The entry of the Venom into RAF Service, however, did not exactly go smoothly. Wing structural failures, engine fires, and other minor problems meant that the aircraft had to be grounded for a while and Vampires re-issued to the squadrons to maintain their operational capability. The last squadron to fly Vampires in Germany was 145 Squadron at Celle, which despite receiving replacement Venoms during early 1954, continued its operational activities

unabated. The Vampires were officially grounded on 20 July, with the last aircraft being returned to the UK at the end of August.

In the Canal Zone, 6 Squadron at Deversoir relinquished its Tempest F.Mk.6s in favour of FB.5s, with two aircraft delivered for pilot familiarization on 17 September 1949. Conversion began the following month and by December 1949 the squadron had received its full complement of sixteen aircraft. Between 1949 and 1952 a total of seven squadrons were to use the Vampire FB.5 operationally in the Middle East. They were 6, 8, 32, 73, 185, 213 and 249 Squadrons.

The RAF's huge commitment in the Middle East frequently stretched its resources to the limits, and the security of the Suez Canal was of paramount importance. Detachments to Iraq and Jordan for army cooperation and air defence exercises were also essential, where the Vampire squadrons operated under desert conditions and with few facilities. By May 1952 the Vampire squadrons had been re-equipped with the FB.9, fitted with the Godfrey refrigerator unit.

The three squadrons of the Odiham Vampire

Two Vampire FB.5s of 185 Squadron, based in the Middle East. (Sqn Ldr P.H.P. Roberts)

Wing Commander (Flying), Odiham, Al Rawlinson on the end of runway 28 during exercise 'Pinnacle', September 1951. The aircraft carries a rank pennant on the nose and a black and white tail unit. (Wg Cdr Al Rawlinson)

High above Aberdeen harbour for the squadron's 1955 Christmas card, WA397 served with 612 (County of Aberdeen) Squadron between July 1951 and March 1957. (Sqn Ldr R. Robertson)

609 (West Riding) Squadron operated a handful of Vampire FB.5s for only a few months before re-equipping with Meteors. VX475 is depicted being taxied by the Squadron Adjutant, Flt Lt P.G. Murton on 2 December 1950 during an acceptance check at Church Fenton. (Sqn Ldr P.G. Murton)

Wing (54, 72, and 247 Squadrons) began their conversion from the F.Mk.3 to the FB.5 in late 1949 and combined to form an eighteen-aircraft formation for that year's Battle of Britain Flypast over London, led by the Station's OC Flying Wg Cdr A.C. Rawlinson DFC.

Following 72 Squadron's departure to North Weald in March 1950, the Odiham Wing was brought back up to strength with the arrival of 421 (Red Indian) Squadron, RCAF, from Chatham, New Brunswick in January 1951 for a period of operational training. Commanded by

Two of a convoy of six OFU Vampires being refuelled at Kanpur, en route to 60 Squadron, Tengah, on 19 December 1950. The three-month operation to reinforce the FEAF fighter squadrons was the longest jet delivery flight made by any air force. The 'shepherd' Mosquito PR 34 from 81 Squadron was responsible for navigation. (Bob Hillard)

The CO of 60 Squadron briefly carried black and silver chequers on the tail-booms of his Vampire, WA258, before lightning flashes were standardized. It is seen here at Butterworth in April 1951, shortly before it carried out the first jet strike during the Malayan Emergency. (Sqn Ldr Joe Warne)

VV689 of No. 226 OCU undergoing maintenance at Stradishall. Note the airframe serial number, which is repeated inside the nose compartment. (via Jim Earnshaw)

The first course to qualify under the Provost/Vampire training sequence poses for the camera at Oakington, August 1954. The aircraft are Vampire FB.5s, which were used for much of the students' solo exercise work. (MoD)

Many Vampire airframes were relegated for ground training purposes following the end of their operational careers. This Vampire FB.5 carries the maintenance serial 7630M, but is in fact VZ304 and is seen at No. 14 MU, Carlisle. It was later restored at Duxford and sold to the Sandy Topen collection in 1983. (P.R. Keating)

Sqn Ldr R.T.P. Davidson DFC, the squadron borrowed sixteen Vampire FB.5s from the RAF and participated in many Wing exercises and detachments before disbanding in December 1951 and returning to Canada to re-form with the F-86 Sabre.

By September 1952 the Vampire squadrons of Fighter Command had re-equipped with the Gloster Meteor. The Auxiliaries lingered on with their Vampires until March 1957, when the flying units of the Royal Auxiliary Air Force were disbanded during a government economy drive following the Suez War.

The mammoth task of re-equipping the Far East Air Force with Vampires in 1950 was undertaken by No. 1 Overseas Ferry Unit at Chivenor. Between November 1950 and February 1951 Vampire FB.5s were flown in convoys of six or seven aircraft on the 7,641 mile trip to Singapore, each trip taking up to eighteen days. The Vampires were escorted for part of the way by 'Big Brother' Mosquitos from Chivenor and the Far East Ferry Flight.

In December 1950 60 Squadron at Tengah received their first FB.5s when four aircraft were collected from Seletar after their ferry flight from the UK. The squadron had been heavily involved in Operation 'Firedog' following the declaration of a State of Emergency in Malaya in June 1948, and had carried out many strikes against Communist terrorist targets with their Spitfire F.18s.

On 26 April 1951 two Vampires from 60 Squadron, WA258 and WA242, flown by the CO, Sqn Ldr Duncan-Smith, and OC 'A' Flight, Flt Lt. 'Jimmy' James, made the first jet strike in the Far East when a terrorist hide-out on a derelict rubber estate in Johore State was destroyed with rockets and cannon fire. By the time the squadron re-equipped with FB.9s in early 1952, it had reverted to an Air Defence Squadron, with a secondary duty of army support.

The second operational squadron in the FEAF to equip with the FB.5 was 28 Squadron at Kai Tak. In January 1951 three aircraft were collected from Seletar and by March 1951 the squadron was considered operational with the Vampire and moved to the recently renovated forward airstrip at Sek Kong, close to the Chinese border. With the Korean War at its height and Hong Kong's

Seventy-five Vampire FB.6s were built at Hatfield for the Swiss Air Force. The aircraft were prepared for service at F+W Emmen and are shown on the finishing line during late 1951, prior to delivery. (F+W Emmen)

northern border under threat of invasion by the Chinese Communist forces, 28 Squadron was kept busy as a quick reaction force.

Single-seat Vampires were also employed by Flying Training Command for solo flight experience and during the weapons application phase of the student's training. Deliveries of Vampire FB.5s began in July 1949 to No. 203 AFS, Driffield, in time to be transferred to No. 226 OCU at Stradishall during a change of identities. Further Fighter Command OCUs to fly the fighter/bomber included Nos 229 at Chivenor and 233 at Pembrey.

The first of the RAF's Vampire Advanced Flying Schools to be formed during the Korean War expansion programme was No. 202 AFS at Valley in April 1951. The unit was later to be joined by No. 206 AFS at Oakington, No. 208 AFS at Merryfield and the civilian-run No. 210 AFS at Tarrant Rushton. All four units operated the fighter version of the Vampire (together with the Meteor T.7 and later the Vampire T.11) until further reorganization of Flying Training Command units in 1954.

Other second-line units to operate the Vampire FB.5 included the Central Flying School at Little Rissington, Nos 102 and 103 Flying Refresher Schools at North Luffenham and Full Sutton respectively, the Armament Practice Stations at Acklington and Sylt, the Empire Test Pilots School at Farnborough, and Nos 2, 3/4 and 5 Civilian Anti-Aircraft Cooperation Units. No. 3/4 CAACU based at Exeter airport became the final unit to fly the

Vampire FB.52 SA219 being moved from the main assembly hall to the paint shop by overhead crane at Chester, March 1951. It was delivered to South Africa on 7 May 1951. (Alan Roach)

Vampire FB.5, relinquishing its last aircraft (WA236) on 5 August 1960 when it was relegated as a non-effective airframe by a working party from No. 49 MU.

A total of 1,123 Vampire FB.5s were built, including some thirty-four aircraft for South Africa and Venezuela. The majority of Vampire production was sub-contracted to the English Electric Company Ltd at Samlesbury near Preston, with 798 aircraft produced for the RAF (including eighteen airframes transferred to Hatfield from October 1948 for conversion to Sea Vampire F.20s), and a further ten aircraft delivered to South Africa in early 1949. Deliveries of FB.5s from English Electric were between May 1948 and October 1951.

Eighty-seven Vampire FB.5s were produced at the Broughton factory, Chester, and delivered between March and November 1951. Hatfield built a further batch of thirty-six FB.5s with deliveries between July 1949 and March 1951. Twenty-four aircraft were built at Hatfield and Chester for Venezuela and delivered between 1949 and 1952.

Foreign air forces were quick to realize the potential of de Havilland's ground attack fighter, and early in 1946 the Swiss Government placed an order for seventy-five of the type to be built at Hatfield, fitted with Goblin 3 engines. Trials were successfully conducted with TG443 fitted with a Goblin 3 by the de Havilland (Engine) Company, and during June 1947 the aircraft served as a demonstrator to a party of Swiss pilots at Hatfield. Two months later, on 18 August 1947, the type was designated the Vampire FB.6 and deliveries to Switzerland began in April 1949. This was followed by a further order of one hundred

In close formation: Vampire FB.5 WA115 of No. 208 AFS, flown by Fg Off. Frith, October 1953. (J.E. Frith via C. Thomas)

FB.6s built under licence at Emmen. In 1948 Sweden also placed an order for ground attack Vampire FB.50s fitted with Goblin 3 engines, and based on the experience gained from the Vampire FB.5/FB.6 and the projected Vampire Mk.7, de Havilland's built 310 of the type under the Swedish designation J.28B.

The main export version of the Vampire FB.6 was the FB.52, of which 193 were delivered to ten countries between December 1949 and October 1953, together with a further 353 built under licence in India and Italy. A variation of

the Vampire FB.52 was the FB.52A built for the Italian Air Force; fifty-one were supplied from Chester between July 1950 and December 1951, followed by a further twenty-seven built by the Macchi Company in Italy.

At the present time, three Vampire FB.5s are preserved in the UK: VV217 is at the North East Aircraft Museum, Sunderland; VX461 is stored at RAF Cosford as part of the RAF Museum's Reserve Collection; and VZ304 is with the Vintage Aircraft Team at Cranfield.

VAMPIRE FB.9

The use of the Vampire in both the Middle East and the Far East, where the aircraft operated in the ground attack role at low altitudes (which also involved long periods on standby) caused particular problems for aircrew. Within the confines of a closed cockpit, where there is virtually no air circulation within a normal flying suit, pilot fatigue and severe physical discomfort was exacerbated by temperatures which could be as high as 165° Fahrenheit. One solution for keeping the pilot cool in the cockpit while on standby at the Egyptian base at Deversoir, was to build sandbagged shelters at the dispersals, with the open ends into the wind. Another form of shelter was the 'Malta canopy', a light, portable fabric-and-metal overhead canvas screen which offered shade for the crews without placing any restriction on aircraft movement.

Windscreen and canopy hood cracking caused by the rapid changes in temperature between sitting in dispersal and climbing to altitude was also a problem, as was the reduction in thrust of the Vampire's Goblin engine in extremes of temperature.

In October 1947 a Vampire F.1 had been dispatched from Boscombe Down to the Tropical Evaluation Unit (TEU) at Khartoum for eight months of intensive flight trials to assess the problems of operating in the Middle East. The subsequent A&AEE report, issued in March 1949, was critical of the Vampire's inadequate ventilation system, for which air was drawn in through a small nose intake, then vented on the starboard side of the cockpit via a 'punkah louvre'. Pilots returned from their evaluation flights at Khartoum with their clothing soaked in perspiration and it was evident that additional ventilation would be required to alleviate their discomfort, but because the air entered the cockpit at a fairly high temperature due to the ram temperature rise, pre-cooling of the incoming air was essential if a satisfactory solution was to be found.

The maximum temperature encountered during the trials at Khartoum was 102° Fahrenheit, which made the Vampire's metal parts too hot to touch, and pilots frequently complained about the intense heat from the sun's rays through the transparent canopy. Painting the top of the canopy white to reflect the sun's rays was suggested, as was a sun blind fitted on top of the canopy, but neither measure was considered acceptable for a fighter aircraft where an unobstructed view was essential.

By 1950 an effective cockpit conditioning system was still not available, although much effort was made by design teams at both de Havilland's and Normalair. Flight trials by de Havilland test pilot John Wilson at Hatfield between February and April 1950 with Vampire VV675 showed significant improvement to cockpit temperatures following various modifications to the ventilation system. In an attempt to produce body cooling by the evaporation of sweat from the skin surface, the air-ventilated flying suit was developed at the RAF Institute of Aviation Medicine (IAM), Farnborough, by the RAF doctor, Wg Cdr A.J. Barwood. Tony Barwood had stressed that pilots directly exposed to the sun for long periods could experience heat exhaustion unless they were provided with adequate cooling facilities. His sleeveless suit used a lightweight nylon liner from a cord-type parachute harness (similar to that manufactured by the GQ Parachute Company), threaded with a network of lightweight flexible plastic tubing (attached to the outer side of the lining) which was connected to the cooling unit's cockpit vent. A series of seventy-two jet orifices were sewn into the suit and projected through the nylon liner, with a pair of holes punched through the tubing immediately downstream of the jet producing a venturi effect which effectively doubled the air circulation. Pressure at the wide bore inlet to the tube system was 5–6 lb psi and the flow could be controlled by a needle valve.

Experimental work at the IAM suggested that effective cooling could be obtained from the suit, and that flight trials should be carried out. The IAM's Vampire 5, VV463, was modified by fitting a ⅝ in tapping from the fifth stage of the Goblin compressor to the cockpit, in which was fitted a small heat exchange tank (which was filled with ice cubes from a domestic refrigerator) to provide cooling, and a water trap to collect the condensation. The cooled air was then passed through a wide bore flexible tube to a quick-release Dunlop connector and thence to the suit, with flow control between the ice box and the suit's flexible tubing. Fitted with the air-ventilated suit system, Vampire VV463 was first flown at Farnborough by the Flying Personnel Medical Officer, Wg Cdr H.P. Ruffel-Smith AFC, and subsequently by other medical and test pilots from the RAE and ETPS. On 9 May 1950 VV463 was flown by Wg Cdr J.S. Howitt AFC of the IAM to the TEU at Khartoum, where the first hot weather trials of the suit were to be conducted.

The extensive series of trials in September 1951, when VV463 was fitted with an experimental ice box to produce cool air, showed fairly encouraging results. Further ground trials were completed in Singapore in the spring of 1952, using air from cylinders, which provided very dry air and therefore more efficient cooling. Finally, in the late spring of 1952, VV463 was again flown to Khartoum for comparison trials with the A&AEE's Vampire FB.9, VV675. The trials showed that the Godfrey cold air unit had a marked advantage over the flying suit, but as it was still under development and a long way from being fitted to the RAF's Vampires it was decided to order fifty of Tony Barwood's suits. During October 1954 pilots of the Deversoir Wing experimented with the air-ventilated flying suit, which was worn over a string vest to encourage the free circulation of air; unfortunately, these suits did not reach the operational squadrons before the Vampire was withdrawn from RAF service.

The Far East presented similar problems, which had been highlighted during the tropical assessment by the Vampire Trials Unit in 1948. In his report, 'Vampire III Tactical Trials in the Far East', published the same year, Flt Lt. John Wilson commented upon operations in Singapore:

Below 5,000 feet at high speed, the cockpit temperature became excessive, rising to 135° Fahrenheit at 500 mph (435 knots) IAS. This heat was the cause of much discomfort to the pilot and must adversely affect his flying ability.

It is thought that nothing can be done to cure this high temperature trouble, which is primarily caused by skin friction heating, until refrigeration equipment is carried.

Arising from an Air Ministry report on the Vampire's operational experience in the Middle East and criticism of the aircraft's inadequate cooling system, a meeting had been held at Hatfield on 31 August 1949 to discuss solutions to these problems. Various methods of cockpit cooling were discussed; the favourite was to use air from the Vampire's existing Marshall Blower (which provided pressurization air which was drawn as bleed air from the Goblin's compressor), and pass it through the compressor side of a mechanical refrigeration unit to an intercooler, thence to the turbo expander side of the unit and to the cabin.

In October 1949 a statement was issued from de Havilland's confirming that the company was to proceed with Mod. No. 784: 'to introduce gear for cockpit cooling for tropical use', and that the cooling unit would be developed and produced by the firm of Sir George Godfrey and Partners (Ltd) of Hanworth, Middlesex. A brochure was issued by the manufacturers which detailed the principle of their cold air unit:

Air supplied for pressurisation and ventilation must be cooled before delivery to the aircraft cabin – the reason being that the process of compressing the air supply may raise its temperature to 350° Centigrade. To reduce the temperature of the air, it is first passed through an air-to-air heat exchanger. Some of the required temperature drop may be obtained in this way, but on leaving the heat exchanger the air temperature is usually too high and it is finally brought to an acceptable level by expanding the air through the heat exchanger.

The Godfrey Cold Air Unit operates on the air cycle principle of refrigeration, using the ventilating air as the working medium. The unit employs an inward-flow radial turbine driven by energy derived from the ventilating air.

The following month, on 10 November 1949, Vampire FB.5, VV675 was taken from short-term storage at Kemble and sent to Hatfield for the installation of the Godfrey Blower and the air conditioning refrigeration equipment (ACRE 8) cold air unit in the aircraft's starboard wing root. The fitment of the cooling unit necessitated structural alterations to the starboard air intake fillet, which was extended by 8 in. On 28 February

1950 the cooling unit was tested in VV675 by de Havilland's test pilot, John Wilson. He flew the aircraft five more times before it was transferred to Boscombe Down for further development testing. His flight test report on the cooling unit, dated 17 April 1950, concluded:

After 30 minutes at 395 knots the cockpit temperature stabilized at 20° C – the volume of cold air is ample, the temperature is cool but pleasant. It is considered that, subject to the pressurisation proving satisfactory, the aircraft is now in a state where further experience must be gained at Khartoum before additional modifications which may be required to produce a lower temperature are tested.

Between 28 August and 21 September 1950 a Service evaluation of the cold air unit fitted in VV675 was carried out at the TEU, Khartoum, followed by hot-dry and hot-humid tests at Habbaniya and Bahrein respectively.

Following these Canal Zone evaluation trials, a statement was issued in December 1950 by Sqn Ldr Yates, on behalf of the C-in-C MEAF, which declared, 'A step in the right direction, the Cold Air Unit is not the complete answer to the requirement for cockpit cooling for fighter aircraft in this theatre.' Yates also criticized the considerable noise from the blower unit, which also provided a noisy background to transmissions on VHF radio frequency.

The A&AEE also sent a critical letter to de Havilland's with regard to the noise from the refrigeration system, to which John Wilson replied:

With flying helmet and oxygen mask in normal use, no unusual cockpit noise was apparent with the refrigeration system working, i.e. admitting cold air: but with full hot, rpm above 9,500 and altitude below 20,000 ft, there was a considerable increase in cockpit noise . . . due to the large quantity of air. It is once more pointed out that the above condition is not a practical one as the cockpit temperature soon becomes unbearable . . . when used intelligently the high flow available should not be admitted to the cockpit, and consequently the noise complaint does not arise.

It was recommended, however, that the cold air unit should be fitted to all future Vampires allotted to the Middle East and that the modification should be retro-fitted to the earlier Vampire 5s.

Between January and February 1951 VV675 was again flown by John Wilson at Hatfield. It was fitted with a new single-skin canopy, and was on test to resolve the problems of canopy demisting, cabin heating and pressurization with a new distribution arrangement which had been designed for Venom aircraft fitted with an ejector seat.

Another comment of John Wilson's report while with the Vampire Trials Unit in Singapore in May 1948 was highly critical of the Vampire's double-skinned canopy and the associated cockpit misting problems:

A more serious trouble was encountered with the canopy sandwich, which invariably misted between two layers as soon as an altitude of 15,000 feet was exceeded, and this opacity persisted throughout a trip while the aircraft was kept above this level, which due to its position it is impossible for the pilot to wipe it away. This trouble occurred irrespective of the newness of the silica-gel crystals and always disappeared by the time the aircraft had descended below 2,000 feet.

When the aircraft was kept above 25,000 feet for more than 15 minutes the misting up became severe when the aircraft carried out either a slow or rapid descent with cockpit heating off. By the time the aircraft reached 5,000 feet the front and side panels of the windscreen were heavily misted and general visibility poor. On the circuit and final approach it was necessary to keep one hand continually wiping the front panel to allow sufficient visibility to carry out a safe landing.

A very considerable reduction in the degree of misting was achieved by moving the cockpit heating control to 'Full Hot' 15 minutes before the let-down was commenced, and playing the heated air from the ventilation louvre forward on to the windscreen.

Trials continued with VV675 fitted with the single-skin canopy at Boscombe Down in April 1951, in an attempt to cure the canopy cracking caused by the temperature variations of operational flying in the Middle East. The high differential temperatures experienced caused high local stress loads in each (thinner) skin of the double-skin canopy, and the attachment of perspex to the metal frame in the redesigned canopy (Mod. No. 727) was soon to show that it provided much greater freedom for differential contraction than was possible in the original design; cold chamber tests and flight trials indicated that the new canopy was a great improvement on the old design. The single-skin canopy was also much stronger than the previous two-skin unit, possessed better visual and optical properties, and would shatter more easily (when fitted to the Venom) if an ejection seat had to go through it, and, in conjunction with a new gallery pipe air system, it was better demisted.

This variant was designated Vampire FB.9, and contrary to accounts previously published, was not a re-engined version of the FB.5; for although de Havilland's had proposed the use of the 3,350 lb thrust Goblin 3 to increase engine performance for low-level operations required in a tropical theatre, the FB.9 continued with the Goblin 2 engine of the FB.5. An exception to this was a batch of

Vampire FB.9s built by Fairey Aviation at Ringway in late 1953 for the Southern Rhodesian Air Force; all these aircraft were delivered with Goblin 3 engines installed.

The prototype VV675 was returned to Hatfield on 20 June 1951 for further tests with de Havilland (Propellors) in an attempt to reduce cabin noise and cure severe elevator overbalance at high Mach numbers. At the completion of the tests, VV675 was sent to No. 19 MU at St Athan in March 1953 for conversion to full FB.9 standard.

Production of the Vampire FB.9 commenced when Contract No. 6/ACFT/5613/CB.7(a), which called for fifty Vampire FB.5s to be built at Preston, was amended to allow the ninth airframe, WG848, built in November 1951, to be the first FB.9. A total of 348 Vampire FB.9s were eventually built, including 255 at Chester, 42 at Preston, and 51 at Fairey Aviation at Ringway. The final FB.9, WX260, rolled off the Ringway production lines two years later, in November 1953.

The first squadron to fly the Vampire FB.9 was 73 Squadron when WL494 and WL496 were ferried to Ta Kali from Abingdon on 23 November 1951 by Wg Cdr Badcoe and Sqn Ldr Gill of the Overseas Ferry Unit. The squadron was fully equipped with FB.9s by February 1952; the other squadrons of the MEAF then began to convert from the FB.5, 6 Squadron at Abu Sueir accepting WL516 and WL546 on 15 February. By December 1952 the remainder of the MEAF Vampire squadrons had re-equipped with the FB.9: 8 Squadron at Deversoir (December 1952), 185 Squadron at Hal Far (May 1952), and 213 and 249 Squadrons at Deversoir (April and May 1952 respectively). Vampire FB.9s were also loaned to 14 Squadron RNZAF at Akrotiri and 78 Fighter Wing RAAF at Ta Kali in late 1952, as part of the joint Commonwealth contribution to the stability of the Middle East.

The last unit to fly the Vampire operationally was 8 Squadron, which had been actively involved in ground attack operations

The main assembly hall at Chester during March 1951. The Vampires on the two lines are FB.9s with VO553/VZ848 in the foreground, which was delivered to the RAF in May 1951. (Alan Roach)

Vampire FB.9s of 249 Squadron from Deversoir during 1952. (via Wg Cdr Roger Boulding)

Surrounded by the aircrew of 249 Squadron, Deversoir's Wing Commander Flying, Wg Cdr 'Buck' Courtney, poses in the cockpit of his 'personal' Vampire FB.9, WG927. Of interest are the three squadron badges, comprising the Deversoir Wing, on the nose of the Vampire. (Paul Sanderson)

High above Malta during 1952, a flight of Vampire FB.9s from 73 Squadron in perfect formation. The squadron transferred to Habbaniya the following year. (Sqn Ldr P.H.P. Roberts)

111 60 lb bombs. The squadron received the first of its replacement Venoms during March 1955, and had completely re-equipped with the type by the following December.

In the Far East the first six Vampire FB.9s arrived at Seletar from the UK on 11 February 1952 and, after air testing, were delivered to 28 Squadron at Sek Kong on 19 February to replace the unit's FB.5s and continue its role as a quick reaction force. Next to receive the FB.9 was 60 Squadron at Tengah on 26 February 1952, when six aircraft were delivered by pilots of Transport Command. Despite decreasing terrorist activities in Malaya, the squadron continued to concentrate on routine training and 'flag-waving' exercises until the spring of 1955, when replacement Venoms were delivered.

AVM Brian Huxley joined 28 Squadron in July 1953, and for the next two and a half years flew Vampires, both in Hong Kong and on detachment with 60 Squadron at Tengah:

against rebel tribesmen in the West Aden Protectorate. In April 1954 eight pilots were detached to Eastleigh in Nairobi in support of anti-Mau Mau operations; during ten days of almost continuous action, 8 Squadron fired 12,740 rounds of 20 mm cannon and released

The unit establishment of 28 Squadron was twelve Vampires and sixteen pilots, plus the CO. We normally worked a five day week, starting the day at 08.00 with a Met and ATC briefing and flew through

No. 78 Wing RAAF operated from Malta between July 1952 and December 1955 with Vampire FB.9s borrowed from the RAF. Devoid of unit markings, the nearest aircraft is WR138. (Nat. War Museum, Malta)

Vampire FB.9 WL607 of 8 Squadron departs Khormaksar in 1954. This particular aircraft ended its days as an instructional airframe at Swinderby. (MoD)

With protection from the tropical heat, Vampire FB.9 WL511 of 60 Squadron is re-armed at Tengah during 1955. (AVM Brian Huxley)

until teatime. Sorties were usually of about one hour duration at high level, or as little as 20 minutes if firing on the air-to-ground range at Port Shelter.

We trained in a variety of roles: interception and air-to-air combat, which were carried out under the control of one of the two radar units; the twice daily low-level reconnaissance sorties around the boundaries of the Colony, noting the progress of junks or gunboats supplying

the garrisons on the outlying islands; and close support for the army and navy.

Our potential enemies, the air force of the Chinese Peoples' Republic, were based in strength around Canton, at the head of the Pearl River estuary. Their main airfield was known as the White Cloud airbase, but there were numerous satellite airfields. They were equipped with MiG-15s, which had gained notoriety in the Korean War. At the time, with all the confidence of

45 Squadron only flew Vampires for twelve months to provide jet conversion for Hornet pilots. Vampire FB.9 WL513 is depicted at Butterworth in late 1955. (No. 45 Squadron Association)

youth and inexperience, we were sure we 'could give a good account of ourselves'. In retrospect, with their vast numerical superiority, more modern aircraft and Korean experience, they might have proved quite a handful.

In order to give a change of scenery, it was the custom for two of us to go down to Tengah for a six week attachment to 60 Squadron. Tactics and procedures were much the same as on 28 Squadron, and there was the opportunity to take part in the continuing internal security operations against terrorists in Malaya – for which we were entitled to a General Service Medal.

An additional benefit of the trip to Tengah was the chance to fly the Venom, which was beginning to arrive in the FEAF. Flying the Venom after the Vampire required no special training: the cockpit layout and controls were almost identical, so after a short verbal briefing one just went out and flew it. Leading a formation of Vampires being 'bounced' by a section

of Venoms at high altitude, I found that by calling the turns at the right moment I could stay out of trouble almost indefinitely, but we couldn't get near the Venoms when they didn't want us to.

The planned replacement of 80 Squadron's Hornet fighters with Vampires in June 1955 did not materialize; however, Vampire FB.9s were delivered to 33 and 45 Squadrons at Butterworth, which merged between March and October 1955 during the conversion of their Hornet crews to jets. Although 33 Squadron returned to the UK to fly Venom NF.2s, 45 Squadron continued to fly Vampires until it re-equipped with Venoms in May 1956.

Due to a shortage of FB.9s, the 2 TAF squadrons were obliged to operate a mixture of FB.5s and FB.9s: 5 Squadron at Wunstorf, 20 Squadron at Jever, and 26 Squadron at Oldenburg all received FB.9s in June 1952. They were followed by 234 Squadron at Oldenburg (August 1952), 4 Squadron at Jever (February 1953), 93 Squadron at Celle

The end of the line for many Vampires at No. 10 MU, Hullavington, 1957. Awaiting scrapping are WR245 (ex-213 Squadron), WA395 (ex-71 Squadron) and WR123 (ex-249 Squadron). (Gp Capt Deryk Maddox)

(November 1953) and 11 Squadron at Wunstorf (March 1954).

In 1954, as deliveries of Canadair Sabres and de Havilland Venoms to the 2 TAF got under way, Vampire FB.9s were gradually withdrawn from the operational squadrons and relegated to training units in the UK. Second-line units to fly the Vampire FB.9 were Nos 226 and 233 OCUs, Nos 202, 203 and 208 AFSs, Nos 1, 4, 5, 7 and 8 FTSs, the Royal Air Force College at Cranwell, and No. 2 CAACU at Langham. In October 1959 the last FB.9 was withdrawn from service with No. 7 FTS at Valley and ferried to No. 19 MU at St Athan.

Although not flown by RAF Fighter Command, eight squadrons of the Royal Auxiliary Air Force operated small numbers of Vampire FB.9s from June 1954 until March 1957. They included 501, 502, 602, 603, 607, 608, 613 and 614 Squadrons.

Some FB.9s were sold for export: Rhodesia bought sixteen aircraft for its air force, and these were delivered between April 1953 and October 1954. Ten ex-RAF aircraft were presented to the Royal Jordanian Air Force between November 1955 and February 1956, and three FB.9s were sold to Lebanon in May and June 1958. Two further FB.9s, WL514 and WR202, were bought from surplus RAF stocks in July 1956 as instructional airframes for the RNZAF and were re-serialled as INST169 and INST171 respectively.

VAMPIRE NF.10

By 1950 the standard night-fighter of the RAF was the piston-engined Mosquito NF.36, which, although possessing an adequate performance and operational ceiling, was still equipped with the wartime AI Mk. 10 radar. Despite the worsening political relationship with the Communist Bloc and the outbreak of the Korean War, the Mosquito's long-overdue replacement, the Meteor NF.11 was still twelve months away. The weakest part of the UK's air defence was undoubtedly the night-fighter force, and it was in an age of jet-propelled enemy bombers carrying atom bombs, and the resulting RAF expansion, that the Vampire NF.10 precipitately entered service with Fighter Command.

It is interesting to note that the RAF's Vampire NF.10s did not originate from an Air Ministry specification or requirement, but were born out of a privately funded de Havilland venture and a subsequent frustrated order placed by the Egyptian Air Force. During their limited operational careers with the RAF, Vampire NF.10s proved themselves to be effective interim night-fighters and were generally liked by all who flew them.

The DH 113 Vampire night-fighter was originally designed as a cheap export aircraft utilizing the wings and tail of de Havilland's proven single-seat Vampire day-fighter. As the diameter of the Vampire nacelle at the cockpit coincided almost exactly with that of the Mosquito night-fighter, the DH 113 retained the latter's side-by-side seating arrangement with the navigator/radar operator sitting in the right-hand seat, offset slightly behind the pilot. A tubular-structured canopy embodied an upward opening rear-hinged lid on the top for crew access, which could be jettisoned in the event of an emergency; no provision was made for ejector seats.

The wooden nacelle was also lengthened by 3 ft 10 in to house the scanner unit of the Mosquito's AI Mk. 10 radar which was mounted behind a one-piece, non-detachable, di-electric nose-cap. The nose-cap was moulded from seventeen laminations of glass fibre impregnated with Nuron resin; access to the scanner was obtained through two detachable panels between the nose-cap and the windscreen; this also provided access to the radar frequency unit mounted on the cockpit bulkhead. The standard Vampire day-fighter armament of four 20 mm Hispano cannon was installed in the floor of the nacelle, with the ammunition tanks fitted behind the rear cockpit bulkhead.

In the compact cockpit a reflector gun-sight and the pilot's controls were located to the port side of the instrument panel. To the right of the panel was the observer's radar equipment, which comprised an indicator, a synchronizer and a control box. Behind the pilot's seat was the R.3121 IFF receiver, and two STR.9X VHF transmitter-receivers were located in the radio bay between the cockpit and the engine bay. To compensate for the increased weight of the radar equipment the DH 113 was powered by the 3,350 lb thrust Goblin 3 engine.

As the night-fighter employed the wings of the Vampire FB.5, fuel tankage was identical – 53 gallons in each of the inner, and 64 gallons in the two outer flexible bag-type wing tanks. A further 96 gallons were carried in a rigid light-alloy fuselage tank and provision was

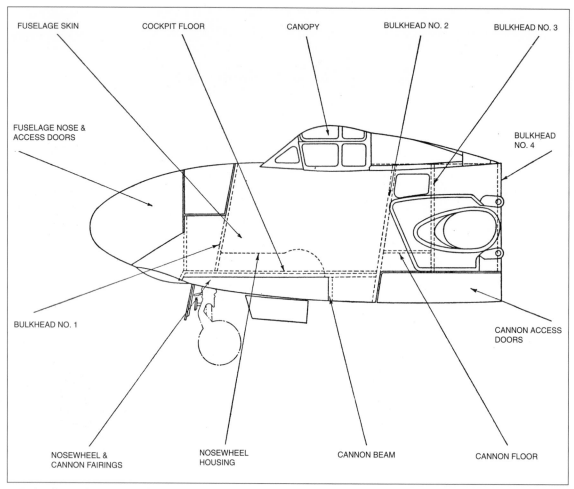

Fuselage diagram of Vampire NF.10. (de Havilland)

also made for two 100-gallon wing drop-tanks, giving a total of 530 gallons.

Two prototypes were built and issued with Class 'B' Registrations G–5–2 (c/n 13001) and G–5–5 (c/n 13002); the first of these, G–5–2 (which was irreverently named 'Pike's Pig'), made its maiden flight at Hatfield on 28 August 1949 with experimental test pilot Geoffrey Pike at the controls. A third prototype, G–5–9, was built and joined the Hatfield test fleet in January 1951 for trials at the CFE, West Raynham. Its civilian career was brief, being re-serialled WP232 during February and delivered to the RAF the following month.

In early flight testing the DH 113 was found to be manoeuvrable and pleasant to fly. Although 270 lb heavier than the single-seat fighter, the DH 113 was slightly faster at high altitude, partly due to the higher-powered Goblin 3 engine, and partly because of the improved fineness ratio of its lengthened fuselage, which improved the 'streamline' and thus decreased the total drag. The DH 113 was, however, slower than the Meteor night-fighter in level flight, and its rate of climb was significantly lower. With drop-tanks, the patrol duration was 2.30 hours at sea-level and 2.70 hours at 30,000 ft, and a maximum range of

Instrument panel of Vampire NF.10. The A.10 radar controller is at the top right of the panel. (de Havilland)

1,220 miles was achieved at altitude. Stability problems were evident in early flight tests of the DH 113; these were resolved by revising the fin shape to the traditional de Havilland outline, extending the tailplane fairings outboard of the booms, and fitting acorn-shaped tailplane extensions.

Nine days after its first flight, the prototype DH 113, G–5–2, made its public debut at the Farnborough Air Show, and the following month Egypt placed an order for twelve aircraft, with an option for more. However, as production of the Egyptian night-fighters at Hatfield got under way, increasing hostility

between Egypt and Israel forced the British Government to impose an embargo on the sale and delivery of arms to the countries of the Middle East. With the shortage of modern fighters affecting the defence of the UK, the government decided to transfer the Egyptian order to the RAF, as an interim type pending the delivery of the Venom NF.2 and an improved version of the Meteor night-fighter.

Although essentially a private venture, the Vampire NF.10 (as the aircraft was designated for the RAF) was covered by a Ministry of Aircraft Production Specification written into the production contracts. This was F.111.P, dated 24 April 1951, and authorized by Operational Requirement No. 265 of 6 February 1951 (which, peculiarly, also applied to the production of the Vampire NF.10's successor, the de Havilland Venom NF.2).

The specification and operational requirement stipulated similar requisites for an interim night-fighter: an endurance at 30,000 ft of at least two hours; accommodation for a crew of two in a pressure cabin; a Goblin 3 engine and a fuel system suitable for aerobatics; four 20 mm Hispano guns; and the retention of standard underwing fittings for the carriage of bombs. An AI Mk. 10 radar set was required, with IFF Mk. 3 and SCR.729 Interrogator. Provision would be made for Gee Mk. 3 (ARI.5816) navigation aid from the twenty-sixth aircraft onwards, and twin ten-channel VHF sets (TR.1934) would be fitted as soon as possible; STR.9X/2M would be accepted on early aircraft. With regard to crew escape facilities, the relevant paragraph stated:

'Ejection seats are not required but urgent consideration shall be given to means of improving the escape arrangements and shall be applied as soon as possible'.

Twenty-five Vampire NF.10s were built at Hatfield with serials WP232–WP249 against Contract No. 6/ACFT/6441/CB.7(a) dated 13 February 1951. Deliveries commenced the following month when WP232 was sent to Boscombe Down for Service trials. Production of the remaining fifty-three night-fighters for the RAF (WM659–WM677, WM703–WM733, WP250–WP252 and WV689–WV691) was transferred to Chester, with the first aircraft (WM659) going to Christchurch in December 1951 for trials.

The Vampire prototype G–5–2 was sent to the A&AEE at Boscombe Down for evaluation trials. Scheduled to commence in February 1950, these trials were briefly interrupted the following month when the aircraft's nose section was badly damaged

The prototype DH 113 Vampire night fighter, G–5–2, in 1949. It was re-serialled as WP256 and served with 23 Squadron and No. 2 ANS, before being scrapped in September 1959. (de Havilland)

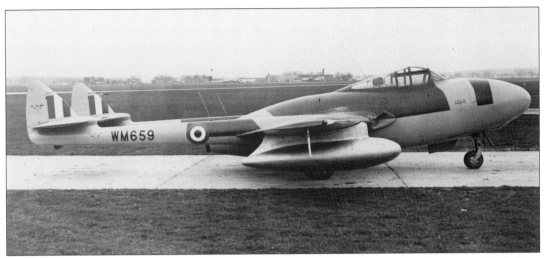

The first production Vampire NF.10, WM659. Apart from service trials with 25 Squadron during late 1952, the aircraft spent most its career at Christchurch before being sold to the Indian Air Force in July 1955 as 'ID593'. (MoS via Mike Stroud)

during a high-speed dive. On completion of the handling and stability trials, G–5–2 was transferred to Hatfield for its tailplane to be fitted to a Vampire FB.5 for spinning trials.

The summer of 1950 proved a busy period for G–5–2 when, between flight tests, the prototype was demonstrated at Hatfield to the representatives of at least ten overseas countries, including Chile, Denmark, Sweden, Australia, South Africa and Canada, and also appeared at the SBAC Show in September.

With the arrival of the first production aircraft, WP232, to join the second prototype G–5–5 at Boscombe Down in March 1951, the radio and navigation acceptance tests were able to get under way. Gun-firing, AI Mk. 10 radar operation, and the revised nose radome tests were completed on WP232 whilst G–5–5 cleared the radio installations, including SCR 729 (Lucero), IFF Mk. 3, twin TR.1934, and Gee Mk. 3.X.

Further trials with WP232 in April 1951 revealed the inability of a pilot of average build to apply 'full up' elevator due to the control stick and column fouling the pilot's

harness release box, and underlined the grossly inadequate facilities for escape in flight. Other criticisms included the need for a retractable foot step instead of the crew entry ladder, and the poor forward vision for the pilot because of the aircraft's radar nose which created a 'dead' area out to about 50 yd straight ahead. Furthermore, as the aircraft seemed prone to spin at the stall, it was recommended that spinning trials should be effected as soon as possible.

De Havilland's experimental test pilot John Wilson was involved in the early test flying of the Vampire NF.10:

I first flew the prototype, G–5–2, on 10th November 1949 and found it delightful in every way. Later, in June 1950, with a new nose, raised canopy and tailplane extensions, I was not so enthralled – though approving of each of the three modifications. Many flights were concerned with improving longitudinal stability by the use of elevator bungees and changing tailplane incidence – a sure sign that stick force per 'g' and trimability were problems.

Vampire NF.10 WP250 was issued to Handley Page at Radlett in November 1951 for boundary layer research, and was fitted with a suction 'glove' over the wings. It was eventually sold for scrap in May 1960. (Handley Page)

25 Squadron at West Malling was the first to receive the Vampire NF.10, in July 1951. WP239 is seen on 21 February 1952, crewed by Flt Lt Roy Bowie and Flt Sgt Dickie Hill. (via Sqn Ldr Roy Bowie)

During the testing of WP232 in early 1951, John Wilson also noted several minor faults which he recommended should be rectified and incorporated into production aircraft as soon as possible. His suggestions included the fitting of ten inches of ¼ in strip to the rudder to cure overbalance, the pilot's oxygen pipe should be lengthened to 5 ft and repositioned, the repositioning of the fire warning light and fire button to a more prominent place on the instrument panel, and the reduction in size of the IFF plate to give a more adequate clearance between itself and the undercarriage selector lever. Also required was a cure for the bad high frequency vibration found on some aircraft which was attributable to the ram air effect on the gun ports.

A few NF.10s were retained for trials purposes: WP240 was used by de Havilland's at Hatfield and Christchurch to test the avionics and nose radome for the DH 110 Sea Vixen in 1955. In November 1951 another NF.10, WP250, was flown to Handley Page Ltd at Radlett for the installation of a wing suction 'glove' and was used for boundary-layer laminar flow experiments. Between 1953 and 1956 it flew with various 5 ft test sections outboard of the port tail-boom, using air tapped from the engine compressor; to avoid asymmetric drag a false section of similar proportions was fitted to the starboard boom. WP250 was eventually sold for scrap in May 1960.

Deliveries of Vampire NF.10s to the RAF commenced on 10 April 1951 when WP236 was sent to the Handling Squadron at Manby for the preparation of Pilot's Notes. Other deliveries to RAF units in early 1951 included WP235 to the Central Signals Unit at Watton and WP239 to the Central Fighter Establishment at West Raynham.

On 2 July 1951 25 Squadron at West Malling became the RAF's first Vampire night-fighter unit when it received WP238 to begin the conversion from Mosquito NF.36s.

Commanded by Sqn Ldr D.C. Furse DFC, the squadron had undertaken jet conversion earlier in the year when Flt Lt. Denis Leete was detached in January 1951 to form a Flying Wing Training Flight with a handful of single-seat Vampires to provide familiarization training:

As the QFI for 25 Squadron, and in fact the only QFI in the West Malling Night-Fighter Wing (25, 29 and 85 Squadrons), I was instructed in January 1951 to form a jet conversion flight, having earlier, in 1949, gained jet experience at the Empire Flying School, Hullavington. I was provided with a Meteor 7 and three Vampire 5s (VV528, VV678 and VV685). I started giving dual instruction to the 25 Squadron pilots in the Meteor on 6th February 1951, and I flew the Vampires myself as often as I could. The 25 Squadron pilots completed their jet conversion in May, and I returned to flying Mosquitos.

On 2nd July 1951 the first Vampire NF.10 (WP238) was flown in by the Station Commander, Gp Capt. George Darley DSO, and after acceptance checks in the Tech Wing, I tried it out on 12th July. The NF.10s began arriving quickly; by mid-August the squadron had changed over from their Mosquitos and became operational on 31st August 1951.

The Vampire NF.10s were originally intended for the Egyptian Air Force, but when they were diverted to the RAF, 25 Squadron at West Malling was detailed to fly them. We were often ribbed about flying 'King Farouk's aeroplanes', and did we understand the dials? etc.

In September 1951 23 Squadron at Coltishall, commanded by Sqn Ldr V.S.H. Duclos DFC (who was replaced by Sqn Ldr A.J. Jacomb-Hood DFC in December 1951), became the second unit to receive the Vampire NF.10

Vampire NF. 10s of 23 Squadron lined up at Coltishall on 10 March 1953 in preparation for a Coronation Review fly-past. (23 Sqn Assce via 'Snowy' Davies)

Rejoining the circuit at Leuchars, Vampire NF. 10 WM705 of 151 Squadron, 1952. (Squadron collection)

when it received WP256 from No. 48 MU at Hawarden on 11 September. Conversion to the Vampire was painfully slow, and until the squadron was fully-equipped the following June, 'A' Flight flew Vampires, while 'B' Flight soldiered on with Mosquitos.

On 15 September 1951 the third and final NF.10 squadron was formed at Leuchars

under the command of Sqn Ldr A.D. Boyle. Initially operating as a cadre unit, 151 Squadron flew a mixture of single-seat Vampires and a Meteor T.7 until it received its first night-fighters (WM660 and WP252) on 8 February 1952.

At its best, in good conditions, the Vampire's simplicity, relatively high speed and manoeuvrability made it an attractive aircraft to operate, and it soon proved itself quite capable of intercepting Bomber Command's 'heavies' – the Avro Lincolns and B.29 Washingtons – and was more manoeuvrable than its Meteor contemporary. One aircrew member recalled that the lowest target he intercepted at night over the North Sea was a B.29 operating at 500 ft, and he was *below* it (to obtain a reasonable radar picture), relying on a pressure altimeter!

The Vampire night-fighter was even known to out-turn (just!) the F–86 Sabre during low-level dogfighting exercises. It was, however, hard-pressed to catch the English Electric Canberra jet bomber, just entering service with the RAF, which soon proved to Meteor and Vampire squadrons that it could with ease fly both higher and faster. Despite its low accident rate there were misgivings among the crews with regard to the Vampire's single Goblin engine; Meteor crews could at least take comfort from the presence of another engine should one fail – especially while operating at night over the North Sea. A single engine, however, enabled Vampire crews to achieve very fast scramble times compared to their Meteor colleagues, and although the Vampire crews approved of the side-by-side seating arrangement of their aircraft (except during formation flying), the lack of ejector seats was heavily criticized; night-fighter aircrew would have to wait for the Gloster Javelin to enter service in February 1956 for that luxury!

Many aircrew considered that the rudimentary aircraft and electrical systems without back-up arrangements meant that the Vampire was not suited to night/all-weather operations; the lack of a radio altimeter and navigation aids (prior to the fitment of Gee Mk. 3) was a major hindrance for a night-fighter.

The Vampire's AI Mk. 10 radar which by then was obsolete, could, when used with efficient Ground Control Interception methods, enable contact to be made with a high-speed, high-altitude target in about eleven minutes. Basically an American radar, designated SCR-720B, the AI Mk. 10 operated on a wavelength of 9.1 cm using a narrow beam, ten degrees in width. The dipole aerial and paraboloid dish scanner in the Vampire's nose was used for both transmitting and receiving, and rotated about its vertical axis at either 360 or 100 rpm. The beam also moved up and down from –20 degrees to +40 degrees, and was controlled by the radar operator. Presentation for the operator comprised two cathode-ray tubes, the right-hand tube giving range and azimuth, the left-hand tube elevation and azimuth. In operational use the maximum range of the AI Mk. 10 was about 6 miles, with a minimum range of 300 ft.

A successful interception required great skill and dexterity from the Navigator (Radar) (Nav/Rad) – or Radar Observers (ROs) as they were later known when the second crew member was trained solely for night fighting. Close cooperation was also required between the crew members and the ground controller who was responsible for putting the fighter into a favourable position for target interception.

Sqn Ldr Ray Follis DFC was a Nav/Rad Leader with 25 Squadron at West Malling, and also flew as navigator for the Commanding Officer, Sqn Ldr Denis Furse. He previously flew Mosquito NF.36s with 141 Squadron at Coltishall and with the Mosquito Training Squadron at No. 228 OCU Leeming, where he was Senior Nav/Rad Instructor. In mid-1951 Ray Follis joined 25 Squadron during its conversion from Mosquitos to Vampires, and his recollections of the role of a Nav/Rad and the complexities of operating the Vampire's AI Mk. 10 are quite explicit:

Conversion from the Mosquito NF.36 to the Vampire NF.10 was, for the Nav/Rad, a relatively easy matter. His interception radar was the same, his principal navigation aid was still Gee (albeit in a miniaturized form –

the Mk. III version) and was still located behind the pilot with its screen pointing towards the navigator and requiring him to have strong neck muscles to see it. The interception technique was also very similar to that used in the Mosquito, but enhanced by the Vampire's responsive handling and increased performance.

The success of any night-fighter crew depended on the rapport between them, and the speed of their reactions. It required the instant interpretation by the Nav/Rad of what was happening on his radar screen, and the immediate translation of this into his commentary and instructions to his pilot. Similarly, it was equally important for the pilot to respond immediately to instructions given and sometimes to anticipate his navigator's next words.

Our practice interceptions were mostly on other Vampires or piston-engined aircraft, and our awareness of the superiority of other jets over us was best illustrated by a Canberra overtaking us with its airbrakes extended! Later confirmation that the Canberra had approached from behind in a dive and that its airbrakes were not all that effective did little to dispel our realization that the Vampire NF.10, together with its obsolete AI Mk. 10 radar, was only a stop-gap fighter.

After flying Spitfires in the Middle East and Vampire fighters at Odiham, Sqn Ldr Roy Bowie flew Vampire NF.10s with 25 Squadron at West Malling between 1951 and 1953:

The Vampire NF.10 was a nice aircraft to fly and possessed a very reliable Goblin engine. It had, however, several disadvantages as a night-fighter: there was only one radio set and generator fitted, the forward view from the cockpit was restricted, and, most seriously, it lacked ejector seats. Eventually

we were given miniature 'Gee', which was a great help whilst flying at night.

Our greatest heart-stoppers were low-level practice interceptions at night over the sea. The Vampire was not fitted with a radio altimeter, and slowing down to 105 knots with two drop-tanks, and at 500 ft or below, waiting to meet the Lancaster's slipstream was quite exciting. However, for real stimulation, Exercise 'Litestrike' helped to raise one's adrenalin level. This was an air-to-sea exercise, undertaken at night, simulating gun attacks against fast patrol boats. We made dive attacks on the targets by the light of parachute flares dropped from MR Lancasters. To extend the length of the sortie we used to operate with underwing tanks and leave about 30 degrees of flap down to improve the handling. Again we had no radio altimeter, and I assumed that I was flying at minimum height when the RO screamed in my ear for me to pull up.

The Vampire NF.10s participated in several Fighter Command exercises including 'Ardent' during October 1952 when, in the ten days it lasted, 151 Squadron scored thirty-one 'kills' in fifty-one sorties – albeit against piston-engined RAF Lincoln and B.29 bombers. During late June 1952 23 Squadron conducted trials in the use of NF.10s for night interdiction for which they undertook low-level simulated attacks against trains, transport and bridges. The following month 23 Squadron was involved in further trials when the Vampires experimented with high quarter attacks at night against RAF Washington bombers.

Venturing further afield, 23 Squadron detached four aircraft to Fassberg in September 1952 for Exercise 'Holdfast', the purpose of which was to assess the Vampire's suitability for night interdiction. Between 3 and 13 November 1952, six of the squadron's Vampires were detached to Ta Kali in Malta under the leadership of Flight Commander Flt

Lt. J.H. Hedger, to participate in the naval exercise 'Longstop' and to provide training for the Malta Air Defence Radar Units. A number of day and night practice interception sorties were flown by the Vampires, and later during the detachment the squadron was involved in searches for naval convoys and attacks on the Royal Navy's fast patrol boats during anti-minelaying sweeps.

Bob Grattan joined 23 Squadron at Coltishall in September 1951 after completing his training as a navigator. He later became the station's Navigation Officer before a posting to 151 Squadron in March 1958 to fly Javelin FAW.5s:

When I joined the squadron in mid-1951 we were known as 23/151 Squadron, but 151 Squadron soon split away to form at Leuchars under Squadron Leader Don Boyle. Four crews went from Coltishall to act as an experienced nucleus.

Jet conversion for the pilots was via the Vampire 5, of which 23 Squadron had three. Long sessions and quizzes with Pilot's Notes were followed by a solo in the Vampire 5. The principal problem was judging the height of the round-out since the Vampire had much shorter legs than the Mosquito! There were no accidents during conversion, however, so the system worked.

23 Squadron had only received its first NF.10 in mid-1951 (there was only one on strength when I arrived) and the replacement Venom was already being discussed. There was a requirement then for a further role for the NF.10 and night interdiction was a possibility. I flew a couple of sorties with the C.O., Jake Jacomb-Hood, in June 1952 which were recorded as interdiction trials, and in September we fired at night against targets on the Holbeach range, illuminated by sodium flares. As a matter of interest, the Vampire NF.10 had the GM2 fixed-ring

sight, which was all right for air/ground firing, but less so for air-to-air work.

On 6th September 1952 four aircraft from 23 Squadron flew to Fassberg for Exercise 'Holdfast'. The Fassberg Wing's Vampires were detached to Sylt for an APC, so only 'Holdfast' aircraft were present during this period. Other aircraft on detachment included four piston Provosts, a couple of Lincolns and probably four Canberras. Our task was to carry out air/ground firing at night against vehicles on the Sennelager range using flares dropped from Lincolns as the source of light; the Provosts used 'Glow-Worm' rocket flares and so looked after themselves.

The build-up for the exercise consisted of a few low-level cross-country flights around West Germany and a daylight air/ground sortie against a beat-up stationary tank. The night sorties began with a recce of the Sennelager range on the 11th and live air/ground attacks on the 13th and 14th. More sorties were flown on the nights of the 19th/20th and 22nd, but these were simulated attacks against army vehicles deploying on a ground exercise. We flew back to Coltishall, via Marham, on 22nd September. Exercise 'Ardent', the annual Fighter Command exercise, began the following month, so our venture into interdiction ended with our return to base.

A highlight of the Vampire NF.10's short operational career with the RAF was the Queen's Review of the Royal Air Force at Odiham on 15 July 1953. Twelve NF.10s drawn from 23 and 25 Squadrons and led by Wg Cdr J.W. Allan DSO, DFC, participated in the massed fly-past of 639 RAF and Commonwealth aircraft in what was one of the largest ever displays of British air power. Operating from Coltishall, the night-fighters flew over Odiham at 700 ft in three boxes of four aircraft at a strictly regulated speed of 305

In its element at Coltishall, Vampire NF.10 WM730 of 23 Squadron, July 1953. (23 Sqn Assce via 'Snowy' Davies)

mph as 'Formation Number Twenty-Three', between three Hastings transport aircraft and twenty-four Vampire single-seaters from Flying Training Command. Timings for the one hour and twenty minute flight from Coltishall were critical to maintain formation in the 34 mile corridor from the 'gate' at Leavesden to Odiham, with a plus/minus of 15 seconds at any point on the route. The Vampires were able to monitor their progress along the route by having one lead navigator, with another reserve navigator in each squadron, who 'map-crawled' with infinite care. In the huge static display on the ground, the Vampire NF.10s were represented by three immaculately polished aircraft (WM676, WM677 and WM703) drawn from No. 10 MU at Hullavington.

The RAF Review at Odiham was, in fact, the Vampire night-fighter's swan-song; 151 Squadron at Leuchars had already received their replacement Meteor NF.11s in March 1953 and had flown their last Vampire sortie on 10 May. Next to relinquish its Vampires was 23 Squadron in January 1954, which converted to Venom NF.2s (the first aircraft was delivered in November 1953), and finally, in March 1954, 25 Squadron became operational with the Meteor NF.12. The final RAF unit to operate the Vampire NF.10 was the Central Signals Unit at Watton, which ferried its last aircraft (WM727) to No. 48 MU in October 1954.

The requirement for a high-speed navigation trainer in 1953 saw a resurgence of interest in the Vampire NF.10, many of which were in storage at various Maintenance Units with minimal airframe flying hours. It was considered that the Vampire could be economical as a training aircraft for navigators who had received their basic instruction in Canada: the syllabus would include high-altitude, high-speed navigation exercises and familiarization in flying and operating over the UK. This would be accomplished by the inclusion in the training programme of timing, tracking and rapid fixing exercises with Gee Mk. 3, and also radar and VHF 'let-downs' and approaches.

The contract for converting the Vampires to navigation trainers was awarded to Airwork General Trading Ltd; the work was carried out at Speke (Liverpool Airport) between March 1954 and December 1955. The AI Mk. 10 radar was removed from the aircraft's nose and replaced by concrete weights, and Rebecca

Mk. IV/BABS was installed to complement the Gee Mk. 3 navigation radar. The night-fighter's four 20 mm cannon arrangement was retained to maintain the aircraft's centre of gravity, and a completely new quick-release clear-view canopy – Mod. No. 3151 – was fitted to replace the heavily framed 'clamshell'. Although this work involved a major redesign of the Vampire's cockpit, provision was still not made for ejector seats.

On 5 March 1954 the first of the thirty-six Vampires to be converted (WM713 and WM729) were flown to Speke Airport and were ready for collection by the end of the year. The serials of the Vampire NF(T)10s involved in the conversion to navigation trainers were WM668, WM670, WM672, WM674, WM677, WM703, WM704, WM705, WM706, WM711, WM712, WM713, WM714, WM716, WM718, WM727, WM729, WM730, WM733, WP232, WP233, WP234, WP235, WP236, WP238, WP239, WP242, WP243, WP245, WP247, WP248, WP249, WP251, WP253, WP255 and WP256.

In May 1955 the fifth aircraft to be converted (WM711) was issued to the A&AEE for flight trials and assessment of the aircraft's navigational equipment. The results were published in August 1955 and concluded that the aircraft fell short of the requirements for a navigation trainer, strongly recommending the resiting of the radar control units and the installation of a folding plotting board for the navigator and a stowage compartment for his maps and charts.

Deliveries of the Vampires in their new role began on 25 May 1955 when WM729 was delivered to No. 2 Air Navigation School at Thorney Island. An average of ten Vampire NF(T)10s was operated by No. 2 ANS until they were phased out in favour of Meteor NF(T)14s in July 1959.

The largest user of the Vampire NF(T)10 navigation trainer was the Central Navigation and Control School at Shawbury. Between May 1954 and May 1957 – when they were replaced by further deliveries of Vampire T.11s to the school – they were used by 'A' Flight. Some aircraft lingered on until September 1959 when they were disposed of by No. 60 MU.

Following a service career with the CFE and 25 Squadron, WP235 was converted to a navigation trainer and delivered to No. 2 ANS at Thorney Island in September 1955. It is depicted here at Upper Heyford in May 1956. (G.A. Jenks)

No. 1 Air Navigation School at Topcliffe became the final unit to receive NF(T)10s and accepted its allotted nine aircraft after the unit reformed on 15 March 1957. The school's main task was to train NCO radio operators and student navigators – who were usually acting pilot officers – for the Javelin all-weather fighter. No. 1 ANS also ran acclimatization courses for Canadian-trained navigators. The intense nine-month course at Topcliffe was later considered inadequate, for of those who eventually graduated, nearly all were 'chopped' during the next stage of their training at Leeming or North Luffenham.

Sqn Ldr 'Joe' Warne was a flight commander with No. 1 ANS, and flew the Vampire NF(T)10 from May 1957 to May 1959:

My time on No. 1 ANS was a 'rest tour' consequent to the Sandys/Boyle fiasco. Inevitably there was a bunch of jet pilots similarly involved, but it was a happy unit, closely connected with the Marathon/Valetta/Varsity staff pilots in all respects.

There were all-through student navigators at both Nos 1 and 2 ANS, in addition to the ex-Canadian acclimatization students and the Cranwell Flight Cadets who came to Topcliffe for their jet training. The Vampires were employed for the final high-speed phase of the students' training after progressing through the piston-engined stages.

The training syllabus included day and night familiarization trips of about one hour, night navexes, and at least one low-level map-reading cross-country flight. There were also two flights simulating 'broadcast control' interception practice where two aircraft would operate together and alternate as fighter and target. The fighter pilot would call a 'split' and subsequently turn in to give a track interception of about 90 degrees. The target navigator would broadcast his position over the R/T in Georef co-ordinates, which the fighter navigator would plot along with his own Gee position, and then vector his pilot onto headings appropriate to effect a visual interception in the most expeditious manner.

The occasional Rebecca homing and BABS approach was done in the Vampire, but the main training on this navaid and

Two Vampire NF.54s, ID595 and ID603, at Hatfield on 30 July 1954, prior to delivery to the Indian Air Force. (Huntings plc)

the ADF was completed in the earlier Valetta/Varsity phase, the course culminating in an overseas trip to Malta, Gibraltar or Idris. The usual fighter recoveries of Gee homing, QGH let-down and GCA were normal.

The original Gee Mk. 3 was retained, positioned behind the pilot's seat and operated by the navigator over his left shoulder. The Gee navigational equipment was unique to north-west Europe and was perfectly adequate, whereas only the Rebecca/BABS could have been used overseas, so the training for high-level navigation was quite satisfactory for subsequent night-fighter duties. The problem was that the students were not selected with any consideration for their aptitude for instant interpretation of the three-dimensional radar picture and interception techniques. In fact, with the full navigator courses, those at the bottom

of the graduation list were automatically sent on to night-fighter duties!

By February 1959 replacement Meteor NF(T)14s had become available and it was decided to dispose of the Vampires at No. 1 ANS, with the majority transferring to the Central Navigation and Control School at Shawbury. By September 1959 the remaining Vampires were finally withdrawn from service.

Many of the surplus RAF Vampire NF.10s held by the Maintenance Units were offered for export. Between July 1953 and January 1954 eighteen of the night-fighters were sold back to de Havilland's and overhauled at Chester; this included the fitting of cold air units. They were then re-sold to the Indian Air Force as Vampire NF.54s. These aircraft were delivered from Blackbushe by pilots of Field Aviation Services between April and October 1954. The NF.54 serials involved were ID592/WM724, ID593/WM659,

Vampire NF.54 MM6016 was built at Hatfield and delivered to Italy in June 1951. (de Havilland)

The second company prototype, G–5–5, was delivered to Switzerland in January 1951 as J–1301 and used for a variety of ECM and radio trials. The 'wasp' markings were created by the paint shop at F+W Emmen to make the aircraft more distinctive. (F+W Emmen)

ID594/WM719, ID595/WM665, ID596/WM721, ID597/WM728, ID598/WM667, ID599/WM720, ID600/WM664, ID601/WM662, ID602/WM660, ID603/WM666, ID604/WM661, ID605/WM675, ID606/WV690, ID607/WV689, ID608/WM715 and ID609/WM710.

A second order for twelve Vampire NF.54s for the Indian Air Force was later received and following a similar refurbishment at Chester, they were delivered between August 1957 and March 1958. The serials were ID1601/WM731, ID1602/WM732, ID1603/WM732, ID1604/WV691, ID1605/WP246, ID1606/WP249, ID1607/WM708, ID1608/WM709, ID1609/WM725, ID1610/WM676, ID1611/WM717 and ID1612/WM707. India used its Vampire NF.54s as operational night-fighters with 10 Squadron at Palam from August 1954 until March 1965. Later in their careers they were relegated as advanced trainers, with the last being struck off charge in September 1966.

The thirty night-fighters delivered to India were not Chester's first export order for the Vampire NF.54, for in October 1949, Italy had ordered fourteen aircraft pending the decision to licence-build a quantity of Venom NF.51s. The first two aircraft, serialled 3–167 and 3–168 (MM6016 and MM6017) were built at Hatfield, and the remainder, 3–169 and 3–170, and 3–211 to 3–220, built at Chester; deliveries took place between July 1952 and March 1953. The Chester-built NF.54s were allocated the military numbers MM6018 to MM6152.

One Vampire night-fighter (the company prototype, G–5–2) was delivered to Switzerland in 1951. Serialled J–1301, this aircraft was used by the Federal Aircraft Factory at Emmen for ECM trials and equipment installation testing for the Swiss licence-built Venoms until August 1958, when it was handed over to the Swiss Air Force for further ECM trials.

To date, only two Vampire night-fighters are known to have been preserved: ID606 (ex-WV690) is displayed at the Indian Air Force Museum at IAF Palam and MM6152 (ex-SCOT, Amendola) with the Museum of Flight at Turin in Italy.

VAMPIRE T.11

It was not unusual for post-war aircraft manufacturers to develop a two-seat training aircraft from a standard fighter: in 1947 the Gloster Aircraft Company had recognized the advantage of a jet trainer and successfully produced the Meteor T.7 from the Meteor F.4 airframe. Although there was no official requirement for a jet trainer for the RAF, interest in the Meteor T.7 was immediate and the Air Ministry issued a specification to cover the RAF version, which entered service with No. 203 AFS at Driffield in early 1949.

Interest in a jet trainer was shown by many countries, as the concept of a proven 'off the shelf' single-seat fighter adapted for training purposes was attractive; pilots could be given training in the use of the fighter they were to fly, training of ground crews could be kept to a minimum, and fewer additional spares had to be acquired.

With Vampire fighters in service with, or on order from, fourteen countries, the need for a two-seat Vampire advanced trainer was obvious, and in June 1950 de Havilland's decided to proceed with the design and construction of prototype Vampire trainer. As the design team at de Havilland's was already heavily committed, the project was given to their associate company, the Airspeed factory at Christchurch, Hampshire.

The design team responsible for the trainer was headed by R.C. Gilbert and R.J.G. Bray, together with R.S. Hammond of the Stress Office. Unlike previous fighter/trainer conversions, the design team decided to opt for side-by-side seating for instructor and pupil. It was believed that this arrangement would benefit not only the pupil, who could learn by watching his instructor's movements, but also the instructor who could anticipate and correct his pupil's mistakes.

Although the Goblin 3 engine (giving 3,350 lb static thrust) was proposed for future developments of the Vampire trainer, the prototype was fitted with a Goblin 33. This engine gave the same power as the Goblin 3, but differed principally in providing air for cabin pressurization by means of bleed air from the engine compressor rather than by driving a blower.

To ensure that the DH 115 Vampire (as the variant was initially known) was attractive to buyers as a weapons trainer, de Havilland's retained the fighter's standard armament and provision for a combination of either eight 60 lb rockets and eight 25 lb practice bombs, or two 500 lb bombs with or without rockets, or two 1,000 lb bombs; this allowed the advanced trainer to be used alternatively as a front line fighter/bomber.

As work got under way on the Vampire trainer at Christchurch, it was planned that the prototype should be exhibited at the SBAC show in September 1950. To speed up the work, the mock-up of the Vampire night-fighter was moved to Christchurch and adapted to serve as the prototype for the trainer version. A set of standard Vampire FB.5 wings, booms and tail unit were brought together, and a Goblin engine collected from de Havilland (Engines) at Leavesden. Working with the night-fighter fuselage nacelle as a basis, the designers found it possible to obtain additional cockpit width (to 44 in at shoulder level) in the trainer by lowering the canopy side rails. This extra width made it feasible to move the position of the navigator's seat forward and obviate the need for the seat-staggered layout of the night-fighter. The night-fighter's canopy was also used, comprising a tubular structure with a rearward-opening entry hatch on the top, which, in the event of an emergency, could be jettisoned by a small hydraulic ram fitted to release the fasteners and then sucked open by the slipstream.

In place of the night-fighter's radome, the trainer's front fuselage incorporated a shaped-sheet nose cap, hinged to fold up, allowing access to a G.45 camera, two five-channel VHF radio sets, four 750 litre oxygen bottles, a glycol container and batteries mounted on an internal shelf. The nose cap was secured by three Napier cowling fasteners on each side and a press-stud

on the front. As with the Vampire fighter, four 20 mm Hispano cannon were fitted in the fuselage belly of the trainer. Because of the extra weight, a slight modification to the Vampire FB.5's nose oleo was found necessary but the main undercarriage legs and wheels were standard Vampire parts.

As the cockpit is the most important feature of an all-purpose trainer, a great deal of thought was given to the arrangement of the Vampire's instruments and controls. Duplicated flight instruments and throttle controls, dive-brake lever and elevator trim were provided for both instructor and pupil. The engine instruments were located in a central panel above which were situated other primary instruments including the Machmeter. To each

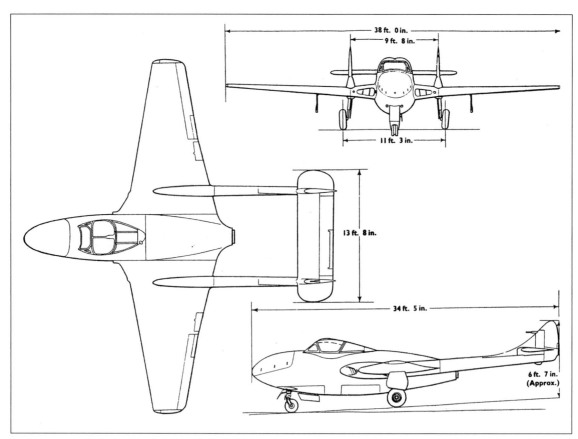

General arrangement drawing of Vampire T.11. (de Havilland)

side of the central panel was a Mk.4E gyro gunsight fitted in a retractable mounting.

The airframe was completed in time to be displayed in the static park of the SBAC show, complete with Class 'B' registration G–5–7, and attracted a great deal of interest. Immediately after the show the trainer was returned to Christchurch to be finished in readiness for its first flight. This took place at Christchurch on 15 November 1950. Apart from problems with the Vampire's wheel brakes, the 35 minute flight by John Wilson was uneventful, as his test report shows:

Prototype G–5–7
15 Nov 1950
WL 9,500 lbs (270 galls fuel)
C.G. .235 at T.O.

First flight – general handling
Stalls, power off, were carried out directly altitude had been gained.
Wheels & flaps up, 8,500 ft, 240 galls.
Pre-stall buffet commenced 105 kts.
True stall, square, with nose drop 76–80 kts IAS.

Wheels down, flaps 60°, 6,000 ft, 230 galls.
Pre-stall buffet commenced 95 kts.
Bad port wing drop at 88 kts (tip stall).
True stall unobtainable as wing drop cannot be held with ailerons.
Port wing tip needs filling for bad stall.

Brakes were not holding above 9,000 rpm (at Hurn), they should hold to 10,250 rpm. Due to this factor, manoeuvring on the

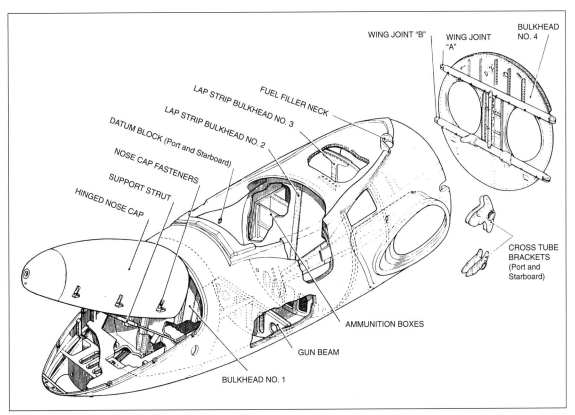

Sectioned diagram of Vampire T.11 fuselage. (de Havilland)

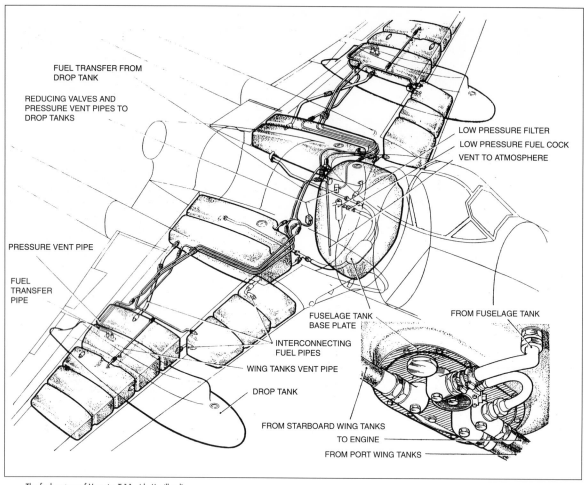

FUEL TRANSFER FROM
DROP TANK

REDUCING VALVES AND
PRESSURE VENT PIPES TO
DROP TANKS

LOW PRESSURE FILTER
LOW PRESSURE FUEL COCK
VENT TO ATMOSPHERE

PRESSURE VENT PIPE

FUEL
TRANSFER
PIPE

FUSELAGE TANK
BASE PLATE

FROM FUSELAGE TANK

INTERCONNECTING
FUEL PIPES

WING TANKS VENT PIPE

DROP TANK

FROM STARBOARD WING TANKS
TO ENGINE
FROM PORT WING TANKS

The fuel system of Vampire T.11. (de Havilland)

ground is difficult, requiring excessive power and speed.

General handling: The aircraft handled in a manner very similar to the standard Vampire 5 and was satisfactory in all respects up to the speed attained of 330 knots (limit 345 knots).

Landing was satisfactory and simple, but could be considerably shortened by more effective brakes. Due to various troubles previously mentioned in connection with the brakes, the port brake overheated at

Hurn whilst taxiing, and it was necessary to change this unit.

John Wilson flew the prototype again two days later and was pleased with the aircraft's high Mach number handling qualities.

The RAF was also pleased with the performance of the Vampire trainer, whose long-term role was envisaged as an advanced trainer for the second half of the standard 'wings' course undertaken by all RAF pilots. In the short term, however, the Vampire was needed to augment the Meteor T.7 at the Advanced Flying Schools, where prospective

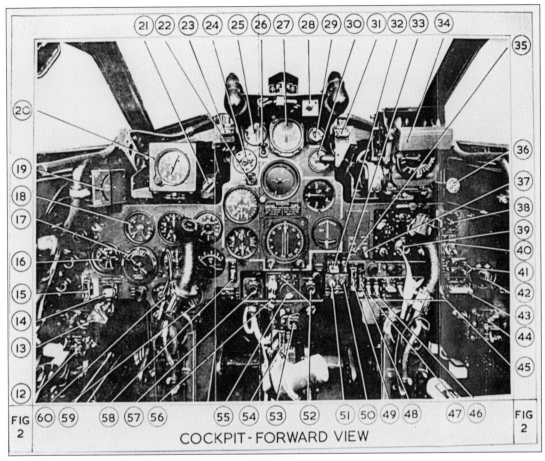

Instrument panel of the Vampire T.11. (de Havilland)

fighter pilots underwent jet conversion after gaining their wings on piston-engined trainers. It was also required both in the short and long term as a gunnery and instrument trainer at the Operational Conversion Units and operational squadrons.

In February 1951 it was decided to evaluate the Vampire trainer at No. 203 AFS at Driffield; to enable the prototype to undergo Service trials it was issued with the serial WW456. Due to armament troubles the delivery of WW456 to Driffield was delayed until 8 March 1951, and four days later it began an experimental training course with two student pilots.

The two students, Pt Off. Michael Warrington and Off. Cadet Kenneth Harvey, had been especially posted to Driffield from No. 6 FTS at Ternhill and No. 7 FTS at Cottesmore, and completed their training on the Vampire on 30 March 1951. Warrington went solo after 6 hours 55 minutes of flying training and Harvey after 8 hours 35 minutes.

On 2 April 1951 WW456 was transferred to the Central Gunnery School for gunnery trials, which finished on 26 April. Three days later the aircraft was sent to the A&AEE for further development testing, and gave a superb flying demonstration at the 1951 SBAC show (11–16 September) with John Wilson at the controls.

Between July 1951 and February 1952 the

Prototype Vampire trainer, G–5–7 during its first flight from Christchurch, 15 November 1950, flown by John Wilson. (John Wilson)

Company test pilots, John Wilson and George Errington in the cockpit of the prototype trainer shortly after the first flight, November 1950. (John Wilson)

trainer prototype (now re-registered G–5–7) was evaluated at Boscombe Down in a series of trials, including in-flight gun and ammunition bay temperature checks, cockpit assessment, and drop-tank and weapons handling tests. During the handling and spinning tests, the prototype's handling characteristics were found to be similar (except for rudder overbalance) to those of the Vampire fighter. In the first two turns of the spin, the trainer's qualities resembled those of the single-seaters, and being less erratic were considered satisfactory; it was recommended that pilots be advised to push the stick well forward in recovery and to ease the aircraft gently out of the dive.

Two pre-production aircraft, WW458 and WW461, ordered against Contract No. 6/ACFT/7075 dated 5 July 1951, were quick to follow the prototype off the Christchurch production line. The first, WW458, took to the air on 1 December 1951 and was delivered to RNAS Culdrose on 21 January 1952. The second was sent to RNAS Culham on 22 May 1952 and following an operational evaluation by various Royal Navy squadrons, orders were secured for the Fleet Air Arm as the Vampire T.22.

To cover the production of Vampire trainers for the RAF, Specification T.111P was issued on 23 September 1951. It required the aircraft to be cleared for four-turn spins, the duplication of undercarriage and flap levers in the cockpit and, in order to fulfil the role as a weapons trainer, provision for eight 60 lb RPs (in practice, only four were normally carried) and two 20 mm cannon – the latter to be installed as a normal training fit, but with the capability for four cannon in an operational emergency.

Production of the RAF's Vampire T.11s commenced with Contract Nos 6/ACFT/7381 and 7382, dated 3 October 1951, which covered the construction of 143 aircraft to be built at Christchurch, Chester and Hatfield. The first production aircraft, WZ414, flew on 19 January 1952, and was retained at Christchurch for company trials until July 1954 when it was transferred to the A&AEE at Boscombe Down for instrument rating assessment. Following storage at various Maintenance Units for the next three years, the aircraft was eventually sold to the Mexican Air Force in 1962.

In March 1952 the second production Vampire T.11, WZ415, was sent to the A&AEE to compare its performance with WW458, which had arrived at Boscombe Down the previous month. They were joined in April 1952 by WZ417, which underwent an engineering appraisal in readiness for the aircraft's release to the RAF. During the next eight weeks the Vampire's suitability as a trainer was assessed, and the A&AEE report concluded:

The general performance capabilities of the Vampire trainer compare very favourably with those of fighter aircraft at present in service, and on this account it could be usefully employed as an advanced, and/or operational trainer. The handling characteristics of the aircraft also render it eminently suitable for this role. It is considered that it would make an excellent intermediate trainer for the more advanced aircraft expected in the near future, and in this role would also be very suitable for armament training.

The only condition in which the aircraft's behaviour is unpleasant (though not dangerous) is in the spin, but this is considered acceptable in an intermediate trainer, and may prove an advantage in that pupils can thereby be introduced at an early stage to the unpleasant spinning characteristics of current fighters.

The side-by-side seating arrangement facilitates demonstration and practice, and aiming and firing guns, rockets, and bombs, since the instructor and pupil have similar sighting systems.

The major disadvantage of the aircraft as a trainer is the lack of ejector seats, without which it is considered that successful emergency exit in flight is unlikely to be achieved. Other less serious disadvantages are the distortion of the curved roof panels which make difficult the closing-in stages of formation flying and turning in formation; and the lack of an undercarriage lever for the instructor, which might on occasion prove embarrassing.

In order that the Vampire T.11 could be evaluated by the RAF as a weapons trainer, WZ418 was sent to the Armament Practice Station at Acklington on 10 June 1952, and then transferred to No. 229 Operational Conversion Unit at Chivenor in July 1952 to continue gunnery trials. Over thirty weapons sorties were flown by WZ418 at Acklington and the aircraft was only rendered temporarily unserviceable when a faulty gun sight necessitated a return to Hatfield for repairs.

On 2 September 1952 the first Vampire T.11 (WZ426) was delivered to No. 202 Advanced Flying School at Valley, and by July 1953 the unit had completed the change-over from the Meteor T.7. One of the squadron commanders at No. 202 AFS was Wg Cdr John Smith-Carington:

Our first Vampire T.11s arrived in September 1952 and I undertook most of the initial air testing.

The aircraft was soon found to be very difficult to recover from an inverted spin. On 8th October 1952, I lost 10,000 feet whilst trying to recover from such a spin and tried to bale out, but the canopy jettison handle was on the floor of the cockpit and it was found impossible to reach because of the negative 'g' forces from the inverted spin. Fortunately the aircraft recovered on its own at a low altitude. I believe that after this incident all Vampire T.11s were modified

with extensions to the fins and outboard of the fin and rudder; the jettison handle was also repositioned.

Together with the Vampires from Merryfield, No. 202 AFS was selected to participate in the massed fly-past of RAF aircraft during the Queen's Review of the RAF at Odiham in July 1953. Vampire T.11 (WZ561 0–55), flown by Master Pilot Sznapka, was in the twelve aircraft formation from No. 25 Group Detachment operating from Oakington. In the static display at Odiham were four more Vampire T.11s: WZ510 and WZ570 from No. 202 AFS, and WZ551 and WZ566 from No. 208 AFS.

Further deliveries to the RAF included four aircraft (WZ422–WZ425) to the Central Gunnery School at Leconfield in September 1952, the APS at Acklington (WZ427 and WZ428) and the APS at Sylt. The work-up at Acklington did not go well when the Vampires were plagued with problems such as flap creep and inaccurate gun harmonization, which meant the aircraft were unserviceable for most of October.

Deliveries to No. 202 AFS, Valley, began in September 1952. One of the original aircraft, WZ446, is seen high above North Wales the following year. (via Gp Capt. A.S. Mann)

Founder members of No. 202 AFS, Valley, in March 1951. Back row, left to right: Flt Sgt Wilson, Flt Sgt Banbury, Sgt Moss, Sgt Hicks. Front row: Sqn Ldr Smith-Carington (Sqn Cdr), Wg Cdr Mann (OC Flying), Gp Capt. Jones (Stn Cdr), Sqn Ldr Horsley (Sqn Cdr), Flt Lt Tebbitt. (Wg Cdr Smith-Carington)

The introduction of the Vampire T.11 into RAF Flying Training Command marked the demise of the Advanced Flying School stage of the student pilot's training. The AFSs had provided an intermediate step for aircrew between the Flying Training School and the Operational Conversion Unit, thereby ensuring a smooth transition from trainer aircraft to operational types. Since 1948 aircrew had completed their basic flying training on the low-powered Tiger Moth or Percival Prentice, and their advanced training to 'wings' standard on the Harvard, Balliol or Oxford. The Vampire trainer allowed the system of pilot training to be radically improved during 1953, by removing the inconsistent Prentice/Harvard /Meteor sequence in favour of a more powerful piston-engined trainer for the initial stage of the pupil's training, and a less powerful jet trainer than the Meteor to allow a smoother transition to jet-equipped squadrons at an earlier stage.

The Percival Provost T.1 was selected to equip the Basic FTSs and deliveries commenced to No. 6 FTS at Ternhill in July 1953; the Vampire T.11 would provide the second half of the pilot training sequence and become the first jet aircraft on which pupils would qualify for their wings.

On 21 April 1954 twenty pupils of No. 101 Course at Ternhill completed their 130 hour basic flying training and arrived at No. 206 AFS Oakington for the advanced stage of their training under the Provost/Vampire sequence. Pt Off. D.J. Clegg became the first student pilot under the new scheme to solo on the Vampire T.11 (closely followed by Pt Offs Hillman and Williams) on 13 May 1954 after some 6.55 hours of dual instruction, and by July the remainder of the course had followed his example. The 110 hour syllabus was divided into 60.10 hours dual and 49.50 hours solo flying, and included such exercises as familiarization, circuits, instrument flying, aerobatics, formation and night flying. Eighteen pilots of the first course at Oakington graduated on 22 December 1954 before the Reviewing Officer, Air Marshal T.G. Pike CB, CBE, DFC.

The first course was considered a success: the students appeared to have the ability to absorb the instruction, and the Vampire seemed to be an ideal aircraft for the task. David Clegg's impressions of the first course are of interest:

I went solo on the Vampire T.11 at Oakington (in XD462) on 13th May – some eight days before my 19th birthday. As young men we thought we were pretty special, but I suppose a point that rates a special mention is the fact that both the Provost and Vampire were side-by-side trainers, as opposed to the Harvard/Meteor, which were tandem. I feel that this was a distinct advantage for both the instructor and pupil.

Further south, No. 208 AFS at Merryfield received its first four Vampire T.11s (WZ457–WZ459, and WZ461) in January 1953, and despite equipment delays, proved itself proficient in a remarkably short time. Later in the year the unit published a report:

In addition to the Meteor T.7s and Vampire T.11s, the unit is equipped with Vampire FB.5s and FB.9s for solo work by the students, who arrive at the School direct from FTS either in the UK, Canada or Rhodesia, with their newly awarded 'wings' and about 200 hours experience.

The first two weeks of the AFS are spent on purely conversion training to jet principles and pupils experience little difficulty; usual solo time is 3–5 hours. In all, 55 hours are flown on the course, which also includes aerobatics, formation flying and general handling, to the proportion of 28 hours dual and 27 hours solo.

Typifying the RAF's Provost/Vampire flying training sequence, Vampire T.11 XD520 of No. 5 FTS, Oakington, and Provost T.1 WV429 of No. 6 FTS, Ternhill. (MoD)

A formation comprising Vampire FB.5s and a T.11 from Nos 202 AFS and 208 AFS, temporarily operating from Odiham for the Coronation Review of the RAF, July 1953. The Vampire detachment was commanded by Flt Lt C.S. McDonald. (Chas E. Brown)

The maximum endurance for a high-altitude sortie on internal fuel with the Vampire T.11 is nearly two hours, and 1½ hours for the Vampire FB.9, while sorties are normally confined to 40 minutes. For long-range work, two Vampire FB.5s are kept with their external wing tanks installed.

The Vampire fighter variants have a critical Mach number of about 0.78, but the longer nose and revised tail of the T.11 have resulted in an increase in critical Mach number to 0.82 or 0.83. Students practise Mach runs up to the critical Mach number of the aircraft, and learn to recognize the symptoms of approaching compressibility – snaking, slight buffeting, and one wing down at the breakaway. Recovery is the standard throttle back and airbrakes out, and is accompanied by a sharp nose-up change of trim.

High-altitude training takes place in the Vampire T.11 up to 42,000 feet, at which height the cabin pressurization maintains a cockpit altitude equivalent to 25–26,000 feet.

The Vampire trainer possesses an extraordinary degree of neutral stability which makes it an excellent machine for instrument flying, and also for armament training when required.

To accommodate the Provost/Vampire sequence there was a complete reorganization of advanced flying training units during 1954, and on 1 June the short-lived AFSs were disbanded and re-formed as Flying Training Schools. Accordingly, No. 202 AFS was renamed No. 7 FTS; No. 203 AFS gave way to No. 8 FTS; No. 205 AFS became No. 4 FTS; No. 206 AFS was renamed No. 5 FTS; No. 208 AFS became No. 10 FTS; No. 210 AFS was disbanded. In July 1954 the organization of the Central Flying School at Little Rissington was also changed to support the new all-through Provost/Vampire syllabus. Responsible for maintaining the high standards of flying instruction (through the Examining Wing) and the training of flying instructors, the CFS had received its first T.11s in the autumn of 1953. On 25 August 1954 eight students of No. 163 Course arrived at Little Rissington from the CFS (Basic) Flight at South Cerney for advanced training with the newly formed

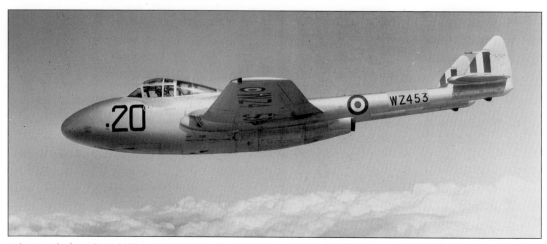

A pleasing study of an early standard Vampire T.11, WZ453 of No. 208 AFS, Merryfield, 20 April 1953. It later served with the RAF College, Cranwell, and was struck off charge in March 1962. (MoD)

Vampire Flight; the course graduated on 3 November 1954.

Also equipped with T.11s were the three Operational Conversion Units which provided tactical training for pupil pilots destined for front-line fighter squadrons: No. 229 OCU at Chivenor received WZ418 in July 1952, No. 233 OCU received WZ464 in February 1953, and No. 226 OCU at Stradishall took delivery of WZ578 and WZ579 in May 1953.

Colin Sloan was a flight commander at Chivenor between February 1952 and November 1953. An experienced Vampire pilot with 32 and 54 Squadrons, Colin claims to be the first RAF pilot to log a thousand Vampire flying hours, which he achieved on 10 July 1953:

I flew the first Vampire T.11 to be delivered to RAF Chivenor, WZ418, on 1st September 1952, with four separate sorties on dual ciné gunnery exercises.

We carried on with the Meteor 7s for a little while, and I next flew a Vampire T.11 (WZ463) on 22nd January 1953 with my squadron commander, Sqn Ldr R.A. Watts

for 'Aerobatics; Spinning'. I had a familiarisation trip in WZ463 on 27th January with my own flight commander on 1 Squadron. Flt Lt. Graham West-Jones, then began normal dual ciné instruction on 16th February 1953. On 19th February I flew two sorties on dual checks for the new

Formation break by four Christchurch-built Vampire T.11s of No. 5 FTS, 9 June 1954. The unit had been renumbered from No. 206 AFS on 1 June. (MoD)

course (No. 28) with Meteor 7s for the last time, and we used Vampire T.11s for dual flights exclusively after that.

We used the live firing ranges off the Pembrokeshire coast, on an east–west line to the south of St Govan's Point. Tempest TT.5s were used as target tugs, taking over from Beaufighter TT.10s. The Vampire T.11s were much better for dual gunnery exercises, as both pilots saw the same target through the gun sights. Initial positioning for quarter attacks could be a little harder if the other pilot obscured the sideways view, but was considered acceptable. The cockpit of the Vampire trainer was inevitably rather cramped, and the later models with ejector seats (which I flew elsewhere) were even worse!

Early production Vampire T.11s suffered from poor spin recovery characteristics, and had a tendency towards rudder overbalance which occurred near full rudder travel at low speeds; limiting rudder travel in turn impaired spin recovery. Also criticized was the restricted visibility from the framed cockpit canopy and the poor escape facilities.

In early 1953 Hatfield-built Vampire T.11 WZ466 was modified at Hurn to overcome rudder overbalance by restricting the rudder travel. The tail surfaces of WZ466 were increased by removing the tailplane fin acorns and extending the tailplane outboard from the fin, and fitting 6 ft dorsal fairings which extended forward along the tail-booms. The aircraft was evaluated at Boscombe Down between February and April 1953 and it was

Vampire T.11s undergoing ejector seat installation and canopy modifications at Marshalls of Cambridge during the mid-1950s. (Marshalls)

concluded that, although the modifications improved the aircraft's spin recovery characteristics, they had little effect on the Vampire's behaviour during the spin. The modifications were successful in eliminating rudder overbalance and the aircraft was considered acceptable for Service use in this form; the modifications were to be incorporated into production aircraft as soon as possible and retrofitted to earlier models at the first opportunity.

Further improvements were made to WZ419 at Christchurch, including a moulded single-piece, upward-opening canopy with direct vision windscreen panels (Mod. No. 3151); a single blind-flying panel (Mod. No. 3167B); duplicate flap and undercarriage controls; and the installation of Martin Baker Mk. 2 manual release ejector seats. Following modification, the prototype made its first flight at Christchurch on 7 April 1953 in the hands of John Hanslip.

In November 1953 WZ419 was sent to Boscombe Down for trials with the A&AEE to assess the improvements. The unit's report, published the following year, was generally favourable, but highly critical of the ejector seats which restricted the rearward stick and control movements in an already cramped cockpit. The rearward view from the cockpit, made worse by the seats' headrests, was also disliked, as was the lengthy 'strapping-in' procedure in the confined space available. The report recommended that the Martin Baker seats be modified or replaced by another type of ejector seat.

Later aircraft fitted with Martin Baker Mk. 3B automatic release ejector seats, which were designed for use above 120 knots and 200 feet, still posed problems: pilots found that they were not the easiest to strap into, were uncomfortable, and restricted the movement of anyone over average height. These modifications to the T.11 were introduced on to the production lines with the 144th aircraft. Earlier

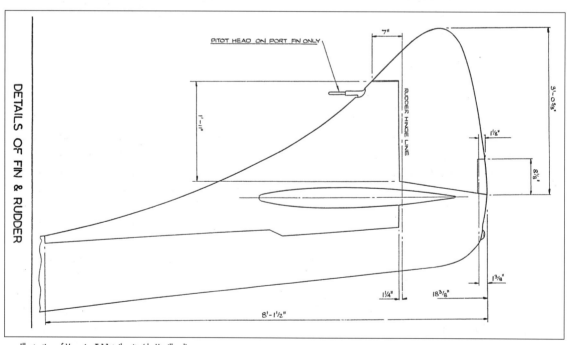

Illustration of Vampire T.11 tail unit. (de Havilland)

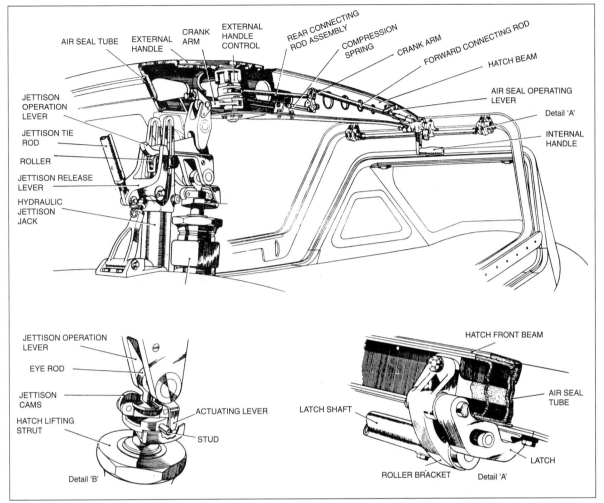

Diagram of hood-locking mechanism of Vampire T.11, fitted with single-piece, upward-opening canopy. (de Havilland)

unmodified aircraft were returned to Marshall Engineering at Cambridge and brought up to the later standard. The three-year modification programme of fitting ejector seats and new canopies began in March 1954 and was completed by December 1957.

On 1 November 1955 the dubious honour of the first double ejection from a Vampire T.11 fitted with Martin Baker Mk. 3B ejection seats went to XE961 of No. 8 FTS at Swinderby. Flown by Master Pilot Evans and student, Acting Pt Off. Jago of No. 101

Course, the aircraft rolled during a stall turn and went into an inverted spin from which it would not recover. Both crew members ejected successfully and the Vampire crashed close to the village of Bardney in Lincolnshire.

A total of 526 T.11s were built for the RAF, with the last aircraft (XK637) coming off the production lines in November 1956. Of these, 257 aircraft were built at Chester, 123 at Christchurch, 114 at Hatfield, with a further 30 subcontracted to Fairey Aviation at Ringway and 2 to Marshalls of Cambridge. In addition, six Vampire trainers were returned

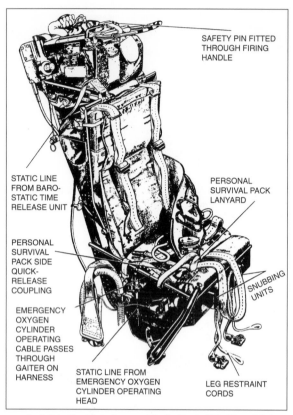

SAFETY PIN FITTED THROUGH FIRING HANDLE

STATIC LINE FROM BARO- STATIC TIME RELEASE UNIT

PERSONAL SURVIVAL PACK LANYARD

PERSONAL SURVIVAL PACK SIDE QUICK- RELEASE COUPLING

SNUBBING UNITS

EMERGENCY OXYGEN CYLINDER OPERATING CABLE PASSES THROUGH GAITER ON HARNESS

STATIC LINE FROM EMERGENCY OXYGEN CYLINDER OPERATING HEAD

LEG RESTRAINT CORDS

Martin Baker Type 3B ejection seat, as fitted to Vampire T.11. (Martin Baker)

completion of their course they were awarded the flying category PAI (Pilot Attack Instructor). On 1 January 1955 the CGS was renamed the Fighter Weapons School (FWS) and continued to fly T.11s until April 1958.

AVM L.W. Phipps CB, AFC, was an experienced weapons instructor. He completed his PAI's course at Leconfield in 1952 and was a Staff Instructor at the FWS between 1954 and 1956:

Mention has already been made of the Vampire T.11 as a weapons trainer. In this role the aircraft contributed much to the operational efficiency of the RAF during the time it was in Service.

Clearly an armed operational mission has failed unless the ordnance which it deploys gets accurately to the target – in the air or on land or at sea. Historically, weapon aiming accuracy was achieved by careful briefing, by having a go and getting close to the target, and hopefully by careful debriefing, using ciné film. With a side-by-side trainer equipped with side-by-side gun sights for both pilots, proper airborne instruction was possible.

The introduction of the Vampire T.11 as a weapons trainer was timely in a special sense. Although Vampires and Meteors had replaced the piston-engined RAF fighters of WWII there was a general view that the ultimate operational capability of the new front line needed sharpening. The new jets flew beautifully in formation but even if the guns worked without stoppages the pilots' scores were low! With the lessons of the Korean war in mind, Commanders-in-Chief ordered renewed emphasis on fighter weapons training, particularly air-to-air gunnery. At this stage the Vampire T.11 arrived, an aircraft in which pupil and instructor could see exactly the same picture on the same target at the same time.

The Vampire T.11 was obviously a

from Norway in 1955 and went back into RAF service re-serialled XJ771–XJ776.

Service use of the Vampire T.11 was extensive, with most operational squadrons and second-line units retaining a few aircraft for continuation training, instrument ratings, or as general purpose 'hacks'. Between March 1953 and January 1960 a total of sixty-nine operational RAF squadrons had at least one T.11 on strength. They were also operated by various station flights, communication squadrons, CAACUs, armament practice camps, air navigation schools, and test establishments.

Vampire T.11s were first delivered to the Central Gunnery School at Leconfield as weapons trainers in September 1952; the CGS was responsible for the training of weapons instructors for operational squadrons, and on

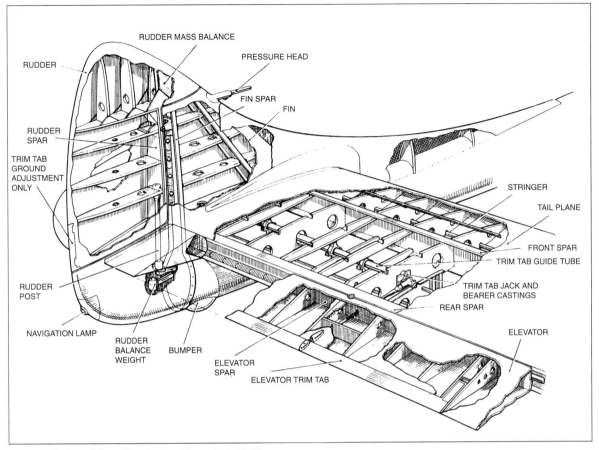

RUDDER MASS BALANCE

PRESSURE HEAD

RUDDER

FIN SPAR

FIN

RUDDER
SPAR

STRINGER

TAIL PLANE

TRIM TAB
GROUND
ADJUSTMENT
ONLY

FRONT SPAR

TRIM TAB GUIDE TUBE

TRIM TAB JACK AND
BEARER CASTINGS

REAR SPAR

RUDDER
POST

ELEVATOR

NAVIGATION LAMP

RUDDER
BALANCE
WEIGHT

BUMPER

ELEVATOR
SPAR

ELEVATOR TRIM TAB

Details of revised shape of fin and rudder of Vampire T.11. (A&AEE)

perfect weapons training vehicle for the Vampire squadrons of the day, for air-to-air and air-to-ground gunnery, for rocket firing and for bombing. And when these squadrons re-equipped with the Venom the Vampire trainer continued equally effectively.

The CGS welcomed their Vampire T.11s. In their task of training PAIs, the aircraft played a prominent role in the achievement of high standards in the Ground Attack Flight, which was equipped with Vampires and later Venoms. The T.11s also raised standards in the Meteor-equipped air-to-air ciné and air-to-air gunnery flights, by means of airborne demonstrations.

Overall, the trainer version of the

Vampire played a significant part in developing fighter weapon effectiveness to a standard which has become the expected norm ever since.

The greatest use of the Vampire T.11 was of course, RAF Flying Training Command, where student pilots were introduced to a syllabus of advanced instruction, which included some weapons training. In the late 1950s T.11s were delivered to more Flying Training Schools: No. 1 FTS at Linton-on-Ouse was equipped with Vampires in January 1958 for the training of naval pilots; No. 4 FTS disbanded at Worksop in June 1958, but was reformed out of No. 7 FTS at Valley in August 1960; No. 5 FTS at

Oakington transferred its last course under the Provost/Vampire scheme to No. 8 FTS in March 1962; No. 7 FTS flew Vampires (apart from a brief hiatus between 1960 and 1962) until November 1966; and No. 8 FTS at Swinderby, which flew a mixture of Vampire variants between July 1955 until disbandment on 19 March 1964.

Air Cdre Roy Crompton's association with the Vampire began in November 1949 when 604 Squadron at Hendon converted from Spitfire 16s. From July 1959 to September 1961 he was OC Flying and Chief Instructor at No. 5 FTS, and from February 1965 to September 1967 he was Station Commander at RAF Linton-on-Ouse. His final flight in a Vampire was of special significance when, as Commandant of the Central Flying School, he flew a batch of 'First Day Covers' in Vampire T.11 XH304 from Little Rissington to Valley on 1 November 1973 to mark the thirtieth anniversary of the first flight of the Vampire/Spider Crab:

During my time at No. 5 FTS, Oakington, we were equipped with some forty Vampire T.11s and six Meteor T.7s. The reason for my having Meteors was entirely the result of a hard fact of life – not every pilot under training could fit into the Vampire, and if overall leg length (and especially thigh length) was outside the prescribed number of inches, the chap would be unable to use his ejector seat safely in an emergency, and would almost certainly lose both knee-caps at the very least during the ejection process!

When I was appointed as Station Commander of RAF Linton-on-Ouse in 1965, the resident No. 1 FTS still possessed a small Vampire Flight. No. 1 FTS was primarily responsible for training pilots for the fixed wing element of the Fleet Air Arm to 'wings' standard in the Jet Provost 3 and 4; the pre-rotary wing element of the FAA were also part of my task, flying some 75 hours on the Chipmunk before going to RNAS Culdrose to start helicopter training (the exact process that Prince Charles followed about twelve years later at Leeming). In addition, however, I was also equipped with six Vampire T.11s. These

Vampire T.11s of the Central Flying School (Advanced), Little Rissington, 1957. (Sqn Ldr M. Biggs)

aircraft were established for the advanced training of foreign nationals who had reached 'wings' standard on graduating from one of our FTSs and would be destined for the 'fast jet' world on return to their own air forces. At that time the RAF were getting to grips with the Gnat as our advanced trainer at RAF Valley. But we (the RAF) were having a whole thicket of teething problems with the aeroplane, with the result that it was decided to restrict Gnat courses to RAF students only. My small Vampire T.11 Flight remained with us at Linton until mid-1966 when we flew them across to nearby RAF Church Fenton.

With regard to the age old argument about tandem versus side-by-side training aircraft, my own belief is that the side-by-side arrangement is probably best at the *ab initio* stage, but that tandem seating probably scores at the later stages, giving the young trainee more of a 'feel' for the single-seat operational model or for the day when he himself is in control as captain/sole pilot, responsible for carrying out a given mission as briefed.

In January 1956, following the completion of Cranwell's south airfield extension, the Royal Air Force College was able to replace its Balliol trainers with Vampire T.11s. Hitherto, Cranwell's cadets had qualified on the Balliol and taken the jet flying stage of their training after leaving the College. After extending the length of the College course from eight to nine terms, No. 69 Course, comprising thirty-two cadets, passed out on 9 April 1957, thus becoming the first to complete the new three year course, of which twenty-four cadets were the first to qualify on the Provost/Vampire scheme. Future flight cadet courses at the College would complete their basic flying training at nearby Barkston Heath on Provosts before transferring to Cranwell during their last year for advanced

flying training to 'wings' standard on Vampires. The courses, of approximately 120 hours (to give a total of 240 flying hours at graduation), were the usual mix of the standard Flying Training Command syllabus.

Following a tour with 266 Squadron at Wunstorf, AVM Sir Richard Pierse completed a CFS course and was posted to Cranwell in August 1956 as a QFI:

I arrived at Cranwell later the same month to find the Balliol had been replaced by a mixed bag of Vampire FB.9s and T.11s – the former being used for solo cadet flying and QFI formation leading and continuation training. This seemed to me (and I think most of my colleagues) an ideal mix for instructional purposes. The T.11s by that time had ejection seats and redesigned canopies and, although a bit cramped, the side-by-side seating made instruction very straightforward. Apart from certain difficulties in prolonged right-hand spins, the T.11 was remarkably free of vices, and for solo flying the cadets gained immeasurably from being able to fly the FB.9.

The cadets flew some 120 hours on this advanced phase with a good syllabus divided into general handling, and instrument, navigation, formation and night flying exercises. As an aside I might mention that night aerobatics were a feature of the training syllabus of those days. In their final night tests (FNTs) cadets would strive to out-do one another with the daring and originality of their aerobatic sequences. As a flight commander I spent many an FNT being alternatively blacked out and/or terrified by some of their efforts. On one memorable occasion the young man was endeavouring to do a stall turn off the top of a prolonged 'Upward Charlie' (i.e., vertical roll) when, passing through a thin layer of upper cloud, he became disorientated. After much stirring of the

Vampire FB.9s and T.11s of the RAF College on the flight line at Cranwell in the late 1950s. (via Mike Hooks)

stick and rudder pedals the aircraft settled into an inverted right-hand spin. I have to say that neither his nor my recovery actions went entirely by the book, but recover we did – somehow! When we eventually pulled out of the bottom of the dive we found ourselves passing below one of Waddington's shiny new Vulcans as it made its stately way around the instrument pattern. Such is life – or nearly the losing of it.

With the arrival of Jet Provost trainers at Cranwell in November 1960, and the reorganization of the College's flying training to the all-through scheme on this aircraft, Vampires were gradually withdrawn, and in March 1962 the last T.11 (WZ548) was dispatched to Swinderby.

Further radical changes within Flying Training Command saw No. 22 FTS at Syerston renumbered No. 1 FTS in May 1955; equipped with Provost trainers, the unit moved to Linton-on-Ouse in October 1957 and became the first to operate both the Provost and Vampire simultaneously when it was merged with the naval element of No. 7 FTS in January 1958. The first 'wings' course in this combined basic and advanced flying school, comprising both RAF and naval pilots, graduated on 3 April 1958.

In November 1962 the Folland Gnat was delivered to RAF Flying Training Command for use as an advanced trainer with No. 4 FTS at Valley, and by September 1963 the Vampire T.11 had been virtually withdrawn from service. The Vampire Flight of No. 3 FTS at Leeming became the final training unit to be equipped with T.11s; originally formed as a lodger unit with No. 1 FTS at Linton-on-Ouse in 1965 for the advanced training of RAF and Kuwaiti pilots, the Flight was commanded by Flt Lt. Richard MacLachlan from 1 October 1966.

The Vampire Flight was transferred to No. 7 FTS at Church Fenton on 4 January 1966, and finally to No. 3 FTS at Leeming on 1 November 1966. Throughout this period the Flight continued to train a mixture of RAF (in parallel with the Gnat courses at Valley) and foreign national pilots from Jordan, Lebanon, Iraq, Kuwait and Saudi Arabia. Each course lasted approximately twenty weeks and the last RAF student (Fg Off. Stevenson) to be trained with the Flight completed his advanced instruction on Vampires on 25 January 1967. The Flight continued to train foreign national students (from where they transferred to an OCU for

Disbandment fly-past of Vampire T.11s from the Vampire Flight, No. 3 FTS, Leeming, 29 January 1967, led by a Jet Provost piloted by AVM Michael Lyne, AOC No. 23 Group. (via Sqn Ldr Reg Drown)

weapons training) until 16 November 1967, when Lt. Shmaisani became the last to complete his final handling test.

Five courses were completed at Leeming before the Flight was officially disbanded on 29 November 1967 – an occasion which was marked by a small ceremony attended by senior RAF officers and a disbandment fly-past comprising four T.11s flown by Flt Lt. Richard MacLachlan (XD515/61), Flt Lt. Reg Drown (XD614/65), Flt Lt. Jim Gregory (XE857/64), and Fg Off. Harry Dyde (XD550/62). The formation was led by a Jet Provost piloted by AVM M.D. Lyne, AOC No. 23 Group. The disbandment fly-past was followed by a public relations flight for Tyne Tees Television and a final aerobatic display over Leeming by one of the unit's QFIs, Flt Lt. Reg Drown.

The Vampire Flight was finally disbanded on 4 January 1968, when Flt Lt. Drown carried out a farewell aerobatic display at Linton-on-Ouse before the aircraft (XD515) was presented to the station for gate guard duties; four days later the unit's last Vampire T.11 (XD550) was flown by the newly promoted CO, Sqn Ldr MacLachlan to No. 27 MU at Shawbury for storage.

The final unit to operate the Vampire T.11 was No. 3/4 Civilian Anti-Aircraft Co-operation Unit at Exeter, whose aircraft flew as high-speed ranging and tracking targets for the Royal Navy and army gunners in Southern England. In 1971 this task was taken over by the Canberras of No. 7 Squadron at St Mawgan and No. 3/4 CAACU was disbanded on 31 December 1971, the last of its Vampires being sold to Exeter Airport in January 1972 for spares recovery.

Most of the Vampire T.11s were scrapped following their retirement from RAF service, although some were preserved as gate guardians at Service establishments. A number were sold to Hawker Siddeley Aviation and following storage at Chester and Woodford, were donated to various

Vampire T.11 XD599 served with the CATCS, Shawbury, from January 1965 until November 1970, when it was presented to Stroud Technical College. (MAP)

museums, schools and Air Training Corps units as instructional airframes.

Between February 1963 and January 1969 sixty-seven Vampire T.11s were sold back to HSA and placed into storage at Woodford and Chester. Many of these airframes were held against anticipated orders for the proposed 'civilianized' Vampires of Jet Craft Ltd at Las Vegas, USA, which was formed in December 1967 by John E. Morgan. In 1968 the company announced its intention to produce a civilian jet trainer, based upon the Vampire T.11 and called the Mystery Jet T.1, which would be built under licence by Marshall's of Cambridge. The design of the Mystery Jet was in fact similar to the projected DH 123 six-seat Vampire trainer development, for which de Havilland's had constructed a mock-up of the fuselage nacelle in the late 1950s, before it was eventually abandoned.

A model of Jet Craft's six-seat executive version with extended front fuselage, the Mystery Jet II, was unveiled in London on 18 February 1969. At the Press Conference which was conducted at the Europa Hotel in Grosvenor Square, it was announced that the company's intention was to remove the original wooden fuselage and Goblin engine of the Vampire T.11 and replace them with a six-seat metal cabin and a Rolls-Royce Viper 522 jet of 3,330 lb thrust. It was also declared that the price of the MJ2 would be in the range of $300,000–$350,000, and that the first flight of the aircraft would be on 1 March 1969.

To coincide with the unveiling of the executive jet model, an announcement by Jet Craft Ltd confirmed that an ex-RAF Vampire T.11, XD527, had been earlier transferred from Woodford to Aviation Traders Ltd at Southend for conversion to the prototype Mystery Jet II. Another ex-RAF Vampire, WZ464, declared to be the prototype Mystery Jet T.1, was also undergoing conversion at Marshall's of Cambridge.

Although Jet Craft planned to purchase thirty-six Vampire T.11s for further conversions, the project came to a halt in December 1970 when the company's founder and president, John Morgan, was declared bankrupt and was found guilty the following year on charges of criminal contempt. Among the company's assets Morgan had listed $500,000 in aircraft engineering and design, but investors never saw the prototype of the Mystery Jet that he had indicated would be in production by 1969. Morgan was subsequently fined, and in April 1971 was sentenced to be jailed for twelve months. The

Partially completed wooden mock-up of the ill-fated Jet Craft MJ.2, a six-seat executive jet based on the Vampire T.11, at the Southend base of Aviation Traders (Engineering) Ltd. (via Mike Stroud)

A model of Jet Craft's Mystery Jet 2, a six-seat executive aircraft based on the Vampire trainer. (via Mike Stroud)

'prototype' Mystery Jet, XD527, was last seen on the Manston fire dump in July 1988.

In late 1989 Jet Craft USA of Las Vegas re-acquired the design and test data of the six-seat Jet Craft Executive Mk. 1 with the ill-founded intention of resurrecting their original project. Based on an Australian-built Vampire T.35, the company planned a completely new all-metal pressurized fuselage with the original wing and tail assembly, and the power coming from a Pratt and Whitney JT15D–5 turbofan. Two other models were envisaged by the company: a Mk. 11 Jet Cruiser with a P&W PT6A–65AR or Garrett TPE331–14 turboprop in the pusher configuration, and the ten-seat Mk III Executive Commuter with a P&W JT15D–4 turbofan.

The earlier sale of single-seat Vampires to the lucrative overseas military market was quickly followed by an interest from many air forces who were likewise keen to obtain the versatile advanced trainer version. A total of 232 Vampire T.55s were built for overseas customers. This figure included 174 Chester-built, 43 Christchurch-built and 15 T.55A aircraft; eight refurbished ex-RAF aircraft were also supplied to foreign air forces. Over 390 Vampire T.55s were built under licence in Australia, India and Switzerland. Throughout the world, twenty-four countries ordered Vampire T.55s as advanced/weapons trainers for their air forces or for evaluation purposes. They included Australia, Austria, Burma, Ceylon, Chile, Egypt, Eire, Finland, India, Indonesia, Iraq, Japan, Jordan, Lebanon, Mexico, New Zealand, Norway, Portugal, South Africa, Southern Rhodesia, Sweden, Switzerland, Syria and Venezuela.

In 1951 Australia became the first overseas customer when it negotiated the purchase of thirty-six Vampire T.33s (built to an early standard without ejector seats), constructed under licence by de Havilland Pty (Australia) at Bankstown Aerodrome, Sydney. The first European customer for the Vampire T.55 was the Royal Norwegian Air Force, which placed an order for six aircraft. Built at Christchurch, the aircraft were delivered via Hatfield between June and November 1952. In 1955 these aircraft were returned to the RAF as a free gift from the Norwegian Government.

The largest order for the T.55 came from India and was for forty-three aircraft; they were built at Chester and flown to Cawnpore between May 1953 and April 1954. A follow-up order for thirteen Vampires (together with a further three which were later assembled from kits) was completed between October 1957 and February 1958, along with five ex-RAF aircraft which were refurbished at Chester. Hindustan Aeronautics at Bangalore built a further sixty under licence in India.

Three Vampire T.55s were built at Chester for demonstration purposes and, as they were owned by de Havilland's, were issued with civilian registrations: G–ANVF (c/n 15485), G–AOXH (c/n 15798) and G–APFV (c/n 15802). All three aircraft were eventually sold to foreign air forces: G–ANVF to Finland as VT–1, and G–APFV to Lebanon in November 1957 as L–160. The third T.55, G–AOXH, was flown by George Errington on its 30,000 mile demonstration tour of South America between December 1956 and April 1957 before it was handed over to the Chilean Air Force as J–04, to join the five T.55s delivered during the first half of 1954.

The final order for Vampire T.55s came from Austria, whose first three T.55s were delivered in March 1957 to form the nucleus of a fighter/bomber training squadron at Horsching. Two more aircraft were delivered in 1961 and were the last T.55s to be built in the main assembly plant at Chester. In July 1964 the final aircraft for Austria (three refurbished ex-RAF T.11s) were delivered from Chester.

The last country to fly the Vampire trainer was Switzerland, which took delivery of three T.11s from Chester between September 1953 and January 1954 for evaluation purposes. An

One of three Vampire T.11s built at Chester and retained by the company as demonstration aircraft. Issued with civilian registrations, G–ANVF was eventually sold to Finland. (de Havilland)

order for seven T.55s, which was completed between January and June 1956, was followed by a further twenty T.55s built under licence at the Federal Aircraft Works at Emmen between July 1958 and June 1959. To supplement these aircraft Switzerland purchased a further nine Vampire T.11s in 1967, which were supplied for ex-RAF stock held at Chester between July 1967 and August 1968.

As an advanced trainer with the Swiss Air Force the Vampire trainer was eventually replaced in 1990 by the BAe Hawk T.66. During a ceremony at Emmen on 12 June 1990, the Vampire was officially retired from service, bringing to an end an association with the aircraft dating back to 1946. The Vampire T.55s were auctioned at Sion on 23 March 1991, when twenty-eight airframes (and eleven Goblin engines), which were listed as 'unfit for combat or fight' (sic), were sold for 1.3 million Swiss Francs in two hours.

A few Vampire trainers were kept airworthy for display on the summer air show circuit. The RAF was represented by XH304 of the CFS's 'Vintage Pair' display team, which had originally entered service in December 1955 and subsequently served with 79 Squadron, Gutersloh Station Flight, and No. 3/4 CAACU before transferring to the CFS in December 1971. In 1972 XH304 joined the newly-formed 'Vintage Pair' at Little Rissington, together with a Meteor T.7. The team moved to Cranwell in April 1976, to Leeming in September 1977, and finally to Scampton in September 1984 when, flown by the Commandant, Air Cdre Kip Kemball, the aircraft, escorted by two Meteors and a formation of sixteen Jet Provosts and nine Bulldog trainers, led the CFS to its new base in Lincolnshire. On 25 May 1986 XH304 was written off when it collided with Meteor T.7 WA669 during an air display at Mildenhall in Suffolk. Although the crew of the Vampire, Sqn

Ex-Swiss Air Force Vampire T.55 U–1216 was presented to the RAF Benevolent Fund at Boscombe Down in June 1990. It was allocated the serial ZH563 in the hope it would be kept flying, but after storage it was eventually acquired by the Royal Jordanian Air Force Historic Flight in 1994. (Author)

Vampire T.11 XH304 and Meteor T.7 WF791 of the 'Vintage Pair' make a last pass over the Officers' Mess at Little Rissington during April 1976, before the unit transferred to Cranwell. The Vampire was destroyed at Mildenhall in May 1986, and the Meteor spun into the ground at Coventry Airport two years later. (Air Cdre Roy Crompton)

Ldr David Marchant and his passenger Sgt Alan Ball, both ejected and landed safely, the crew of the Meteor were killed when the aircraft hit the ground.

A privately owned Vampire T.11, WZ507/G–VTII, flies with the Vintage Aircraft Team at Bruntingthorpe in the markings of 43/151 Squadrons. Receiving a civilian registration in January 1980, WZ507 first flew as such on 17 March 1980.

After the sale of the Swiss Air Force Vampires during 1991, several aircraft have made a welcome appearance on the European air show circuit. Jet Heritage at Hurn have repainted T.55 G–HELV/U–1215 in RAF markings, while three more trainers (G–DHVV/U–1214, G–DHWW/U–1212 and G–DHZZ/U–1230) were purchased by Lindsay Wood Promotions and flown by the Source Classic Jet Flight at Hurn.

A handful of Vampire trainers still remain airworthy as civil registered aircraft and make regular appearances at air displays. In 1970 Westfield International of Broomfield, Colorado, USA, bought fourteen ex-RAAF T.55s which were reregistered N11920–N11933. A few of these original aircraft were lovingly restored to flying condition: N11926 (ex-A79–631) is owned by Mission Motors of Universal City, Texas, and flown in the markings of the Rhodesian Air Force. Another Vampire, N11930 (ex-A79–645) was bought and restored by Ed Stead of Stead Aviation Corporation, Bedford, New Hampshire. In July 1984 the Vampire flew again in the colours of the RAF's Central Flying School, with the spurious serial 'ES930', and won the 1986 Oshkosh Best Jet Warbird Category Award.

Several ex-Indian Air Force T.55s have also appeared on the civil register in the USA, and include BY385–N172LA, IB882–N173LA, and IB1686–N174LA of Lance Aircraft of Dallas, Texas. Also in the USA is the Vampire Centre, a wholly owned subsidiary of the Ogden Jet Centre, located in Ogden, Utah; it is the only organization in the world that specializes in the acquisition, restoration, maintenance, and flight operation of Vampire aircraft. Included in the fleet of six Vampire trainers are ex-RAF T.11 N70877 (ex-XD538), former RAAF T.35 N11921 (ex-A79–613) and ex-Irish Air Corps T.55 186, reregistered as N4861K. Catering for the boom in jet 'warbird' operations, some of the aircraft have undergone extensive restoration, including a solid state starting system and fuel quantity power supply, and (in the case of N11921) a sophisticated avionics/instrument panel.

SEA VAMPIRE

In early 1944, after closely studying the development of the Vampire and Meteor fighters, the Admiralty called for an assessment of the feasibility of operating jet aircraft from the decks of aircraft carriers. Many factors had to be taken into consideration: the limited endurance and high fuel consumption of the early jets, crash barrier and hydraulic catapult compatibility, and the improvement of current arrestor techniques.

The unit responsible for evaluating jet aircraft for naval use was the Aerodynamics Flight of the Royal Aircraft Establishment at Farnborough, commanded by Wg Cdr H.J. 'Willie' Wilson. In mid-1944 the Flight, which already had various aircraft on strength, including a Gloster E.28/39 (W4041/G), a Bell YP–59A Aircomet (RJ362/G) and two Meteors, one of which was the Metropolitan Vickers F.3/1 prototype DG204/G, was joined by the second Vampire prototype LZ551/G. One of the unit's tasks was to recommend which type of jet aircraft should be used for deck landing trials and, despite the fact that its twin tail-boom layout could cause problems during catapulting and arresting, the Vampire was considered the better choice when the Gloster E.28/39 became unavailable.

In May 1945 the Aerodynamics Flight's Commanding Officer and chief naval test pilot Lt. Cdr Eric 'Winkle' Brown, carried out a deck landing assessment with LZ551/G at Hatfield. The aircraft had earlier undergone a series of modifications to increase the drag provided by the flaps and air brakes; this had been achieved by increasing the standard flap area by 40 per cent by extending the chord and the span under the engine nacelle, and also extending the chord of the dive brakes by 8 in. These modifications also served to lower the stalling speed and eliminate float caused by the ground effect of the Vampire's low wing and short undercarriage; in later marks of the Sea Vampire, lengthened undercarriage oleos were fitted as standard which also provided a better absorption of the high vertical velocities incurred during deck landings. At the conclusion of the trials, subject to a satisfactory arrestor hook being incorporated, Lt Cdr Brown recommended that the Vampire was satisfactory for deck landing trials.

LZ551/G was returned to Farnborough on 1 October 1945, complete with a faired V-form arrestor hook which had been designed and fitted at de Havilland's Christchurch factory. Deck trials officially commenced on 10 October, and during proof testing on the RAE's runway arrestor gear the hook unfortunately separated from the wing root at a retardation of 3.35 'g', which necessitated another return to Christchurch for strengthening. While at Christchurch the aircraft was further modified with the replacement of its 2,700 lb Goblin I engine with a 3,000 lb Goblin 2. Before its return to Farnborough for the conclusion of the arrestor proofing trials, a teardrop canopy was fitted, and the pitot tube was transferred from the fin to the port wing to avoid a large position error at high angles of attack.

At this time, rumours began to circulate that the US Navy had declared its intention to fit an arrestor hook to a Lockheed P–80A Shooting Star fighter and that preparations for a first deck landing were at an advanced stage. Although the

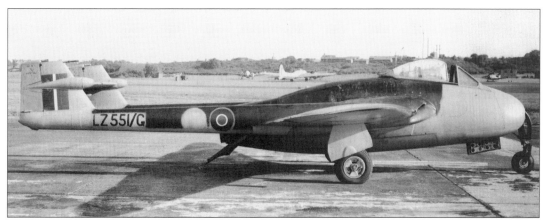

The second prototype Vampire, LZ551/G, at RAE Farnborough during proof testing of the arrestor hook, October 1945. (RAE)

development of the 'navalized' Vampire was well ahead of that of the Americans, it was thought necessary to press on without delay, and on 26 November 1945 Lt Cdr Brown flew the Vampire down to RNAS Ford for a series of Aerodrome Dummy Deck Landings (ADDLs) in preparation for the first-ever landing on an aircraft carrier by a pure-jet aircraft.

On 3 December 1945, in less than perfect weather conditions with a moderate swell and overcast sky, the 14,000-ton light fleet carrier HMS Ocean, commanded by Capt. Caspar John, was off the Isle of Wight when the instruction to proceed with the landing was received by Lt Cdr Brown. Taking off from Ford at 11.05 hrs, Eric Brown made one low pass over the carrier before a final turn in at 100 knots. As he crossed the round-down of the carrier's pitching deck, Brown eased the Vampire's throttle back and picked up the carrier's No. 1 arrestor wire, which brought the aircraft to a satisfactory halt.

Having successfully landed the Vampire, Eric Brown took off and made a further two relatively uneventful landings. On the fourth landing the Vampire touched down with the port wing slightly low and the trailing edge of the flaps hit the deck and sheared the hinge brackets. The flaps were subsequently

modified by cutting away an area of 4 sq. ft. to provide an increased wing-down ground clearance, and were tested satisfactorily during further landings on HMS Ocean.

During June 1946 a deck landing assessment of LZ551/G was conducted on board HMS Triumph by the pilots of 'C' Squadron of the Naval Test Squadron; the unit's commanding officer during this assessment was Cdr J.A. Ievers (now a retired Rear Admiral). He wrote:

After the first set of deck landing trials had been completed in December 1945, there was a brief lull while the Ministry of Supply considered whether or not to pursue trials to the Service acceptance stage. There was a body of opinion at the RAE which thought that the Vampire was unsuitable for deck landing by the average pilot. Lt Cdr 'Winkle' Brown spelt this out in his official report. However, at a high level meeting in the Ministry at which the RAE and Boscombe Down were represented, it was agreed that the Naval Test Squadron at Boscombe Down should carry out a deck landing assessment, and on 19th February 1946, LZ551/G arrived for that purpose.

From the start all the pilots involved in the

Detail of the V-form arrestor hook fitted to the second prototype Vampire, LZ551/G. (MoS)

trials were enthusiastic about the aircraft's deck landing potential. They felt that the deficiencies of the engine response which had become apparent in the first set of trials would be more than compensated for by the combination of tricycle undercarriage and perfect deck landing view. It was decided from the outset to make full use of the tricycle undercarriage by flying the Vampire onto the deck without throttling back, though this technique would have led to disaster with a tailwheel configuration, with the aircraft ballooning over the wires. The pilots had, of course, to operate within the limitations of the hook and undercarriage strength, but in the event, both stood up well to the additional speed of impact.

Cdr S.G. Orr DSC, AFC, served as a lieutenant with the Royal Navy Test Squadron at Boscombe Down between January 1946 and September 1948. In June 1946 he was involved with initial deck landing trials with the Sea Vampire:

In the spring of 1946 we were asked by the Admiralty and MoS for a second opinion on the feasibility of deck landing jet aircraft in general and the Sea Vampire in particular. Previously Lt Cdr Eric Brown of the RAE had carried out deck trials with the same Vampire but had concluded that the exercise would be too difficult for the average pilot with the aircraft in its present state and therefore design developments and modifications, such as lift spoilers, would have to be built into future aircraft. The main argument was that on a sinking

On 3 December 1945 the second prototype Vampire, LZ551/G, made history when it carried out the first ever deck landing by a pure jet aircraft on HMS *Ocean*. It was piloted by Lt Cdr Eric 'Winkle' Brown. (de Havilland)

approach deck landing technique, the engine RPMs were below that required for immediate throttle response if it was necessary to open quickly to stop sinking or to go around again.

On receiving the Sea Vampire, LZ551/G, at Boscombe Down in May 1946, the CO, Cdr J.A. Ievers, Lt. Cdr Randolph Pearson and myself carried out a programme of ADDLs to ascertain the best technique to use for deck landings. It quickly became apparent that the jet aircraft as such had some marked advantages, from a landing point of view, over piston-engined aircraft when, for the first time, the pilot was presented with a completely unobstructed view of the deck, with no engine cowlings or propellers in front of the windscreen.

Therefore a straight approach could be made as opposed the curving flight path normally employed on deck landings in order to see sideways. Further, the tricycle undercarriage much reduced the possibility of bouncing over all the arrestor wires.

In order to overcome the problem of engine response it was decided to carry out a low flat approach so that the engine RPMs could be kept in the range where throttle response was immediate if required.

The deck landing trials, which comprised some sixteen landings spread over two days, were carried out by Cdr John Ievers and Lt. Cdr Randolph Pearson during the first week of June 1946 on HMS *Triumph* in the English Channel. I also carried out a take-off and landing at the end of these trials.

Detail of the extended dive brake and flap area, as fitted to the second prototype Vampire, LZ551/G.

The consensus of opinion was that the deck landing of the Sea Vampire was simple and straightforward, and providing the right technique was used there were no problems.

During the next six months further deck landing trials were conducted on board HMS *Ocean* by pilots from the Naval Test Squadron of the A&AEE when further modifications to the Vampire were found necessary, including an improvement to the Goblin's throttle response, longer-stroke undercarriage oleos, and an interconnected throttle and landing flap to improve lift control.

In September 1946 LZ551/G was passed to the Service Trials and Carrier Trials Unit, 778 Squadron, at RNAS Ford for general evaluation trials and pilot familiarization until November 1946, when it was damaged on HMS *Illustrious*. Following repairs at Hatfield, the aircraft was sent to the RAE in January

1947 for barrier trials at Farnborough. On 15 September 1947 LZ551/G was sold to de Havilland's and then placed into store with the Science Museum at Waddon, Surrey in October 1949; finally, in recognition of its significant contribution to the development of naval aviation, the aircraft was loaned to the Fleet Air Arm Museum at RNAS Yeovilton in March 1966 as a permanent exhibition.

Because of critically slow engine acceleration response and a limited fuel capacity that would restrict carrier operations, the Admiralty decided that the Vampire could never be considered as a front-line naval fighter. However, because of its operating and maintenance record, the navy was interested in acquiring the Vampire as a cost-effective means of introducing its pilots to jet flying.

To cover the design of the Sea Vampire by de Havilland's, Specification 45/46P was issued on 14 January 1947; as the work was

Following storage with the Science Museum, the second prototype Vampire, LZ551/G, was loaned to the Fleet Air Arm Museum at Yeovilton in March 1966 as a permanent exhibit. (P.R. Keating)

to be subcontracted to the English Electric Company at Preston, Specification 46/46P was issued simultaneously, and both were distributed under Contract No. 7/ACFT/1512. Both specifications were also governed by Operational Requirement 240 which, among other design requirements included an improved undercarriage, increased area dive brakes and landing flaps, an arrestor hook with a maximum retardation of 3.0 'g', and replacement of the TR 1464 VHF radio set with an ARI 5272.

Three months after the specifications had been issued, on 21 March 1947, an order for thirty Sea Vampire F.20s was placed under Contract No. 6/ACFT/1053/CB.7(a) in the serial range VV136 to VV165. In January 1948 the order was cut back to eighteen aircraft, VV136 to VV153. Originally built at Preston as Vampire FB.5s, these aircraft were flown to Hatfield for conversion to F.20 standard; this included a V-frame arrestor hook housed in a small fairing above the jet pipe, long-stroke undercarriage legs (embodying a vertical velocity energy absorption of 16ft/sec. which made it the strongest undercarriage in any naval

aircraft to date), and clipped wings fitted with 'accelerated take-off' hooks. The standard Vampire air brakes were increased by some 36 per cent in area by forward and rearward extensions; the split trailing edge flaps were also increased in area by 31 per cent by a rearward extension and by the addition of plates, shaped to the tail-booms, joining the inboard and outboard sections.

On 1 May 1947 Vampire F.3 VF317 was delivered to Hatfield for conversion to the first prototype F.20, after which, from November 1947 until January 1948, it was retained at Hatfield for manufacturer's tests. Deliveries of the Sea Vampire F.20 commenced on 6 October 1948 when VV136 was sent to the A&AEE for handling and deck landing assessments; the F.20 conversion programme was finally completed by July 1949. The prototype VF315 was released to the RAE in January 1948 for arresting and catapult trials which were interrupted in May when the aircraft was returned to Hatfield for preparation for an overseas tour with 806 Squadron's aerobatic team.

This unique Royal Navy team was formed

at RNAS Eglinton on 3 May 1948 when 806 Squadron was equipped with two Sea Furies and two Sea Hornets for a tour of North America and Canada. Commanded by Lt. Cdr D.B. Law DSC, the unit also received Sea Vampire VF315 when it was delivered from Hatfield to RNAS Sydenham in Belfast by John Cunningham on 20 May 1948 as the squadron embarked on HMCS *Magnificent* for Dartmouth, Nova Scotia.

The squadron went ashore on 2 June and gave its first show on 17 June, but without the Sea Vampire which was undergoing repairs following a start-up fire. Throughout the next three months the team gave thirty planned demonstrations, including the International Air Exposition in New York (31 July–8 August 1948) to celebrate the opening of Idlewild Airport by President Truman. Although most of the Vampire demonstration flying was undertaken by Lt. Cdr Law, it was also flown on occasions by the squadron's senior pilot, Lt. A.B.B. Clark. On 25 August the squadron returned to Canada for the Canadian National Exposition at Toronto, with the final display of the tour at Ottawa on 11 September where they performed as a

squadron with the Royal Canadian Navy.

During the period the Sea Vampire had completed forty flying hours and flown over 4,000 miles, and despite being dogged with starting and other problems – including an engine fire, dirty fuel, and a cracked canopy – it had performed well during the impressive high-speed, low-level routines; on 20 June 1948 VF315 became the first British jet to fly in the USA when it landed at Floyd Bennett Field, New York. The success of the tour was due to the skill and showmanship of the squadron pilots, and the dedication of the maintenance crews, spurred on by the knowledge that the squadron represented British Naval Aviation before an extremely critical audience. On 12 September 1948 the squadron was officially disbanded and the aircraft were shipped back to the UK.

The A&AEE's arresting and catapult assessment of the Sea Vampire was continued with the first production aircraft, VV136, between September 1948 and July 1949. Particular attention was paid to the Sea Vampire's air brakes which, over the speed range tested, were considered among the most effective ever evaluated by the establishment

The aerobatic team of 806 Squadron at Sydenham, Belfast, during the work-up period for the tour of North America and Canada, May 1948. Left to right: Lt Cdr Dick Law, Lts Nigel Fisher, Dick Reynolds and Bruce Clark. (Capt Bruce Clark)

Between 1947 and 1950 Vampire F.1 TG314 was used by the RAE and A&AEE for interconnected throttle and flap system trials. It was eventually used as a ground instructional airframe at RNAS Arbroath. (RAE)

and offered a significantly higher deceleration in level flight than that of a standard Vampire 1 (TG338) used in the tests. It was suggested that the enlarged air brake could easily be fitted to all later marks of the Vampire.

Carrier trials were also required to clear the Sea Vampire for Service operation. These trials were preceded by a brief deck landing assessment with VV136, and followed by landing trials on HMS *Illustrious* in November 1948 by pilots of the A&AEE and 703 Squadron NAWDU/CTU, who completed about sixty landings in VV137 and VV138. For the purpose of the trials, 703 Squadron was detached from its parent base at RNAS Lee-on-Solent to Tangmere between August 1948 and February 1949, where it was joined by two 'hooked' Sea Meteor F.3s for a similar assessment. Although the A&AEE report was generally favourable to the Sea Vampire carrier trials, it pointed out that future operations would be limited by poor take-off performance and recommended that a more powerful version of the Goblin engine should be fitted.

In April 1949 702 Squadron re-formed at RNAS Culdrose as the Naval Jet Evaluation and Training Unit under the command of Lt.

A.B.B. Clark, with an establishment of six Sea Vampire F.20s (VV144–VV148 and VV150) and two Meteor T.7s. To provide experience of naval jet operations on board ship, the squadron was detached aboard HMS *Implacable* from 21 September to 11 November 1949. Six Sea Vampires and pilots were embarked, including the CO, Lt. Bruce Clark, the Senior Pilot, Lt. Peter Perrett, and Qualified Flying Instructors (QFIs), Lt. Nigel Ovenden and Lt. Theo Theobald. Operations proved difficult on the carrier, with its straight flight deck and lack of a suitable crash barrier.

Between 2 May and 30 June 1950 the squadron embarked again with six pilots for further trials on the light fleet carrier HMS *Theseus*. During these trials, on Monday 19 June 1950, two F.20s, flown by Lt. Bruce Clark and Lt. Peter Perrett made the first jet night landings on a carrier. The landings were made while HMS *Theseus* was steaming some 20 miles south of the Isle of Wight and were achieved without the aid of a floodlit deck.

As the carrier could not produce the necessary wind speed over the 200 yd flight deck to allow a free take-off, the Sea Vampires were launched by catapult. First away was Lt.

Sea Vampire F.20 VV149 airborne from Hatfield, November 1948. It was delivered to 703 Squadron in May 1949 and subsequently served with 700, 702 and 771 Squadrons, before being struck off charge in January 1960. (RAFM)

Clark (in VV138) who was quickly joined by Lt. Perrett (in VV145), both aircraft circling at 1,000 ft, burning off fuel to reduce the landing weight. Perrett was 'downwind' when cleared for landing and came straight in, catching the wire on the first attempt, to be brought to a halt on the middle of the deck. As soon as the flight deck was cleared (by recatapulting Lt. Perrett), Lt. Clark repeated the landing procedure. A routine of catapulting and landing then followed, until Perrett had completed three cycles, and Clark two.

The embarkation on board HMS *Theseus* by the Sea Vampires of 702 Squadron was considered a great success and both pilots commented that they had experienced few problems with approach and touch-down; Bruce Clark had given prior instructions to the Deck Landing Control Officer (DCLO) or 'batsman' to signal a 'cut' as the Sea Vampire crossed the rounddown as an additional aid

to landing. The unobstructed view from the cockpit of the Vampire, its excellent handling characteristics and the tricycle undercarriage had made deck landing uneventful.

The training of pilots with 702 Squadron had begun with a handful of senior and experienced naval officers who required jet experience for future appointments. By the time 702 Squadron had embarked on HMS *Implacable* the first official jet conversion course was under way, with the principal syllabus compiled by the unit's Vampire QFIs. The first course comprised their primary jet conversion on the Meteor T.7s, followed by tactical training on the Sea Vampires.

In May 1951 Lt. Bruce Clark was replaced as CO of 702 Squadron by Lt. Cdr Pete Perrett, with Lt. Len Jeyes as his Senior Pilot. With courses similar to those operated by No. 226 OCU at RAF Stradishall and the Day Fighters Leaders School at RAF West

During June 1950 702 Squadron deployed its Sea Vampires to HMS *Theseus* for sea trials. It was during this embarkation that the squadron made the first jet landings at night on a carrier. (Capt Bruce Clark)

Aircrew of 702 Squadron involved in the sea trials onboard HMS *Theseus,* June 1950. Left to right: Lts Robertson (Air Engineer), Theobald, Clark, Perrett, Burnett, Battison and London. (Capt Bruce Clark)

Raynham in mind, Lt. Cdr Perrett revised the training programme and wrote a syllabus for a jet operational flying school based on the squadron's complement of eight Sea Vampires and four Meteor T.7s, with courses planned for 120 flying hours. Great emphasis was placed upon weapons training and tactics and, apart from dual instruction, regular checks and instrument flying in the Meteor T.7s. The course comprised familiarization on type, snake climbs to and descents from altitude, battle formation drills, fighter tactics, carrier descents, battle formation flying, ADDLs, deck qualification, quarter attacks at varying altitudes, navigation and cross-country flying. Another service provided by 702 Squadron was the jet conversion of experienced fighter pilots destined for the original Attacker squadrons, and for almost a year the squadron operated short conversion courses. On 26 August 1952, under a reorganization of Royal Navy fighter training units, 702 Squadron was renumbered 736 Squadron.

Sea Vampire F.20s were also used by the Fleet Air Arm for jet familiarization and training duties in second-line squadrons; other naval units to fly the aircraft included 700 Squadron (Trials and Requirements Unit), RNAS Ford; 728 Squadron at RNAS Hal Far; 759 at RNAS Culdrose; 764 (Jet Fighter Pilot Pool), RNAS Ford; and 771, 778, 781 and 787 Squadrons. This latter unit, in its role as the Naval Air Fighting Development Unit, based at West Raynham, was responsible for the Service trials of naval aircraft prior to their introduction into the fleet and the development of naval air tactics. An example of the trials conducted by 787 Squadron included the development of techniques for assembling formations of aircraft at altitude (to conserve fuel) as opposed to the standard piston-engined procedure of orbiting at low level, and the conduct of high-speed interceptions. In addition to its Sea Vampire F.20s, 787 Squadron also flew the Vampire FB.5s allocated for naval use, which included VV548, VV631, VV635, VX973, VZ142, VZ143, VZ145, VZ146, VZ148 and VZ823.

In August 1948 the Service Trials Unit, 778 Squadron at Lee-on-Solent, was disbanded and re-formed as 703 Squadron. Using a variety of Vampires and Sea Vampires, 703 Squadron became actively engaged in flexible deck trials and moved to Ford in April 1950 where it was involved in an essential range of duties. Cdr David 'Shorty' Hamilton served as a lieutenant with 703 Squadron at Ford from July 1953 to July 1955:

I joined 703 Squadron in August 1953,

A number of Vampire FB.5s were issued to the Fleet Air Arm, including VZ148 of Yeovilton Station Flight, which is seen at Bramcote in July 1954. (M.P. Marsh)

which used the old WW1 hangars on the far side of the Ford airfield. The squadron carried out many trials, from radio and radar to deck landing trials for new aircraft, 'wire-pulling' (arrestor gear trials for carriers following refit), angled deck trials, as well as training and general flogging around the countryside.

In the Sea Vampire we tested the first production deck landing mirror system which was fitted on board HMS *Illustrious*. I started by doing ADDLs at Boscombe Down using a mirror and then, on 25 November 1953, six deck landings on HMS *Illustrious* in VT802.

The Sea Vampire was a delight to land on carriers – the forward view was excellent. Deck take-offs, however, were another matter. We had to do 'free take-offs', i.e., no catapult, and as the Sea Vampire was not over-endowed with thrust, we were pushed to the very stern of the flight deck, applied full throttle, released the brakes and trundled slowly along the deck. We always got airborne but were inclined to fall off the front end of the carrier a bit!

Another Fleet Air Arm unit to fly Sea Vampires was 771 Squadron, the Southern Fleet Requirements Unit, which operated the aircraft between March 1952 and August 1955 while based at RNAS Ford. The squadron used a variety of aircraft to perform a range of tasks for ships of the Fleet and RN shore establishments. Two Sea Vampires (VV138 and VV149) were used as target aircraft for gunnery training at the ranges at Eastney and as target aircraft for Radar Director training in the Portland exercise area when ships were working-up in the anti-aircraft gunnery role. In September 1954 the aircraft were detached to RNAS Lossiemouth to exercise with ships in the Moray Firth area, and in June 1955 a larger detachment was sent to Gibraltar to assist in the work-up of the carrier *Ark Royal*. On 17 August 1955 771 and 703 Squadrons merged to form 700 Squadron.

On 15 June 1953, with Vampires borrowed from 703 and 759 Squadrons, and flying a mixture of FB.5s and F.20s, 787 Squadron commanded by Lt. Cdr S.G. Orr DSC, AFC, participated in the Queen's Review of the Fleet

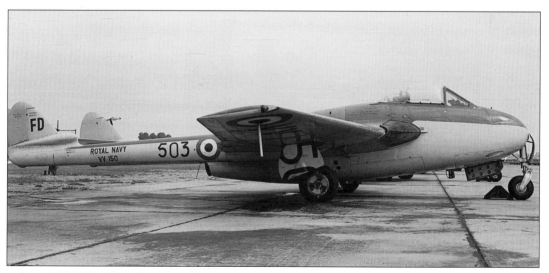

Sea Vampire F.20 VV150 of 771 Squadron – the Southern Fleet Requirements Unit – at RNAS Ford, July 1953. It served with the squadron between March 1952 and April 1955. (John Rawlings)

Air Arm. The massed fly-past of 327 aircraft drawn from forty naval squadrons, was led by a single Sea Vampire from the Admiral's Flight, piloted by Rear Admiral W.T. Couchman DSC, OBE, Flag Officer Flying Training, and took place after the Queen had reviewed the assembled fleet of 279 warships in the Solent from the frigate HMS *Surprise*. Following the formations of piston-engined aircraft, the groups of jet aircraft participating in the Coronation Review, which included Meteor T.7s, Attackers, Sea Hawks and Sea Venoms, were led by the Sea Vampires of 787 Squadron (which had temporarily detached eight aircraft to RNAS Ford for the event), led by Lt. Cdr Stan Orr (who flew Vampire FB.5 VV548).

Between 1956 and 1957 the majority of the single-seat Sea Vampires were put into storage at RNAS Lossiemouth, and were struck off charge in January 1960 and sold as scrap.

FLEXIBLE DECK EXPERIMENTS

In an attempt to improve upon the poor range and endurance of the early jet fighters, many possibilities were considered by the aircraft manufacturers and the Ministry of Aircraft Production. In early October 1944 the Director of Technical Development, Mr N.E. Rowe, wrote to his contemporary at the RAE, Mr W.S. Farren, about a report concerning the Messerschmitt Me 163B rocket-propelled fighter. The report highlighted the fact that the German fighter was able to jettison its undercarriage soon after take-off, allowing the weight saved to be available as extra fuel; in turn this gave the fighter the higher rate of climb necessary to intercept high-flying Allied bombers.

By December 1944 the practicability of an undercarriage-less jet fighter was being considered for naval aircraft and the feasibility of operating from a suitably adapted landing base sought from various companies within the aircraft industry. At a meeting of the RAE in January 1945, chaired by the then Deputy Director W.G. Perring, nine schemes were submitted for consideration; these included wires suspended from towers, 'pick-a-back' aircraft, a flexible surface which would float on water, and landings on a high velocity jet of air! The RAE committee settled on two proposals:

Photographed from a Grumman Avenger in December 1953, Sea Vampire F.20 VV139 together with a Sea Hawk F.1 WF152 of 703 Squadron, RNAS Ford. (Lt Cdr David Hamilton)

the Naval Air Department's use of an air bed as a landing surface and Major Fred Green's radical idea of an undercarriage-less aircraft landing on a rubber carrier deck.

A former aero-engine designer at Farnborough and with Armstrong Siddeley Motors, Green suggested that the removal of the undercarriage would result in a saving of 7 per cent of the aircraft's all-up weight; utilizing this saving as extra fuel or for greater payloads aroused considerable interest among the RAE committee members. To absorb the shock of impact Green proposed that the carrier deck itself would consist of five layers of vulcanized rubber above three layers of readily available surplus fire hoses which would be inflated to a low pressure. It was also proposed that the aircraft would be catapult-launched and arrested by a single wire located at the rear end of the carpet. Tests with ⅛th and full-scale models were promising and in the spring of 1946 a full-scale flexible deck measuring 200 ft by 60 ft was laid out at Meadow Gate, Farnborough, in readiness for the preliminary trials.

To measure impact velocities of up to 20 ft/sec., a steel bottle weighing 2,800 lb was dropped onto the mattress from varying heights. This was followed by a Hotspur glider (BT752) weighted with 8,000 lb of concrete and dropped from a crane from differing heights to test the level of energy absorption. The glider was then fitted with wings and a tail unit and fired from a rocket-powered catapult trolley located behind the flexible deck to prove the arrestor gear. The results of thirty-four launchings and landings from the trolley onto the flexible deck were encouraging, and in August 1945 the Director of Technical Development approached both the de Havilland and Supermarine companies to cooperate in the development of the rubber deck. Although the latter company eventually dropped out, de Havilland decided to proceed with the project and subsequently 'navalized'

three Vampire F.1s (TG286, TG328 and TG426) for the intended trials. The aircraft were further modified during the trials to include an interconnected throttle and flaps to ensure that the pilot could make his approach at comparatively high thrust and, in the event of a wave-off, was able to obtain full power quickly, simultaneously reducing drag by retracting the air brakes.

In May 1947 Vampire F.1 TG286 was converted at Hatfield for the mattress trials and dispatched to Farnborough in November, where it was flown by Lt. Cdr Brown on a series of low and slow passes along the dummy deck which had now been resited to the centre of the airfield, checking the average hook height and deck landing speed (which incidentally, were 26 in and 101.5 mph respectively).

On 29 December 1947 everything was ready for the first landing. As Lt. Cdr Brown made his approach over the inclined Jersey Brow site to the deck at the controls of Vampire F.1 TG426, the aircraft began to sink and despite an increase of power, was slow to respond. The arrestor hook was now trailing on the ground and despite corrective action by the pilot, the hook and tail-boom hit the approach end of the deck, causing the Vampire to pitch violently onto the carpet; the hook jammed in the 'up' position, and the damaged booms restricted the movement of the elevators. During the second bounce the Vampire struck the steel fixing drums at the forward edge of the mat and split the cockpit structure. As the aircraft cleared the forward edge of the ramp, Lt. Cdr Brown closed the throttle and slid onto the grass; he was fortunately unhurt despite the Vampire being damaged beyond repair.

The subsequent investigation concluded that an increase of 10 knots on the final run-in was necessary, as was avoidance of the wind turbulence over Jersey Brow by increasing the height of the approach. Modifications incorporated to assist the pilot on his final run-in included an airspeed indicator at windscreen height to reduce the pilot's need to constantly refocus from instruments to deck, and a Deck Landing Control Officer (DCLO) positioned forward of the wire, equipped with a VHF radio set to inform the pilot of his approach height.

The trials continued on 17 March 1948 with a second Vampire, TG328, which was joined in June 1948 by the first Sea Vampire F.21, VG701. Both these aircraft, which were fully navalized, unarmed versions of the Sea Vampire F.20, incorporated all the modifications required for deck landings, and were serialled VG701, VT795 and VT802–VT805. The airframes had been removed from the Vampire F.3 production line at Preston and sent to Hatfield in September 1947 for modification to F.21 standard. The conversion work undertaken at Hatfield was in accordance with Specification No. N.18/47, 'Design of Vampire for Flexible Deck Operation', which was issued on 2 October 1947 and covered the alterations to the Sea Vampire F.20 airframe: reinforcing the Vampire's belly and jet pipe fairing; reducing the internal fuel capacity from 330 gallons to 203 gallons by blanking off the outer wing tanks; installation of an accelerometer; and the fitting of an arrestor hook, which was lowered by an electric motor (as distinct from the gravity system) and equipped with a 'trigger' within the bill which ensured that once the hook caught the wire and the trigger was depressed, the flaps and dive brakes were automatically retracted. With the resumption of the deck trials it was necessary to replace the arrestor hook attachment bolts which had shown signs of shearing.

On 15 July 1948 the RAE's Aerodynamic Flight achieved the first catapult launch of a jet aircraft in the UK; the Sea Vampire F.21 involved in the trials also achieved the first catapult take-off of a British tricycle-undercarriaged aircraft. A peak of 4.9 'g' was recorded on the Sea Vampire during the catapult-launch, representing an end speed of 89.4 knots which, at the time, was a record for a piloted aircraft in Great Britain during a catapult take-off.

At the beginning of November 1948 preparations were completed for the first flexible deck landing on the converted light fleet carrier HMS *Warrior*. The deck had been transferred from Farnborough earlier in the year, and was situated close to the carrier's swivelling crane which would be used to hoist the Vampire for transportation after landing. The carrier put to sea on 2 November, and two days later, on 4 November, the first landing was made by TG286 after two practice dummy runs over the deck; the aircraft then went on to make another three landings; all subsequent landings were made by Sea Vampire F.21s VT795, VT803 and VT805.

Between November 1948 and the completion of the trials on 31 May 1949, the nine pilots involved (of whom only Lt. Cdr Brown and one RAF test pilot were from the Aerodynamics Flight) made a further 200 successful landings on HMS *Warrior* using Sea Vampire F.21s VG701, VT803 and VT805. The trials had been relatively free of major accidents and resulted in a few alterations carried out to the Sea Vampires' arrestor hooks and the installation of airbags to the forward edge of the flexible deck.

In October 1951 the proofing of the hydraulically operated arrestor hook and damper gear fitted to the four Sea Vampires of the Flight was successfully carried out using VT804. Having successfully completed the flexible deck trials programme, the two naval pilots of the Experimental Flying

Several Sea Vampires were employed for flexible deck trials on board HMS *Warrior* during February 1949. Here, F.21 VT802 is seen having just picked up the wire. It was removed from the deck by a crane. (RAE via Ray Sturtivant)

Department at Farnborough, Lt. W.H. Noble DSC and Lt. A.G.H. Perkins, began to extend the work of Lt. Cdr Eric Brown, with the eventual aim of using Sea Hawks rather than Vampires. It was planned to launch and recover the Sea Hawk without using the undercarriage (as opposed to the Vampire which after making a conventional take-off, landed 'wheels up'). It was also planned to launch the Sea Hawk from a German cordite catapult used originally for V-1 missiles, and to recover it on the flexible deck. Defence cuts eventually hit the programme and only one pilot, Lt. Bill Noble, was allowed one launch and recovery cycle in a Sea Hawk prototype VP143 during the autumn of 1953.

DECK LANDING MIRROR SYSTEM TRIALS

702 Squadron's experience of jet operations on board ship during 1949 and 1950 suggested that as aircraft became bigger and faster, the approach speed of naval aircraft to the ship would be too fast to be compatible with the human reactions of the pilot or the 'batsman'. The batsman had long been responsible for guiding aircraft safely to the deck by indicating its landing path with a system of hand signals.

In November 1951 the Deck Landing Mirror System (DLMS) – an instantaneous indication of the aircraft's angle of approach – was first proposed by Cdr (E) H.C.N. Goodhart, a Technical Secretary to the Chief Naval Representative in the Ministry of

A Sea Vampire F.21 of the RAE (VG701) being hoisted by a crane during rubber deck trials aboard HMS *Warrior*, 17 February 1949. (via Ray Sturtivant)

Supply. Simple and effective, the system comprised a concave mirror mounted beside the flight deck in such a way that it reflected the light of a group of spot lamps towards the pilot as he made his landing approach. The pilot saw the reflected lamps as a point of light on the mirror, and provided he flew the aircraft so that the point remained central – in line with a bar of green lights each side of the mirror – he should touch down on the correct spot.

The DLMS had to be gyro-stabilized to rotate through half the instantaneous pitch angle of the carrier to keep the elevation of the 'beam' constant. Fortunately, British carriers tended to pitch about a point two-thirds from the bow, close to where the mirror was mounted; thus the line defined by the mirror maintained its angle relative to the horizon and moved up and down only to the extent that the carrier heaved.

Following conversion to a Sea Vampire F.21 VT795 was employed by the RAE for flexible deck and approach aid trials. The markings on the nose were for sighting measurements. (RAE)

The angle and height of the mirror could be set for the approach characteristics of the aircraft concerned: the critical factor was the height of the pilot's eye above the wheels in the approach attitude and to adjust for this the whole mirror was moved vertically. The angle of the mirror was varied only slightly for different aircraft since the hook had to touch down at least by the second wire; the wheels had to clear the round-down by a reasonable margin and the vertical velocity had to be within the undercarriage limits.

Most of the development work for the DLMS was carried out at RAE Farnborough by a team headed by Mr Danny Lean, a scientist with the Aerodynamics Division, with later trials performed at RAE Bedford. The system was as effective by night as it was by day and was later installed at the side of the runways at naval air stations to provide deck landing practice; the shore-based version was not gyro-stabilized, and a reflected light source used to keep the physical height of the system to a minimum.

The Naval Air Section of the Aerodynamics Flight was formed on 1 January 1952 and became actively involved (using Sea Vampires) in the development of the deck landing aid equipment during May 1952. Much of the initial work was completed by the unit's CO, Lt. Cdr T.G. Innes AFC and Lt. A.E. Facer. The Section had also completed twenty landings on HMS *Illustrious* during March with Sea Vampire F.20s VV142 and VV149 in connection with the 'no cut' landing trials. During 1952 the NAS completed 192 deck landings and 160 flexible deck landings.

In May 1953 the work of these two officers was further developed by Lt. Bill Noble and Lt. Geoff Perkins, who also experimented with an early form of 'head-up' display in their Vampires. Fitted into VT802, this display was used in conjunction with the DLMS to assist the pilot (who frequently experienced difficulty when constantly shifting eye focus and angle from his airspeed indicator to the mirror during the final approach), by projecting a series of flashing lights from within the cockpit onto a darkened panel on the windscreen. The lights showed red, amber and green, according to whether the speed was low, high or correct, and were driven by the ASI.

Lt. Geoff Perkins qualified as a test pilot with the Empire Test Pilots School and between January 1953 and February 1954 was one of two naval test pilots with the RAE, before transferring to the Naval Test Squadron, A&AEE Boscombe Down:

I first flew a Sea Vampire 20 when visiting RNAS Culdrose in August 1951 with some RAF colleagues from 226 OCU. Later, in October 1951 I spent a short period with 702 Squadron to experience deck landing jet aircraft so that I could pass on that knowledge to fellow instructors at Stradishall.

In January 1953 I moved to the RAE's Experimental Flying Department at Farnborough, where we were equipped with Sea Vampire 21s for the flexible deck landings, including VT795, VT802, VT804 and VT805. In association with Deck Landing Mirror trials, we also experimented with an early form of 'head-up' display of air speed readings on the windscreen. During our initial work on this display, the boffins failed to check the flashing light air speed indicator for light leaks, so on our first attempt at night landings the windscreen was covered in white light! The display trials were not altogether successful as the system did not feature any angle of attack input.

The 'prototype' mirror was about seven feet high and comprised a highly polished aluminium sheet mounted on a slightly concave wooden frame. This configuration necessitated an approach to the deck which had more 'straightway' than the more usual curved approach. The height of the mirror was too great, and Bill Noble and I found that in exploring the upper and lower limits we would have overshot all the wires at one extreme and clobbered the round-down at the other! As a result we agreed to blank off the top and bottom quarters of the mirror with Pusser's canvas, which gave us nearly enough the ideal height for the mirror – approximately four feet. It was recognized that the mirror 'meatball' needed to be picked up earlier in the approach to avoid the lengthened 'straightway' problem. The version used for the night trials met this need by having a greater depth to the concave surface – the material used was (I believe) cast aluminium, which was then highly polished.

In June 1953 came the great moment to try out the Mirror System at sea. This was at the time of the Coronation Review of the Fleet on 16th June. HMS *Indomitable*, with the mirror shrouded in canvas to avoid the prying eyes of foreign navies, slipped anchor that evening and we landed aboard later (with Sea Vampires, VT795 and VT804), completing five landings each between that date and the 18th June. The Vampires performed well, the only snag being that the ship's catapults could not launch us. Thus, every take-off was 'free' and, starting with the tail-booms hanging out over the rounddown, we prayed that the chocks and brakes would hold! Then as we set off down the deck the slow acceleration of the Vampire became apparent, with the ASI only just flickering as the island was passed!

Then Bill Noble and I turned our attention to proving that the Deck Landing Mirror could be used afloat at night. If Bill and I could do it as a couple of Day Fighter/Ground Attack pilots, then anyone could do it! On 19th November 1953 we flew to HMS *Illustrious*, and after a few day landings each to ensure that the mirror was set up properly we carried out our first night landings on 23rd November – I flew Sea Vampire VT795; more night landings followed on the 26th. On the latter occasion the weather in the Channel was somewhat 'crinkly' and the Commander (Air) observed that 'he would not have allowed experienced night-fighter pilots to operate that night!' Our point had been made – the Vampires had helped us prove the system. They may have also been the last fixed-wing aircraft to land on *Illustrious* before she was placed on the reserve and eventually scrapped.

The Deck Mirror Landing System was publicly announced on 15 March 1954, when newspapers including the *Daily Express* reported that 'hundreds of secret landings on the carriers *Illustrious* and *Indomitable* using the robot signaller have proved that any airman can now land on a pitching, rolling flight deck'. The papers also went on to report that all aircraft carriers and naval airfields ashore were to be fitted with the new system. Following a programme to equip all Royal Naval aircraft carriers, the device was also likely to be adopted by the US and NATO navies which were already fitting their carriers with two other recent British inventions – the steam catapult and the angled flight deck.

The radical concept of the flexible deck had been proven, and although it had been focused on the use of mid-wing aircraft such as the Vampire or Sea Hawk, there were schemes for up-grading the operation to include the Canberra bomber! The flexible deck was not adopted, on the grounds that it would be both impracticable and too costly; a widespread requirement for installations,

Mirror Landing Sight ashore at RNAS Brawdy for deck landing practice, December 1956. (via Pat Dobbs)

both ashore and afloat, for a comparatively small gain in range and fuel saving by eliminating the Vampire's undercarriage could not be advantageous. Many also considered the flexible deck a waste of valuable development resources, and the advantages to the aircraft greatly outweighed by the loss of deck and airfield handling management. Sea Vampires had, however, brought the Fleet Air Arm into the jet age, and made an important contribution to the development of future carrier deck technology as well as to the training of many first-generation naval jet pilots.

SEA VAMPIRE T.MK.22

With the experience gained from their single-seat Sea Vampires, and from the success of the Vampire T.11s as advanced jet trainers with the RAF, the Royal Navy were keen to obtain their own version of the de Havilland two-seaters. As basic and advanced flying training up to 'wings' standard was provided for all Fleet Air Arm student pilots by the RAF, the navy envisaged the use of Vampire trainers for jet conversion and operational flying training which would include weapons, instrument and Aerodrome Dummy Deck Landing (ADDL) circuit instruction.

In early 1952 two pre-production Vampire trainers, WW458 and WW461, were delivered to the navy for evaluation. The first, WW458, went to RNAS Culdrose on 21 January 1952, but was transferred to the A&AEE at Boscombe Down for brief handling tests conducted between February and April. A sharp wing drop when the stick was held fully back at the stall and a tendency to spin with very little warning were evident during the tests. The report recommended that the stalling characteristics should, if possible, be rectified before release to the Service and that further tests should be made by naval pilots if the Royal Navy intended to use the type for ADDLs. The second, WW461, was delivered to RNAS Culham on 22 May 1952, and with WW458 was evaluated by 759 Squadron at RNAS Culdrose and 781 Squadron at RNAS Lee-on-Solent, before both were withdrawn from flying duties in early 1954 and relegated for use as instructional airframes.

In April 1952 Specification T.111 P.2 was issued to cover the production of Vampire trainers for the Royal Navy at de Havilland's Christchurch factory. The aircraft were to be built to the earlier Specification T.111 P (which covered the RAF's Vampire T.11s), but would require modifications to adapt it for naval use, including a TR 1936 VHF radio, A.1271 and ZBX radio beacon equipment, a pilot-operated signal discharger, and anti-G fittings. This equipment was introduced on the Christchurch production lines following trial installation in a standard Vampire T.11 (WZ414) at the A&AEE Boscombe Down. Specification T.111 P.2 also stated that arrestor hooks or wing folding mechanisms were not to be prerequisites as the aircraft would not be required to operate from aircraft carriers.

On 19 February 1952 Contract No. 6/ACFT/7704/CB.7(a) was contingent to an Instruction To Proceed letter (ITP) for a batch of fifty-three Sea Vampire trainers, and also assigned their serial numbers: XA100–XA131 and XA152–XA172.

Designated Sea Vampire T.Mk.22 on 16 June 1952, the first production aircraft, XA100, was ready for collection on 23 April 1953, but was retained by the manufacturers for company trials before being passed to the A&AEE in February 1954 for radio acceptance trials. Next off the Christchurch production line was XA101, which was transferred to the A&AEE in August 1953 for assessment of the new clear-view canopy. The redesigned canopy (Mod. 3151) had not been made available by de Havilland's until mid-1953, and the navy had agreed to accept

The first pre-production Vampire trainer, WW458 was delivered to the Royal Navy for evaluation in January 1952. Following trials with 759 and 781 Squadrons it became an instructional airframe. (de Havilland)

their first production aircraft fitted with the older unmodified hood. The third production T.Mk.22, XA102, was sent to the Handling Squadron at RAF Manby on 11 August 1953 for the compilation of the Pilot's Notes.

In September 1953 the Sea Vampire T.22 received its CS(A) release, which stipulated a maximum weight of 11,710 lb for normal flying, a maximum permissible speed of 455 knots in 'clean' condition and 390 knots when fitted with underwing tanks, with or without the standard armament of 3 in rockets (with 25 lb or 60 lb heads) with No. 8 Type 14 projectiles carried on shortened front struts. Underwing bombs were not required to be carried by the Sea Vampire.

Deliveries to the Aircraft Handling Unit at RNAS Stretton commenced on 18 September 1953. Here, the first batch of aircraft was prepared for service and issued to the Junior Air Officers Course of 781 Squadron at RNAS Lee-on-Solent in October 1953. The following month T.22s were delivered to 736

Squadron and 759 Squadron at RNAS Lossiemouth, which conducted operational conversion courses for pilots destined for front-line squadrons.

Between August 1951 and May 1953 759 Squadron was commanded by Lt. R.D. Lygo (later Admiral Sir Raymond Lygo, Chief Executive of British Aerospace). His first flight in one of the two pre-production Vampire trainers used for evaluation by the Royal Navy was in August 1952; in November 1953, he was sent to RNAS Lossiemouth to assist in the jet conversion of the resident Sea Fury squadrons:

Jet flying was still relatively new in the Fleet Air Arm and was being used in some quarters as an excuse for proclaiming one's excellence. It was also still considered something of an art.

My first flight in the Sea Vampire trainer was on 15th August 1952, for a local flight around Culdrose with Flt Lt. Johnny Pinnington, who was on attachment from the RAF at the time. In those days it was still the practice to set the clock in the control tower every time a jet took off, so that a close watch could be kept on the endurance of the aircraft in the prevailing weather conditions!

My first recorded flight in a Sea Vampire T.22 was with Bill Newton at Lossiemouth on 25th November 1953, when we formed the Jet Conversion Unit, which converted 802 and 804 Squadrons. With two Sea Vampires we continued without mishap until April 1954, and I see the last flight recorded by me was on 9th April when the unit was disbanded.

The introduction of the Sea Vampire T.22 into the Fleet Air Arm gave everybody a better appreciation of jet aviation. Not only was the aircraft simple to fly, it also had the advantage of having the instructor alongside, and it quickly became the favourite vehicle for senior officers to demonstrate their own flying skills! As a Qualified Flying Instructor, I spent a lot of time flying around with various senior officers, as they acquainted themselves with flying a jet aircraft.

It was somewhat longitudinally unstable, because of its width to length ratio, and barrelled along a bit, but it was an excellent training aeroplane and I happen to be a believer in the advantage of side-by-side training – the perpetual debate that goes on with all QFIs.

Sub. Lt. (E) Paul Cross completed his National Service in the Fleet Air Arm and, after training at the Royal Navy Engineering College, Manadon, was posted to RNAS Lossiemouth in November 1952. He was attached to 759 Squadron, which at the time was in the process of converting from Meteor T.7s to Sea Vampire T.22s. 759 Squadron's role of jet conversion and fighter pilot training was continued until October 1954, when it was disbanded and absorbed into 736 Squadron, also at Lossiemouth.

At the time I joined 759 Squadron, pilot training was still mainly piston-engined orientated, with Sea Furies, Fireflies and Avengers in mind. Therefore, all pilots destined for Attackers, Seahawks and, later, Sea Venom NFs went through 759 Squadron, then on to 736 Squadron (with which I spent a little time during their 'deck party' on HMS *Illustrious*) for fighter training on Attackers.

All serious training prior to the Sea Vampires was on Meteor T.7s, which the students flew 'one up' when they went solo. The squadron began equipping with Sea Vampire trainers in November 1953, and had fully equipped with the type by the following February. We also had a few single-seat Vampires (probably ex-RAF machines, and not navalized F.20s with hooks), but my recollection is that they were used for odd jobs only.

After the Meteor, the Sea Vampires were marvellous aircraft to handle and maintain. The pilots complained a little of the cramped cockpit, but generally the aircraft was regarded as a 'real jet' and worthy to train future Seahawk pilots on.

As mentioned previously, all basic and advanced flying training of naval students up to 'wings' standard was undertaken by the RAF. On 1 June 1954 No. 7 FTS was formed at RAF Valley from No. 202 AFS with a mixture of Vampire FB.5s and T.11s. The first intake of four lieutenants and eleven upper yardsmen comprising No. 40 Course commenced training on 10 August 1954. During their course the students received 110 hours of advanced flying training before receiving their 'wings' on 16 February 1955 and went on to RNAS Lossiemouth as potential day or all-weather fighter pilots, or to RNAS Eglinton for conversion to the Fairey Gannet.

With the reduction in the number of students by February 1957 due to the disbandment of the RNVR squadrons, the courses at No. 7 FTS were reduced to make more efficient use of naval training. With the final passing out parade at Valley on 17 January 1958, when eight officers graduated from No. 64 Course, the training of naval pilots was transferred to No. 1 FTS at RAF Linton-on-Ouse, thereby ending an association which had resulted in 225 naval pilots receiving their 'wings' with No. 7 FTS.

One of the naval instructors with No. 7 FTS was Sub. Lt. Brian 'Schmoo' Ellis, who had been a member of the flight of Sea Furies from 802 Squadron at the time (9 August 1952) when Lt. Peter Carmichael shot down a North Korean MiG-15, while operating from HMS *Ocean*. 'Schmoo' Ellis's first experience with the Vampire was at Lossiemouth in early 1954 when 802 Squadron re-equipped from Sea Furies to Sea Hawks: jet conversion consisted of several flights in a Vampire trainer before progressing to the Sea Hawk. After completing an instructor's course with the CFS Brian Ellis went on to instruct with No. 7 FTS at RAF Valley between 1954 and 1956:

Most of my Vampire flying was clocked up when I was on loan to No. 7 FTS, and during that time I flew both the Vampire FB.5 and T.11.

Sometime in late 1955/early 1956, we were involved with the training of the first batch of *Luftwaffe* officers earmarked to re-establish German military flying. They were all hand-picked, highly decorated, ex-World War Two *Luftwaffe* pilots (one was said to have 152 Allied aircraft to his credit – mostly Russian!), and arrived at Valley after receiving a period of refresher flying in Florida. Our job was to train them to White Card instrument rating standard. The fighter ace had the misfortune to trundle off the runway at Valley and end up in the creek – thereby claiming his 153rd Allied aircraft!

In 1960 the Vampire again figured when I completed an Instrument Rating Examiner's course at Yeovilton and was posted to 831 (Electronic Warfare) Squadron at Culdrose. This squadron flew a mixture of specially modified Gannets, Avengers and Sea Venoms. The job of renewing the instrument ratings of a bunch of pilots qualified on all three types was something of a challenge. For the Gannet pilots we used a Gannet trainer, for the Avenger it was the Balliol, and for the Sea Venom pilots the Vampire. About this time I can recall acting as safety pilot for a well known naval flier who had lost a leg in Korea. The day I flew with him I had my right arm in plaster. I can still remember the landing run at Culdrose with me controlling the rudder and he the brakes. It was a lot more difficult than you can imagine!

In 1962 I joined 890 Squadron as Senior Pilot, flying Sea Vixens from Yeovilton and HMS *Ark Royal*.

As the original batch of Sea Vampire trainers were built to the early RAF standard, with framed canopies and lacking ejector seats, they were returned to Chester between 1956 and 1957 for a retrofit modification programme. Meanwhile a second batch of twenty T.22s, XG742–XG748 and XG765–XG777, was ordered from Christchurch to Contract No. 6/ACFT/10521/CB.7(a) dated 24 June 1954. The first aircraft, XG742, was delivered to RNAS Stretton on 3 November 1954, with the final Sea Vampire to be built, XG777, arriving at RNAS Lossiemouth from Christchurch on 25 May 1955.

Between August 1954 and May 1964 Sea Vampire T.22s were used by the following FAA second-line squadrons for instrument rating and as continuation trainers: 700 and 702 Squadrons at RNAS Ford; 727 Squadron at RNAS Brawdy; 728 (Fleet Requirements) and

Sea Vampire T.22s at Hawarden, c. August–December 1956. The aircraft are undergoing a modification programme, which included the fitting of ejector seats. (de Havilland via Darryl Cott)

Seen undergoing a first-line inspection at Little Rissington in May 1966, Sea Vampire T.22 XA115 belonged to the Station Flight, RNAS Brawdy. It was scrapped at Brawdy two years later. (Author)

750 (RN Observer School) Squadrons at RNAS Hal Far; 766 Squadron at RNAS Yeovilton; and 831 Squadron, an Electronic Warfare Unit, at RAF Watton. Sea Vampires were also operated by No. 700X Trials Flight at RNAS Ford, and 718 Squadron at RNAS Stretton for the jet conversion of RNVR pilots. During 1954 and 1955 Sea Vampire trainers were also issued to 809, 890, 891, 891X and 893 Squadrons at RNAS Yeovilton during their work-up period with Sea Venoms, and 1831, 1832 and 1836 Squadrons of the RNVR; 808 Squadron Royal Australian Navy was loaned a Sea Vampire T.22 during their work-up period with Sea Venoms at RNAS Yeovilton during 1955, as was 300 Squadron Indian Navy at RNAS Brawdy as it equipped with Sea Hawks in 1960.

Sea Vampire trainers were also employed as 'Admiral's barges' by the Flag Officer Flying Training (FOFT) and senior naval officers, and between 1954 and 1970 at least one example was flown by various naval Station Flights including Abbotsinch, Brawdy, Culdrose, Ford, Hal Far, Lee-on-Solent, Lossiemouth, Stretton and Yeovilton. Between December 1955 and October 1957 Rear Admiral W.D. Lang was Flag Lieutenant and personal pilot to the FOFT at RNAS Yeovilton:

When I joined the staff, the FOFT Flight consisted of a Sea Prince and a Sea Balliol, but shortly after I joined, Rear Admiral C.L.G. Evans CBE, DSO, DSC took over as FOFT and arranged for the Sea Balliol to be replaced by a Sea Vampire trainer, XG773. Although this aircraft was in a standard colour scheme, it was eventually repainted dark blue all over, with a Rear Admiral's flag painted on the side, below the cockpit. In October 1956 XG773 was replaced as the 'Admiral's barge' at Yeovilton by XA129, until this aircraft was, in turn, replaced by XG774 in August 1957.

Apart from checking out the Admiral to fly solo, the majority of the flying was routine communications duties. I suppose that the most noteworthy flight during my time as Flag Lieutenant was the occasion of the presentation of the Colours to the Fleet

The last Sea Vampire T.22 to be operated by the Royal Navy, XA129 of the Air Directors School at Yeovilton was placed into reserve storage for the Fleet Air Arm Museum in July 1970. (Mike Hooks)

Air Arm by HM the Queen which took place at RNAS Lee-on-Solent on 30th July 1956. Admiral Evans led the fixed-wing fly-past, accompanied by the six captains of his Air Stations in four Sea Vampires. Every squadron of the FAA took part so there must have been at least 150 aircraft participating. The fly-past was in three sections: first, helicopters, which operated separately from the rest; second, the slow stream led by the four Sea Vampires, and consisting of, if memory serves me right, Fireflies, Gannets, Wyverns, Skyraiders, etc., which formed up over Yeovilton; and then the jets from Ford, including Sea Hawks, Attackers, Sea Venoms and Meteors. On the day of the fly-past, despite half a gale blowing, there were no problems and the timings were impeccable.

The four Sea Vampires were piloted by Rear Admiral Evans, FOFT, accompanied by myself as his Flag Lieutenant and personal pilot. The other three aircraft were piloted by Capt. P.D. Gick OBE, DSC (RNAS Lossiemouth), Capt. D.C.E.F.

Gibson (RNAS Brawdy), and Capt. L.E.D. Walthall DSC (RNAS Ford). The other crew members were Capt. D. Vincent-Jones DSC (RNAS Culdrose), Capt. H.J.F. Lane (RNAS Yeovilton) and Capt. I.G. Jameson (RNAS Eglinton) – probably the most senior flight ever flown in the Fleet Air Arm!

In 1959 four ex-naval T.22s, XA101, XA167, XG766 and XG770, were sold to the Royal Australian Navy for use with 724 Squadron RAN, an Operational Flying School based at RNAS Nowra, New South Wales. The four aircraft were withdrawn from service between 1969 and 1972 and sold to various museums in Australia.

Six further Sea Vampire T.22s, XA107, XA128, XA166, XG769, XG772 and XG777, were delivered in crates to Chile from Chester in November 1972 and flown with Group 4 at Antofagasta and Group 8 at Los Condores until December 1980, with serials in the range J306–J311.

Following their withdrawal from service with the Royal Navy in the early 1960s some

Sea Vampire trainers were stored in the open at RNAS Brawdy, until they were scrapped. The final Sea Vampire T.22 to be used by the Fleet Air Arm, XA129, was flown by the Airwork-operated Air Directors School at RNAS Yeovilton until July 1970, when it was placed into storage at Wroughton on behalf of the Fleet Air Arm Museum. The nose and cockpit of Sea Vampire T.22 XA127 is also exhibited at the Fleet Air Arm Museum RNAS Yeovilton, XA109 is preserved at the Museum of Flight at East Fortune, while XG743, which was stored with the Imperial War Museum collection at Duxford, was transferred to Wymondham College in Norfolk in June 1993 for restoration to static condition.

FOREIGN SALES

Britain was quick to realize the potential of a lucrative, post-war overseas market, and supplied large numbers of surplus wartime aircraft to countries anxious to rebuild their depleted air forces; with an industry already producing jet aircraft in quantity, it was able to supply many air forces with their first jet fighters, often in exchange for raw materials or food, including cotton, beef and tomatoes.

De Havilland's, already experienced in the overseas military and civil market since the mid-1920s, took advantage of the RAF's decision to adopt the Meteor as its standard day fighter and achieved considerable success by offering their Vampire, either direct from their factories or built under licenced contract – a figure of £22,000 was quoted for a standard Vampire FB.5.

In February 1946 Sweden became the first country to place an order for Vampires, and between that date and August 1968, when Switzerland took delivery of the final Vampire trainer from Chester, thirty countries had either ordered or acquired the fighter or trainer version for their air forces or navies.

The more urgent requirements to equip emergent post-war air forces with Vampire fighters were met by diverting aircraft from existing production contracts: the major export versions of the fighter were the Vampire FB.6, FB.50 or FB.52, fitted with a Goblin 3 engine. Switzerland and Sweden were the only countries to operate the FB.6 and FB.50 respectively, whereas nine countries eventually flew the FB.52, two of whom built large quantities under licence in their own factories. Additionally, nineteen countries decided to purchase the Vampire T.55 trainer, which was built at Chester between May 1953 and May 1961.

To boost their sales drive during the mid-1950s, de Havilland's temporarily retained three Vampire T.55s with the civilian registrations G–AOXH, G–ANVF and G–APFV to demonstrate the multi-role, advanced trainer to potential customers. Although offered in the original configuration with framed canopies and DH tailplanes, by 1954 the export version resembled the modified RAF aircraft, with one-piece canopies and dorsal fairings; ejection seats could be installed if required.

AUSTRALIA

In August 1945 de Havilland (Australia) proposed that the need for Vampire fighters for the Royal Australian Air Force (RAAF) should be met by building the aircraft under licence at their factory at Bankstown, Sydney, New South Wales. The RAAF considered the Vampire an ideal replacement for their CAC Mustangs and, notwithstanding de Havilland's argument that the Goblin's single-sided impeller was a more efficient compressor, specified that the aircraft should be fitted with a Rolls-Royce Nene engine, with the double-sided impeller.

The RAAF's decision recognized that the 5,000 lb s.t. Nene engine embodied a number of magnesium-alloy components to save weight and was about 50 per cent more powerful than the Goblin, resulting in a notable increase in the Vampire's performance. The licensed production of the Nene 2-VH engines would be undertaken by CAC Pty at Fishermans Bend, Melbourne.

In September 1946 the RAAF placed an order for eighty DHA 100 Vampire F.30s. To enable the RAAF to assess the potential of the Vampire, and to gain jet experience, three ex-RAF aircraft were obtained: the first, Vampire F.1 TG431, was delivered to No. 1 Aircraft Depot at Laverton on 20 May 1947. This was followed by the Nene-powered, ex-trials Vampire F.II TX807 on 27 August 1948, and Vampire FB.5 VV465 on 9 May 1949; in service with the RAAF they were renumbered A78–1, A78–2 and A78–3, respectively.

The first Australian-built Vampire, A79–1 (DHA 4001), flew on 29 June 1949 with de Havilland (A)'s chief test pilot, Brian 'Blackjack' Walker, at the controls, and was delivered to the RAAF on 26 September 1949. Of the eighty aircraft ordered, the first fifty-seven (DHA 4001–4057) were delivered as Vampire F.30s between September 1949 and July 1952, and the remaining twenty-three aircraft (DHA 4058–4080) as FB.31s between September 1952 and August 1953, featuring clipped and strengthened wings. The last twenty-eight Vampire F.30s (DHA 4030–4057) were retrospectively modified to FB.31

standard during 1956, leaving twenty-nine F.30s (DHA 4001–4029) in service with the RAAF. The RAAF's Vampire F.30/FB.31s carried the serial numbers A79–1 to A79–996, which were 'scrambled' for security reasons.

An FB.32 variant was planned with enlarged wing air intakes and fitted with an ejection seat: two Vampire F.30s, A79–227 and A79–737 were employed as trials aircraft at the ARDU Laverton from October 1951 to April 1953, when the project was abandoned.

In service with the RAAF, handling difficulties were encountered when the aircraft approached its critical Mach number. This problem had been encountered earlier during the Nene/Vampire trials in England, and it was clear that the position of the 'elephant's ears' intakes affected the elevator control during dive recovery. Repositioning these intakes to the underside of the aircraft caused the aircraft to 'pitch up' more strongly than the standard aircraft at the critical Mach number; a modification programme was introduced to convert the RAAF Vampires as soon as possible.

Regular units to operate the Vampire included 75 (F) and 76 (F) Squadrons, which

Vampire F.30 A79–942 of 23 (City of Brisbane) Squadron RAAF during annual camp in April 1956. The aircraft was taken on charge in August 1951 and served with 21 and 23 Squadrons before being converted to a FB.31 in 1956. It was issued to No. 2 (F) OTU and struck off charge in November 1959. (Sqn Ldr John Parker)

The distinctive yellow and black stripes on this Vampire FB.31 (A79–333) denote that it was flown on target-towing duties. It is seen here at No. 2 (F) OTU, Williamtown, in January 1956. (AVM John Price)

formed in May 1952 at Williamtown, New South Wales, as elements of 78 (F) Wing. In July 1952, as part of Australia's response to the military commitment in the Middle East, the Wing personnel sailed to Malta where they were provided with Vampire FB.9s on loan from the RAF. As representatives of their country in the Coronation Review at Odiham in June 1953, the Wing deployed twelve Vampires to Horsham St Faith to participate in the massed fly-past. The Wing returned to Australia on 24 January 1955.

Also equipped with Vampires at Williamtown was No. 2 (F) Operational Training Unit, which formed on 1 March 1952. The unit was redesignated No. 2 (F) Operational Conversion Unit from September 1958 to January 1961, when it became a training squadron within 81 (F) Wing.

Between 1955 and 1956 some fifty-four Vampire fighters were adapted for use as target tugs, with those based at Williamtown painted with distinctive yellow and black bands to aid identification.

During 1951 Vampire fighters were also issued to the squadrons of the Citizen's Air Force to replace their CAC Mustangs, including 21 (City of Melbourne) Squadron, based at Laverton, Victoria; 23 (City of Brisbane) Squadron, Amberley, Brisbane; and 25 (City of Perth) Squadron, Pearce, Western Australia.

Sqn Ldr John Parker flew a Vampire for the first time in November 1951, following a tour in Korea. He went on to log over 1,000 hours on the type at the CFS, East Sale, and as 'A' Flight Commander with 23 Squadron, CAF:

23 Squadron was comprised of eight or ten Vampire F.30s and two Vampire T.33s, and we operated by flying every second weekend. Each year the squadron participated in an operational exercise of two to three weeks duration, usually at another operational base.

Pilots completed their *ab initio* training on Wirraway (and later Winjeel) piston-engined aircraft, and subsequently gained their 'wings' along the same programme appropriate to RAF pilots. Upon graduation, the new pilot officers were immediately introduced to the Vampire T.33 conversion course. After ten to twelve

A pair of Vampire FB.31s of 21 (City of Melbourne) Squadron CAF, RAAF, lift off the runway at Laverton in November 1953. The unit markings on the nose were in red. (Sqn Ldr W.H. Brook)

Originally delivered as a Vampire T.33 to the ARDU at Laverton in June 1955, A79–831 was converted to a T.35A in February 1956. The radio compass under the nose is of interest. (de Havilland (A))

hours, the students were sent solo before transferring to the F.30 to follow a standard training programme.

The Vampire 30 was a delightful, generally forgiving, yet efficient aircraft, and was in contrast to our previous 2,000 hp,

sixteen-cylinder, propeller-driven, vision-obscuring Mustangs. It was quite a change.

By late 1961, as the RAAF's fighter squadrons began to re-equip with Sabres, the Vampires were finally withdrawn from service.

Some airframes were used for instructional purposes at RAAF bases; most were scrapped at Tocumwal and Wagga, New South Wales, and some sold privately for display purposes.

In 1951 orders were placed with de Havilland (A) for thirty-six Vampire T.33s for advanced flying and weapons training for the RAAF, to be powered with a 3,500 lb s.t. Goblin 35 engine. Based on the RAF's Vampire T.11 to the original standard, the serials for the T.33s were A79–801 to A79–836 (DHA 4081 to 4121).

On 16 October 1952 the first Vampire T.33, A79–801, entered service with the RAAF when it was accepted by No. 2 Aircraft Depot at Richmond, New South Wales. Deliveries were completed by September 1955.

The last production Vampire T.33, A79–836, was modified at Bankstown to incorporate a clear-view canopy, dorsal fairings, and ejector seats. With these modifications, together with an increased fuel capacity, the aircraft was renumbered A79–600 and became the prototype for the 68 DHA Vampire T.35s ordered for the RAAF in 1955 as A79–601 to A79–668 (DHA 3122/4131, 4133/4190), with deliveries between September 1957 and June 1960. With the exception of the increased fuel capacity, these modifications were retrospectively incorporated into the RAAF's T.33s, which were redesignated T.35As.

Among the units to fly the Vampire trainer were No. 2 OTU/No. 2 OCU and No. 5 OTU at Williamtown; the Central Flying School, East Sale, Victoria; No. 1 Applied Flying Training School (which equipped with Vampires following its move to Pearce in May 1958); and 21, 22, 23 and 25 Squadrons of the Citizen's Air Force.

In June 1969 the final Vampire course was completed at No. 1 AFTS and on 18 September 1970 the final Vampire sortie was flown by No. 5 OTU. The Vampire trainers were withdrawn from service and replaced by Macchi MB.326Hs. Thirty-one Vampires were written off during the eighteen years' service with the RAAF, and many of the survivors were placed into open storage before disposal as instructional airframes or sold to various museums around Australia. In 1970 fourteen ex-RAAF Vampire trainers were purchased by Westair International of Broomfield, Colorado, for resale in the USA, and at least four have been restored to flying condition.

Airworthy Vampires in Australia consist of a T.35, VH–HLF/A79–636, which flew again in February 1988 following a lengthy restoration programme, and an ex-Zimbabwean T.11, R4221, which flies in its original colour scheme at Melbourne. There are, however, similar projects under way to restore many more Vampires, including seven bought from the Zimbabwean Air Force.

ROYAL AUSTRALIAN NAVY

During the production of the RAAF's initial batch of Vampire T.33s at Bankstown, the Royal Australian Navy (RAN) placed an order for five trainers, to be known as the T.34 and serialled A79–837 to A79–841 (DHA 4105 to 4109). Suitably adapted for naval use, the Vampire T.34s were to be used to train crews for the Sea Venom all-weather fighters, with deliveries commencing in 1954. In 1958 these aircraft were modified to T.35 standard, and became known as T.34As.

Deliveries of the RAN's Vampire trainers commenced on 18 June 1954 when A79–837 was flown by Lt. P. Goldrick RAN, from Bankstown to 723 Squadron, a communications and fleet support unit, based at RNAS Nowra, New South Wales. Further deliveries to the RAN were A79–838 on 18 July 1954; A79–839 on 11 August 1954; A79–840 on 8 September 1954; and A79–841 on 11 October 1954.

With the loss of A79–839 in a flying accident at RNAS Nowra in August 1956, the RAN ordered a replacement T.34A,

Vampire T.34s of 724 Squadron, Royal Australian Navy, from RNAS Nowra, New South Wales. (via Lt Cdr R.E. Geale)

A79–842, which was delivered on 8 March 1957. In addition, four ex-Royal Navy Sea Vampire T.22s, XA101, XA167, XG766 and XG770, were imported; XG770 was taken on charge at RNAS Nowra on 8 August 1957, with the remainder (which arrived in Australia on board the SS *Canopic Star*) being received by the RAN on 18 June 1959.

During October 1956 it was decided that all the RAN Vampires should be transferred to 724 Squadron which had been formed at RNAS Nowra in June 1955 as an operational flying school and aircrew conversion unit, and used both the Vampire T.22 and T.34A for pilot training.

During 1964 the RAN Vampires were renumbered with the type identification code N6– (N indicating Naval aircraft, and 6 the aircraft type), and it is interesting to note that, because of the time period involved, the 'N6' prefix never caught up with the Vampires and most records continued to use A79– or XG–.

On 5 October 1970 the final flight of a RAN Vampire was made by A79–842 (N6–842) at RNAS Nowra, by which time the type had been replaced by Macchi

MB.326Hs. The Vampire trainers were finally disposed of in March 1970: four had been lost in flying accidents and the rest sold off to various museums.

AUSTRIA

The post-war Austrian Air Force was reconstituted in December 1955, and the following year consideration was given by the Austrian Defence Ministry to the formation of a fighter/bomber squadron, for which the Swedish Government offered a quantity of surplus single-seat J28A Vampires. A total of twenty-three Vampires, plus engines and spares, were bought by a Belgian aircraft broker in May 1956, with the eventual destination given as Austria.

Despite being overhauled by Svensk Flygtjanst AB, only three of the airframes were delivered to Geneva Airport on 27 June 1956 and given the civil registrations, OE–VAB (ex-28026), OE–VAC (ex-28017) and OE–VAE (ex-28065), the OE–V registration series being allocated for aircraft in the experimental and evaluation classes. Very little is known of their

Three J28A Vampires were sold to the Austrian Government from Sweden in 1956 for evaluation: OE–VAC was ex-28017 and originally delivered to Sweden in November 1946. It is shown at Contrin/Geneva in May 1960, prior to being broken up. (P.R. Keating)

subsequent histories, but all three aircraft are thought to have been disposed of at Geneva by June 1960.

Following the collapse of the negotiations with Sweden, Austria immediately placed an order for three Vampire trainers to form the nucleus (together with six Fouga Magisters) of the Jagdbomber-Schulstaffel (Fighter/Bomber Training Squadron), No. 2 Wing at Graz/Thalerof. Following a reorganization of the Austrian Air Force the unit later moved to Linz/Horsching. The three aircraft, Vampire T.11 5C–YA (c/n 15770), and two T.55s, 5C–YB (c/n 15795) and 5C–YC (c/n 15797), were delivered on 20 March 1957 and handed over during a ceremony at Schwechat airfield.

One of the original aircraft, 5C–YA was lost during a post-maintenance test flight from Hawarden on 18 April 1966, when it crashed on the Berwyn mountain range, Snowdonia, killing the pilot, Alan Brandon, and his observer, Anthony Chalk. A Vampire T.55 (ex-RAF XD598) was later delivered as a replacement.

Five additional Vampire trainers were supplied to Austria, including the last two T.55s to be built in Chester's main assembly plant in 1961: 5C–YR (c/n 15814) and 5C–YS (c/n

15818). In late 1964, following refurbishment at Hatfield, three ex-RAF T.11s were delivered to complete the order: 5C–VD (ex-WZ618), 5C–VE (ex-XK634), which crashed on 4 October 1968, and 5C–VF (ex-XH320).

The Vampires were withdrawn during April 1972, having been replaced by SAAB 1050E light attack trainers. One aircraft, 5C–VF, is preserved at Linz/Horsching.

BURMA

Burma ordered eight Vampire T.55s in 1954. The aircraft, UB501 to UB508 (c/ns 15476–15483) were all built at Chester and delivered by air from Hatfield to Mingaladon Air Base, near Rangoon. The first four, UB501 to UB504, were delivered on 7 December 1954, with the balance following in February 1955.

Burmese Air Force Vampires are known to have been used in action during the civil war in the north of the country, and several of them were reported to have been shot down by ground fire from the various rebel guerrilla groups during the protracted ground-strafing operations.

One aircraft, UB503, is curently preserved at the Defence Services Museum, Yangon.

Three Vampire T.55s await delivery to the Austrian Air Force outside the service department hangar at Chester in July 1964. (Alan Roach)

CANADA

Following the extensive cold weather trials of Vampire F.1 TG372 at the Winterization Experimental Establishment, Edmonton, in Alberta between November 1946 and October 1949, any doubts that the aircraft could operate in severe Arctic conditions as required by the Royal Canadian Air Force were dispelled.

Although the Canadians had planned to build their own Vampire F.1s in May 1946, following a change of heart the Canadian Government ordered 150 Vampire F.3s from de Havilland's. To speed up deliveries, it was decided that the aircraft would be built at Preston and shipped to Toronto, where they would be reassembled by de Havilland of Canada's plant at Downsview. This order was subsequently amended and only eighty-five of the original allocation were built: VP674–VP786, with RCAF serials 17001–17085; of these, VP732/17043 crashed

during an aborted take-off at Samlesbury in November 1947 following an engine failure, and was replaced by VP787/17086.

The first Canadian Vampire flew at Preston on 3 June 1947 and shipment began in September 1947 with eight aircraft, 17001–17008; the order was completed in February 1948 with the delivery of 17045. The first aircraft to be assembled at the Downsview plant, 17014, was flown by de Havilland's chief test pilot Russ Bannock on 7 January 1948.

Deliveries to the RCAF commenced to the Central Flying School at Trenton, Ontario, on 19 January 1948. Further deliveries were made in August 1948 to No. 1 (F) Operational Training Unit at St Hubert, Quebec, which officially formed the following month to train single-engine jet pilots; moving to Chatham, New Brunswick, in November 1949, No. 1 (F) OTU flew Vampires until 1952, when they were exchanged for Canadair Sabres.

On 1 December 1948 410 (F) 'Cougar'

Squadron formed at St Hubert, and became the first post-war Regular Force fighter unit within the RCAF to fly the Vampire. The squadron became operational the following January, and between 1949 and 1951 flew its own aerobatic team, the Blue Devils, which regularly toured throughout Canada and the USA, culminating with the annual Canadian National Exhibition at Toronto. Before being re-equipped with Sabres in May 1952, the squadron sent twelve Vampires to Whitehorse in the Yukon Territories in February 1950 to participate in Exercise 'Sweetbriar', a joint Canadian/US winter training operation along the Alaska Highway. Returning from Whitehorse on 1 March, two Vampires beat Canada's coast-to-coast air speed record when they flew from Vancouver to Montreal in four hours and 55 minutes. The 2,300 mile flight was completed at an average speed of nearly 460 mph, and cut nearly two hours off the previous record. Of the two pilots, only Flt Lt. Don Laubman was able to complete the course, the other, Fg Off. Mike Doyle, being forced to land at North Bay, Ontario with fuel problems.

Mike Doyle had originally joined the RCAF in 1942 and flew Spitfires operationally with 411 Squadron. Following a conversion course at St Hubert, he joined 410 (F) Squadron in January 1949:

The Vampire conversion course at No. 1 OTU was a very casual affair: a few lectures, a brief reading of the Pilot's Notes, and a slap on the back before going out to the aircraft for the first solo.

Most of the pilots on 410 Squadron were experienced wartime fighter boys, so there was nothing new about flying single-seat aircraft; the only novelty was its unaccustomed power and speed.

The Canadian Vampires behaved extremely well in the cold temperatures. In fact, its performance was considerably enhanced during take-off and climb

Vampire F.3 17063 of 410 (F) 'Cougar' Squadron RCAF, in the snow at Whitehorse, Yukon, during exercise 'Sweetbriar', 19 February 1950. (DND)

conditions. It was, however, somewhat uncomfortable to sit in whilst on runway readiness, as we did on Exercise 'Sweetbriar', because there was no way of getting heat into the cockpit without the engine running. We were equipped with bulky, nylon pile flying suits, but this made the cockpit more cramped than ever.

The second RCAF squadron to receive Vampires was 421 (F) 'Red Indian' Squadron, which re-formed at Chatham in September 1949 under the command of Sqn Ldr R.T.P. Davidson DFC. Work-up was slow, and aircraft were pooled with No. 1 (F) OTU to remain operational. Lt. Cdr (then Flt Lt.) Doug Warren commanded 'B' Flight, 421 (F) Squadron, between September 1949 and July 1950:

I was temporarily attached to 410 (F) Squadron, where I awaited the formation of 421 (F) Squadron. The Vampire was an excellent choice of aircraft to introduce the RCAF to jet fighter operations, and proved ideal for Canadian winter flying. At first it was thought that slushy snow or water thrown up from the runway might damage the engine, or even cause it to flame out, but that never occurred to my knowledge. The Goblin engine would just 'grunt' and carry on. A decided handicap was the lack of instrument lighting, especially at night, and better cockpit heating would have been an advantage.

In October 1950 421 (F) Squadron was selected as the first post-war RCAF fighter squadron to be based in the UK, '. . . on a rotational basis, for the purpose of obtaining training, in close co-operation with the RAF units, in operational techniques under European operating conditions'. The squadron was also informed that their own Vampire F.3s were to be left behind and, upon arrival at Odiham, they would be loaned Vampire FB.5s. Reassembling at Odiham in mid-January 1951, the squadron flew over 4,000 hours and participated in twenty-eight Sector or Group exercises before returning to St Hubert the following November.

From March 1948 until October 1956 six RCAF auxiliary squadrons also flew

Vampires: 400 (City of Toronto) Squadron at Downsview; 401 (City of Westmount) at St Hubert; 402 (City of Winnipeg) at Stevenson Field, Manitoba; 411 (County of York) at Downsview; 438 (City of Montreal) at St Hubert; and 442 (City of Vancouver) at Vancouver, British Columbia.

Similarly equipped was the Flying Instructors School at Trenton, and the Experimental & Proving Establishment at Rockcliffe, Ottawa. The latter unit was renamed the Central Experimental Proving Establishment and supported the Climatic Detachment at Namao, Edmonton. Several Vampires were flown to Namao for experimental purposes, including 17007, which between April 1948 and June 1954, was used for cold weather trials of the Goblin engine.

The RCAF Vampires were finally struck off charge in June 1958. Of the many airframes put up for disposal, some twenty-six (plus four spares) were sold to the Formetal Division of Fliteways Inc., West Bend, Wisconsin, in 1958 for possible use in the US civil market as executive jet or fast private 'hacks'. The airframes were 17002/N6865D, 17007/N6880D, 17012/N6882D, 17016/N6870D, 17017/N6873D,

Vampire F.3 17030 of 421 (F) 'Red Indian' Squadron RCAF at Chatham, 27 October 1950. The aircraft was taken on charge in April 1948 and served with 421 and 438 Squadrons and the CFS at Trenton, before being struck off charge in March 1958. (RCAF)

The personnel of 421 (F) 'Red Indian' Squadron RCAF were transferred from Chatham to Odiham in January 1951 and, with borrowed Vampire FB.5s, underwent twelve months of operational training with the RAF. (de Havilland)

17018/N6881D, 17019/N6874D, 17020/N6863D, 17030/N6861D, 17036/N6884D, 17038/N6876D, 17039/N6871D, 17040/N6875D, 17044/N6866D, 17047/N6872D, 17058/N6860D, 17065/N6862D, 17067/N6879D, 17068/N6860D, 17069/N6877D, 17070/N6870D, 17071/N6883D, 17072/N6878D, 17078/N6867D, 17085/N6868D and 17031/N41J. The four spare airframes were 17006, 17021, 17055 and 17062. Very little is known of their subsequent histories after 'civilization', but Paul Mantz, the Hollywood film pilot, was known to have operated two, one of which was 17071/N6883D.

The severe restrictions imposed by the American Federal Aviation Administration upon the use of the Vampires effectively

438 'City of Montreal' Squadron (Auxiliary) in formation over St Hubert, September 1955. The squadron flew Vampire F.3s from April 1948. (DND)

Many ex-RCAF Vampires were sold to Fliteways for use in the civilian market. Originally serving with 400, 401 and 442 Squadrons, 17036 was renumbered N6884D and was last noted with Airplanes Inc., Wyoming, in 1967. It is seen here at Vancouver in April 1958. (P.R. Keating)

closed any possible market in the US. However, fifteen of the former Fliteways Vampires were sold to the Mexican Air Force in 1950 to form the basis of that country's first jet squadron, 200 Squadron at Santa Lucia, numbered FAM–1 to FAM–15.

CEYLON

In the autumn of 1954 five Chester-built Vampire T.55s, CF–501 to CF–505 were delivered by sea to Colombo and transported to Katunayake air base. However, the Commander of the Royal Ceylon Air Force considered that, as the air force was still in its infancy, the Vampires were too advanced for his Cadet pilots and that the technology required to support jet flying was not yet available. The order was subsequently cancelled in favour of Boulton Paul Balliols and the crated Vampires were returned to Chester, unopened. Three of the airframes, CF–501 to CF–503 were reassembled at Chester and sold to Finland in July 1955 as VT–4, VT–3 and VT–2, respectively; the other two were thought to have been used for spares, but Sri Lankan sources also suggest that they were sold to Burma.

CHILE

On 22 October 1953, following the collapse of negotiations with the US Government to purchase jet aircraft, Chile placed an order for five Vampire T.55s. The first aircraft, J–01 (c/n 15414), was flown to Hatfield on 29 December 1953 for acceptance trials, and by the end of the following January had joined J–02 (c/n 15415) and J–03 (c/n 15452) for shipment to Chile. Under the supervision of de Havilland engineering pilot George Errington, the Vampires were reassembled at El Cerrillos Airport, Santiago, and the first aircraft (J–03) was test flown by Errington on 28 April. The following day, Wg Cdr Ianiszewski flew the same aircraft, becoming the first Chilean pilot to fly a jet aircraft in that country. The second aircraft, J–02, was completed on 10 May 1954, followed by the third, J–01, which flew on 15 June 1954. By this time, the remaining two Vampires of the order, J–04 (c/n 15470) and J–05 (c/n 15475), had also been shipped to Valparaiso.

The Vampires entered service with the newly formed Group 7 at Los Cerrillos, under the command of Wg Cdr Ianiszewski, and the first

Officer's Fast Jet Course commenced on 8 November 1954 with five students. One Vampire (J–04) was written off on 7 September 1954 when it crashed at Quilicura, near Santiago, after entering an inverted flat spin; the pilot was able to bale out, unhurt.

In November 1956 Vampire T.55 demonstrator G–AOXH arrived at Buenos Aires docks, and after reassembly, embarked on a 3,000 mile tour of South America in the hands of George Errington. The tour of Argentina, Peru, Uruguay and Chile lasted from December 1956 to April 1957, when it was handed over at Los Cerrillos to replace J–04.

When the Chilean and US Governments signed a Military Aid Agreement in 1957, which provided funds to purchase low-cost Lockheed F–80 and T–33 jets, the Vampires were progressively grounded by 1962; by this time they had also been renumbered J301 to J305. The following year, however, they were given a new lease of life as ground

attack fighters when, following refurbishment, they were transferred to Group 8 at Cerro Moreno, Antofagasta. They were finally grounded in December 1971 when their structural life came to an end, leaving only J301 in airworthy condition.

The Chilean Air Force still had a requirement for ground attack fighter trainers for pilots destined to fly Hawker Hunters, and in 1972 bought a further four ex-RAF Vampire T.11s (WZ512, XD614, XE857 and XJ774) and six ex-FAA Sea Vampire T.22s (XA107, XA128, XA166, XG769, XG772 and XG777) 'as seen' from de Havilland's. Following their removal from store the aircraft were shipped to Antofagasta in December 1972, becoming J302 to J311.

Once in service, the Vampires served with Group 8 at Cerro Moreno, Antofagasta from 1973, until transferred to Group 4 at Los

J310 was an ex-Royal Navy Sea Vampire T.22, delivered to Chile for use with Group 8 at Cerro Moreno airbase, Antofagasta. It was finished in a brown and cream/yellow camouflage, with light blue underneath. (Alberto Douoso)

Condores, Iquique, the following year. Vampires in service with the Chilean Air Force during this period were:

Vampire T.55 J301   (ex-J-302)
Withdrawn Dec. 1980
Vampire T.11 J302   (ex-XD614)
Withdrawn June 1977
Vampire T.11 J303   (ex-XJ774)
Withdrawn June 1977
Vampire T.11 J304   (ex-XE857)
Withdrawn June 1977
Vampire T.11 J305   (ex-WZ512)
Vampire T.22 J306   (ex-XG777)
Withdrawn Dec. 1980
Vampire T.22 J307   (ex-XA166)
Withdrawn Dec. 1980
Vampire T.22 J308   (ex-XG772)
Withdrawn Dec. 1980
Vampire T.22 J309
Withdrawn June 1977
Vampire T.22 J310
Vampire T.22 J311

Some of the Vampires were withdrawn during June 1977; the remainder were struck off charge on 31 December 1980 following a ceremony at Cerro Moreno. Three are preserved: J302 is a gate guard at Los Condores Air Base; J304 is at Cerro Moreno; and J305 is displayed at the Chilean National Aeronautical Museum at Los Cerrillos.

DOMINICAN REPUBLIC

In May 1953 the Royal Swedish Air Force asked various companies for offers on their J28As (Vampire F.1s), which were due for retirement. Despite some interest from Spain, India and Nicaragua, the aircraft remained unsold. In 1955 the Swedish company Henry Wallenberg & Co. bought twenty-five J28As on behalf of the Aviacion Militair Dominicana (AMD). The aircraft were dismantled and shipped to the Dominican Republic at the end of 1955. The serial numbers of the ex-Swedish J28As sold to the AMD were 28013, 28021, 28022, 28025, 28027, 28028, 28030, 28032, 28036, 28038, 28040, 28041, 28042, 28044, 28046, 28047, 28049, 28055, 28057, 28058, 28059, 28061, 28062 and 28067.

Following their arrival in the Dominican Republic in early 1956, the Vampires were transported to the main AMD base at San Isdrio where they were reassembled by Swedish mechanics and handed over to the Escuadron

Ex-Swedish J28A Vampires of the Escuadron Caza-Bombardero, Aviacion Militar Dominicana at San Isdrio in 1956. The large unit badge on the nose is of interest. (Lennart Engerby)

de Caza-Bombardero, supplementing the unit's F-47D Thunderbolts.

In service, the Vampires were renumbered 2701–2725, but the serial tie-ups between the RSwAF and AMD are largely unknown, and only 28028/2720 has been positively identified.

The AMD wished to use its Vampires as fighter/bombers, and designed and installed its own electric bomb release gear. Unfortunately the design of the equipment was sadly wanting and, on the first occasion that bombs were carried, they were dropped onto the apron when the electrics were switched on!

Although the AMD was reasonably satisfied with its Vampires, the US Government tried desperately to persuade it to buy Lockheed T-33As. However, the AMD approached Sweden for a follow-up order for more Vampires, which, although it had disposed of its remaining J28As, had large numbers of surplus J28Bs (Vampire FB.50s) available. Seventeen Vampires were purchased by the AMD in mid-1957, with Henry Wallenberg again acting as the intermediary for the sale. The aircraft were delivered by sea in January 1957. The serials of the ex-Swedish J28Bs were 28152, 28174, 28176, 28183, 28202, 28227, 28279, 28332, 28346, 28347, 28365, 28370, 28374, 28379, 28406, 28408 and 28409. Again the serial tie-ups are unknown, and mystery surrounds the actual quantity delivered, with informed sources stating that eighteen aircraft were assembled, and that one of the aircraft sold as a spares source was indeed flown by the AMD. The J28Bs were given the serial numbers 2726–2742, but unconfirmed sources also quote a '2746', which was probably the 'spare' aircraft.

The new aircraft were issued to the Escuadron de Caza-Bombardero and operated alongside the original Vampire F.1s as first-line equipment of the AMD (renamed Fuerza Aerea Dominica (FAD) in the early 1960s) for many years.

In June 1959 a Castro-supported invasion was made by some 400 revolutionaries at Puerto Plata; after being surrounded in the hills, the rebels were bombed by P-51D Mustangs and Vampires flying from San Isdrio.

During the 1965 civil war the Vampires were again used as fighter/bombers, alongside Mustangs and B-26 Invaders, attacking rebel positions with the loss of several aircraft. By the time the civil war had finished some thirty-four Vampires were in service with the FAD, and some, if not all, of the F.1s had been relegated to training duties.

Because of a lack of spares and problems with serviceability, the Escuadron de Caza-Bombardero and the Escuadron de Caza 'Ramfis' combined to form the Escuadron de Combate in late 1969, and flew a mixture of six Vampires and a quantity of P-51Ds.

By the early 1970s most of the Vampires had been withdrawn from service, and in October 1974 the last three FB.50s (which had been used as trainers and were seen wearing a mottled green and tan camouflage with white undersurfaces) were disposed of. During 1988 at least two airframes were on display at San Isdrio and the Headquarters Fuerzas Armadas at Santo Domingo.

EGYPT

Egypt was the first Middle Eastern country to order Vampires; after the 1948 War of Independence with Israel, Egypt needed to re-equip and modernize its air force. In October 1949 the Egyptian Government ordered twelve Vampire NF.10s, with the option for further aircraft. However, in an attempt to suppress the increasing hostility between Israel and its Arab neighbour, the deal was cancelled when the British Government placed an embargo on arms to Middle Eastern countries. For some unknown reason, an Egyptian order for a batch of single-seat Vampires survived this embargo, and deliveries started with one FB.5, No. 1500 (c/n V0095) in November 1949, and continued with a further fifty FB.52s, Nos 1501 to 1550 (V0092 to V1185) from March 1950.

With the lifting of the British Government's arms embargo in August 1953, the EAF acquired fifty-eight reconditioned Vampires from Italy. As early as June 1952, the Italian Chief of Air Staff had discussed the possibility of selling twenty British-engined, Italian-built Vampires to Italy; the British Government refused permission on the grounds of contractual agreements.

In March 1955 the British Foreign Office received reports that a quantity of Italian Vampires had been sold to Egypt; this was confirmed the following November when Italy officially announced its sales to Middle Eastern countries (which would have included Egypt). Of the order for reconditioned Vampires, forty-three aircraft were flown via Brindisi–Athens–Cairo, and the balance dispatched by sea, in crates marked 'Fragile – Murano Glass'.

Between 1952 and 1956 Vampire fighters (and T.55 trainers) equipped four units and formed the mainstay of the REAF/EAF's tactical offensive strength following the RAF's withdrawal from the Canal Zone. The units were:

2 Squadron Kabrit (1952–56) Vampire FB.52 & T.55
30 Squadron Almaza (1952–56) Vampire FB.52
31 Squadron Kabrit (1955–56) Vampire FB.52 (probably ex-Italian)
Fighter Training Unit Almaza (1955?–56) Vampire FB.5, FB.52, T.55

In the spring of 1955 Egypt placed an order for twelve Vampire T.55s to provide advanced training for pilots destined to fly MiG-15 and MiG-17 fighters. The British Foreign Office had earlier obstructed the sale of the aircraft as they could have been used in combat, which resulted in Egypt making tentative approaches to Norway. The Egyptian T.55s, Nos 1570–1581 (c/ns 15721–15760) were delivered from Hatfield to Fayid between July 1955 and March 1956.

Continued fighting over Sinai saw frequent clashes between Egyptian Vampires and Israeli Meteors: on 29 August 1955 four Vampires

Deliveries of Vampire fighters to Egypt began with a single FB.5, 1500, in November 1949. Further deliveries from Hatfield and Ringway took place between March 1950 and March 1955. (Hawker Siddeley via Philip Birtles)

were intercepted by two Meteor FR.9s near the Gaza Strip, and one Vampire was claimed as shot down. Three days later, another flight of Vampires was intercepted by Meteors after strafing the Kibbutz Carmia in the Gaza Strip; one Israeli pilot was able to shoot down both Vampires (1567 and 1569) during the ensuing action. A further Vampire was shot down near the Gaza Strip in April 1956.

On 26 July 1956 President Nasser announced his intention to nationalize the Suez Canal Company, which prompted Britain and France to mobilize their forces to project their joint interests. Estimates of the number of EAF Vampires vary, mainly because of re-equipment with Soviet aircraft. It is probable that 31 Squadron based at Kabrit and Kasfareet, whose main role was to support the garrisons in the Sinai with detached flights at El Arish in the Gaza Strip, had twelve operational Vampires, with a further six in reserve. The FTU at Fayid and 2 Squadron at Cairo West may also have been operational units.

On 30 October Vampires of 31 Squadron attacked Israeli forces in the Mitla Pass; the following day four Vampires of the same squadron were 'bounced' by six IAF Mysteres while making an attack on ground forces in the same area. Two Vampires were shot down with the loss of their pilots, and a third badly damaged, causing the pilot to abandon his aircraft.

At dawn on 1 November 1956 the British and French bombed Egyptian airfields, including Fayid and Kasfareet. Claims were made of nine Vampires destroyed and five damaged. A further aircraft of 31 Squadron was also lost while operating against the advancing Israeli forces inside Sinai. The following day the Egyptians withdrew from the area leaving behind several wooden mock-ups of Vampire aircraft; one discovered by the Israelis at El Arish was serialled '1562', which was out of any known allocated sequence. A cease-fire came into effect from 6 November 1956.

With the formation of the mutual defence pact with its Arab neighbours, seven ex-EAF Vampires were presented to Jordan in October 1956, and a further seventeen to Saudi Arabia during 1957.

Vampire T.55 1577 at Hurn in December 1955, awaiting delivery to Egypt. (John Havers)

Wooden mock-up of a Vampire FB.52 '1562', was destroyed and abandoned at El Arish during the Suez War, 1956. (D. Nicolle)

FINLAND

In 1952, in common with its two Scandinavian neighbours, Finland ordered six Vampire FB.52s for its air force to replace the Messerschmitt Bf 109Gs of 2 Lennosto (Wing).

Deliveries to HavLv 11 (Fighter Squadron 11) at Pori Air Base, 150 miles north of Helsinki, started on 22 January 1953 with VA–1 to VA–3 (c/ns V0691 to V0693), flown by company pilots George Thornton, Derek Helmore and Michael Hill-Jones. The remaining three aircraft, VA–4 to VA–6 (c/ns V0694 to V0696) were delivered by Finnish pilots in April 1953, and operated alongside the Valmet Vihuri trainers of HavLv 13.

Although maintenance proved more difficult than expected in the Arctic conditions, and a ban on spinning had been imposed, the Vampires lived up to the Finns' expectations. Early experiments with the carriage of air-to-ground rockets were abandoned after government intervention, and a few FB.52s were later transferred to

HavLv 31 at Utti Air Base for winter trials with the especially adapted ice runway.

In March 1955 the Finnish Air Force placed a further order for four Vampire T.55s to serve as advanced trainers, and later as jet conversion trainers for the Folland Gnat trainers which were delivered in 1958. To expedite the order, a company demonstration aircraft, G–ANVF was renumbered VT–1 and three other Vampires were taken from the cancelled Ceylon contract: VT–2 (ex-CF–503), VT–3 (ex-CF–502) and VT–4 (ex-CF–501). The first two aircraft were flown to Pori AB on 15 July 1955 by Finnish Air Force pilots.

The order for T.55s was later increased to nine, and the additional aircraft, VT–5 (15755), VT–6 (15756), VT–7 (15718), VT–8 (15719) and VT–9 (15720), were delivered for use by HavLv 11 at Pori and HavLv 31 at Utti by March 1956.

Between 1956 and 1957 all Vampires were transferred to HavLv 21, 1 Lennosto, based at Luonetjarvi, Jyvaskyla Airport, and in 1957 the Wing was renamed Hameen Lennosto.

Vampire FB.52 VA–3 was delivered to Finland in January 1953 for use with HavLv 11 at Pori. (E. Ritaranta collection)

Three Vampire T.55s of the Finnish Air Force. The trainers served with HavLv 11, HavLv 21 and HavLv 31 between July 1955 and July 1965. (Finnish Air Force)

One Vampire FB.52 was written off in a flying accident when VA–1 crashed near Pori AB on 3 December 1955, killing the pilot. Two Vampire T.55s were also lost: VT–4 was destroyed in a mid-air collision with VA–2 near Luonetjarvi on 29 July 1958, and VT–3, which crashed on final approach to Oulu Airport on 18 April 1963.

Most of the Vampires were withdrawn from service in 1965; the last flight of the FB.52 was made by Capt. Lenni Vaintola in VA–6 on 2 February 1965, before preservation at Pori AB. On 15 July 1965 Vampire T.55 VT–8 made the last flight of the type in Finland and is now exhibited at the Aviation Museum of Central Finland at Luonetjarvi.

In 1960 an additional Vampire (whose identity remains a mystery) was donated to Finland by the arms dealer, Interarmco; it was used as an instructional airframe at Kauhave until 1963, when it was scrapped.

FRANCE

Eager to re-equip its post-war fighter squadrons, France signed an agreement with de Havilland's in 1948 to supply the Armée de l'Air with the readily available Vampire. The deal included the delivery of some thirty ex-RAF Vampire F.1s for pilot conversion, and the training of a number of aircrew. In October 1948 French pilots were sent to Hatfield for conversion and on 16 December these pilots ferried the first five aircraft to France. The principal unit to receive Vampires was the Centre de Transformation sur Avions a Reaction at Mont de Marsan, which was responsible for pilot training.

In May 1949 the first of ninety-four ex-RAF Vampire FB.5s were supplied to the 2eme Escadre de Chasse (EC) at Dijon; by the following October it comprised four escadrons: EC 1/2 'Cigognes', EC 2/2 'Alsace', EC 3/2 'Cote-D'Or' and EC 4/2 'Coq Gaulois'. Further deliveries were to 3eme EC at Rheims and 4eme EC at Friedrichshafen in Germany; during July 1950 this latter unit sent six Vampires to Odiham to participate in the RAF Display at Farnborough.

Earlier that year the Societe Nationale de Constructions Aeronautique du Sud-East (SNCASE) successfully negotiated with de Havilland's to build sixty-seven Goblin-powered Vampire FB.51s under licence at their Marignane plant, with components supplied from de Havilland's. A further 120 airframes were to be assembled from components built in France, and powered by Rolls-Royce Nene engines, also to be built under licence at Hispano-Suiza. The first Vampire FB.51 (10001) made its maiden flight at Marignane on 27 January 1950, followed by the first of the wholly French-built machine (10068) on 21 December 1950, flown by test pilot Jacques Lecarme.

The Mistral was a development of the

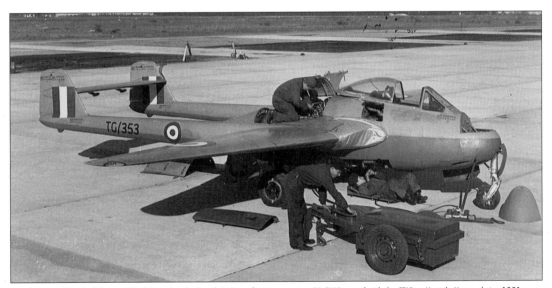

One of the initial batch of Vampire F.1s delivered to the French Air Force for jet conversion, TG/353 served with the CTAR at Mont-de-Marsay during 1951. (via P.X. Henry)

Originally built at Preston, Vampire FB.5 VX965 was delivered to France in July 1949 and issued to EC 2/2 at Dijon. It was destroyed in a flying accident in Morocco in April 1958. (via P.X. Henry)

Built under licence in France, Vampire FB.5 10042 served with EC. 1/5 at Orange from February 1952 until December 1953, when it was written off. (Sud-Aviation)

standard Vampire airframe, powered by the Hispano-Suiza-built Rolls-Royce Nene 104B engine. Original flight trials of the Nene-Vampire F.2 had been unsatisfactory until their 'elephant ears' intakes were removed and the wing root intakes redesigned and enlarged. Further improvements by SNCASE included the fitting of an ejector seat, refining the wing shape (which was made necessary by the relocation of the fuel tanks), and the installation of an air conditioning system –

which was essential for the aircraft's intended operations in North Africa.

Four prototypes of the Mk. 53 Mistral were built and the first ('01') was flown on 1 April 1951 by Jacques Lecarme. The first aircraft were designated SE.532s and did not possess ejector seats (but these were retrofitted at some stage). From No. '98' onwards the ejector seat became standard and the aircraft was redesignated SE.535 Mistral; on 23 January 1953 No. '98' was destroyed in a crash, and

The fourth prototype SE.535 Mistral over the French Alps, flown by Jacques Lecarme. It was issued to SNCASE at Marignane for Nene engine trials in July 1952, and eventually presented to the Musée de l'Air for preservation. (SNCASE)

the pilot Jean Boulet became the first Frenchman to use an ejector seat.

A month after receiving its first Vampire in July 1951, the 1eme EC at Sidi Ahmed in Tunisia began flying 'dissuasion missions' against native forces rebelling against the French Government. On 15 October 1951 the 1eme EC was renumbered the 7eme EC, and in May 1953 became the first unit to convert to the Mistral.

Between 1955 and 1961 three Mistral-equipped escadres were flown against the rebels in Algeria: 6eme EC at Oran, 7eme EC at Sidi Ahmed and 8eme EC at Rabat Sale. Because of their short endurance the Mistrals were employed in the ground support role, attacking targets with a combination of rockets, bombs, napalm and 20 mm cannon fire.

Vampires were also operated by 57.S of the Aeronavale based at Khouribga in Morocco which, between 1954 and 1961, operated the aircraft alongside SNJ-4s and Hellcats in the training of French Marine pilots. Other units included the Le Centre d'Experimentations Aeriennes Militaires at Mont de Marsan and the Centre d'Essais en Vol at Bretigny. The latter flew Mistrals and four Vampire F.1s (TG284 'NJ' 'Porthos', TG310 'PV' 'Aramis', TG344 'AN' 'D'Artagnan' and TG379 'AY' 'Athos') as radio-controlled drones between 1955 and 1967. These aircraft were used in trials involving MATRA air-to-air missiles, and the results of the firings were recorded on cameras fitted in the underwing tanks.

In 1951 SNECMA developed and fitted a reverse-thrust Goblin engine to Vampire FB.5 No. 10119, which was displayed at the twentieth Salon d'Aeronautique at Le Bourget in July 1953. Mistrals '02' and '61' were also fitted with experimental oleo-pneumatic skis on the mainwheels for STOL trials, which were conducted on an especially constructed ski-slope between September 1954 and March 1956.

Remarkably, on 12 May 1951 Mme Jacqueline Auriol was able to establish a new women's world speed record of 515 mph over a 100 km closed-circuit course (Istres/Avignon/Istres), flying a Vampire FB.5, No. 10061.

The serials of the French aircraft were as follows:

SE.535 Mistral 114 of EC 1/7 taxiing at Sidi Ahmed in 1959. (via P.X. Henry)

Vampire F.1:
Thirty aircraft delivered, ex-RAF stock, between 15 December 1948 and 8 January 1950:
TG284, TG288, TG294, TG310–311, TG331–333, TG335, TG339–344, TG347, TG350, TG353–355, TG378–379, TG383, TG422–423, TG425, TG428, TG430 and TG433.

Vampire FB.5:
Ninety-four aircraft, ex-RAF stock, between 31 May 1949 and 9 March 1950:
VV568, VV718, VV720–723, VV725–736, VX950–952, VX954–972, VZ120, VZ129–130, VZ132–141, VZ144, VZ152–154, VZ161–169, VZ172, VZ176, VZ191, VZ196–197, VZ207–209, VZ211, VZ215, VZ217–221, VZ223, VZ226, VZ257–258, VZ270, VZ282, VZ284–285, VZ810, VZ814–815, VZ817 and VZ820.

Vampire FB.5:
Fifteen aircraft assembled at SNCASE, delivered between August 1949 and June 1950:
Nos 1–15.

Vampire FB.5:
187 aircraft built by SNCASE.
Nos 10001–10187.

SE.532/535 Mistral:
Four pre-production aircraft, Nos 01–04, delivered between June 1950 and October 1951.
247 production aircraft, Nos 1–247, delivered between June 1953 and February 1954.

INDIA

Following Independence in 1947, and occasioned by Pakistani aggression in Khashmir which underlined existing military deficiencies, India became a major overseas customer for both the fighter and trainer versions of the Vampire. During 1948 a contract was negotiated by the Indian Government for 286 single-seaters: an initial batch of 39 Vampire FB.52s produced at Hatfield, and the remaining 247 built under licence by Hindustan Aeronautics Limited (HAL) at Bangalore. To provide jet experience, three additional Vampire F.3s, VV209 to VV211 were diverted from the Preston production lines and delivered to the newly formed No. 1 Aircraft Testing Unit at Kanpur as HB544 to HB546 on 6 November 1948. The flight was made by Roger Jamieson, George Thornton and Leo DeVigne, and the aircraft were temporarily given the civilian registrations VT–CXH to VT–CXJ.

The first operational unit to fly Vampires

Three Vampire F.3s were delivered to India in November 1948 for pilot training. All three aircraft carried dual military and civilian registrations, as well as the short-lived 'Chakra' national markings. (de Havilland)

was 7 Squadron at Palam; the aircraft were delivered to 'A' Flight in November 1948 to replace its Tempest IIs. The squadron completed its conversion in July 1949 when it absorbed the Aircraft Testing Unit, and was declared operational in June 1952. A total of sixteen Regular and four Auxiliary IAF units operated Vampires by the time the last squadron was formed in February 1963.

Deliveries of the Hatfield-built Vampire FB.52s, HB732 to HB770 were made between September 1950 and June 1951, by which time India was producing its own licence-built aircraft in the IB200–IB1707

and BB431–448 serial range. The first HAL-built Vampire flew on 21 February 1952.

Two further orders were also signed for Vampire T.55 trainers, and in December 1953 Field Aviation Services at Croydon Airport was awarded the contract to ferry forty-three aircraft, IY467 to IY552, to the Armament and Aircraft Testing Unit at Cawnpore (now Bangalore); the first four, IY467 to IY470, departed in May 1953, and the final aircraft (IY552) left Hatfield in April 1954.

The second order, for ten Vampire T.55s, BY377 to BY386, was delivered between October 1957 and February 1958; in the

The first Vampire T.55 for the Indian Air Force was IY467, seen at Hatfield in May 1955. It was eventually struck off charge in November 1969. The Vampire T.11 in the background is WZ575, destined for the RAF. (de Havilland)

meantime, as with the single-seaters, a further batch of sixty Vampire T.55s was built under licence in the IY1591–IY1600 and BY390–BY478 range. Two T.55s (BY1008 and IY1591) and two FB.52s (BB431 and IB797) were later transferred to the Indian Navy to train pilots for Sea Hawk shipboard fighters, which were purchased from Britain in 1958.

Between the late 1950s and mid-1960s, India took advantage of the many surplus Vampire trainers offered for sale by foreign air forces: in 1957/1958, eight aircraft, J–701 to J–708 were purchased from Indonesia and renumbered BY601 to BY608. Seven more ex-RAF Vampire T.11s were acquired in July 1963; two of these, WZ467 and XE953, had seen previous service with 28 Squadron at Sek Kong, the other five were refurbished at Chester and delivered as BY1005 to BY1009 (previously having been XE983, WZ498, XD532, XE945, and WZ471 respectively). Finally, three Vampire T.55s were assembled from components after the production at Chester had ceased, and sold as BY996 to BY998. Most of the aircraft served with the Armament Training Wing at Jamnager, the Fighter Training Wing at Hakimpet, and the Flying Instructors School at Tambaran.

Between April and October 1954 Field Aviation Services ferried a further batch of eighteen refurbished ex-RAF Vampire NF.54s, ID592 to ID609, to India for service with 10 Squadron at Palam, which was tasked with the all-weather air defence of Delhi. A follow-up order for an additional twelve night-fighters, ID1601 to ID1612, was delivered from August 1957, some of which were issued to the newly formed 37 Squadron at Poona. In October 1962, however, following a drastic reduction in serviceability, all Vampire night-fighter operations were transferred to 10 Squadron.

IAF Vampires went into action for the first time during Operation 'Vijay', the action launched to liberate the Portuguese enclaves of Goa, Daman and Diu on 18–19 December

1961, when two 45 Squadron aircraft attacked and destroyed a patrol boat. In 1963 Vampires were also used in close support of the army counter-insurgency operations against Naga hostiles and in the Mize hills.

Of interest was the handful of Vampire trainers (including BY426, BY477, IY521, IY526 and IY531) adapted to carry cameras and designated PR.55s. This version was delivered to 101 Squadron at Adampur in October 1954 to replace its Spitfire XIXs, and 108 Squadron at Halwara in November 1959. Both units were active during the Indo-Pakistan conflict in 1965, providing armed photo-reconnaissance support for the army, especially in the disputed Rann of Kutch. The IAF Vampires suffered badly during the war with Pakistan, being easy prey to the superior, more manoeuvrable F-86 Sabres. During August 1965 many of the IAF Vampire FB.52s were distributed between six operational units: 24, 45, 108, 121, 220 and 221 Squadrons.

On the first day of hostilities (1 September 1965) a section of Vampires from the combined 45/220 Squadron was detailed to bomb an armoured regiment of the Pakistan army in the Chhamb battle area, inside Kashmir. Despite poor visibility, all four Vampires (BB445, IB432, IB875 and IB1688) were intercepted by Pakistani Sabres on combat patrol, and shot down with the loss of their pilots. A further two FB.52s (IB344 and IB614) were destroyed at Kalaikunda on 7 September during an air raid by Pakistani B-57 Canberras. Four days later a taxiing Vampire PR.55 (BY413) of 108 Squadron was lost during a strafing attack by F-86 Sabres at Baghdogra. Subsequent limited day offensive support missions were undertaken by Vampires, totalling forty-three operational sorties during the war.

By the time the third Indo-Pakistan conflict broke out in 1971, Vampires had been largely replaced in first-line service by Hawker Hunters and Dassault Toofanis, and had been relegated to the training role. However, as hostilities became imminent, an operational squadron of sixteen aircraft, 121 Squadron, was formed at Hakimpet. A detachment of six aircraft (four FB.52s and two T.55s) was attached to No. 12 Wing on 10 November, primarily as close air support for the army. Their role was quickly switched to that of night interdiction, and during fifteen days of operations the detachment carried out attacks against railway yards, fuel dumps and troop concentrations. A total of fifty-six operational sorties were carried out during the war for the loss of one aircraft (a T.55, BY925), which was destroyed on the ground during an air raid on Srinagar airfield on 15 December 1971.

The Vampire continued to serve in the training role with the FTW, FIS and ATW until 1 April 1975, when the type was officially retired from service. The IAF maintains one airworthy Vampire FB.52, IB799, with the Vintage Aircraft Flight at Palam. It was last flown by Sqn Ldr Pawan Arora on 3 October 1989.

INDONESIA

Eight Vampire T.55s, J–701 to J–708 (c/ns 15729–15734, and 15750–15751) were purchased by Indonesia in 1955. The first aircraft, J–702 was flown to Hatfield on 23 September 1965 for acceptance by government representatives. All the aircraft were dismantled and packed for shipping, via London docks, on 23 December 1965. After their arrival at Djakarta, they were reassembled and test flown by de Havilland pilot George Errington, before being officially handed over to the Indonesian Air Force at Hussein Airport, Bandung, on 20 February 1956.

Following the Indonesian Government's decision to re-equip the air force with Soviet-supplied aircraft in the late 1950s, the Vampires were put up for disposal and sold to India. The Vampires were renumbered BY–601 to BY–608 by the Indians, and were noted staging through RAF Butterworth on their delivery flight during 1958.

IRAQ

Established in 1931, the Royal Iraqi Air Force (RIAF) was the third largest air force in the Middle East, and was supplied exclusively with British military equipment. By Rights of Treaty, Britain's interests in Iraq were protected by units of the RAF, including the important

Eight Vampire T.55s were bought by Indonesia. J–707 is shown at Hatfield in November 1955, a month before they were crated and shipped to Djakarta. (de Havilland)

staging posts at Habbaniya and Shaibah. The RIAF had also adopted the RAF flying training programme, continuing in the early 1950s to progress from the Chipmunk/Harvard syllabus to that of the recently introduced Provost/Vampire sequence.

On 25 May 1953 six Vampire FB.52s (336 to 341) and a Vampire T.55 (333) were flown to Iraq, where they formed the basis of the country's first jet fighter unit, 5 Squadron based at El-Rashid, near Baghdad, and commanded by Lt. Col. Sadiq Al-Azawi. During August a further three Vampire FB.52s (342 to 344) were flown from Ringway to Hatfield for dispatch to Iraq.

Six more Vampire trainers were ordered later in the year, and the first three (334 to 336) were delivered in early December. Unfortunately during the first leg of their ferry flight to Hatfield on 16 December, one of the aircraft (334) crashed on high ground near Mold in North Wales, killing the pilot, Fg Off. M. Hills-Jones. A further three Vampire T.55s (386 to 388) were delivered in November 1955, together with three Vampire FB.52s (389 to 391).

Vampire conversion for Iraqi pilots was undertaken by Maj. A.L. Mahmood, the squadron's flight commander, with assistance from Flt Lt. Mercer, an RAF officer loaned to the squadron. The squadron moved to Habbaniya in April 1954 because of the disastrous flooding caused when the River Tigris burst its banks; the move also served to relieve the overcrowding of the airfield caused by the presence of 1 and 7 Squadrons, the Flying College and a communications flight.

With the signing of the Baghdad Pact with Turkey in April 1955 which called for mutual cooperation and defence, Britain agreed to the termination of the Anglo-Iraq Treaty. After the subsequent withdrawal of British forces from the country, Habbaniya was handed over to the RIAF, who then assumed increased responsibility for air operations in the region.

In August 1955 Maj. A.L. 'Paul' Mahmood was appointed as commanding officer of 5 Squadron following a temporary position with 6 Squadron, which had formed the previous March with Venom FB.50s. He retained this post until 1958 when, following the Iraqi revolution, he returned to the UK.

Built at Christchurch, Vampire T.55 333 was the first of a batch of trainers ordered by Iraq, and was delivered in May 1953. (de Havilland)

Vampire FB.52s 390 and 391 at Hatfield in November 1955, prior to delivery to Iraq. (de Havilland via Mike Hooks)

A formation of Vampire FB.52s of 5 Squadron, Royal Iraqi Air Force, over Habbaniya in May 1956, led by the CO, Capt. A.L. Mahmood. (de Havilland via Major A.L. Mahmood)

At the time of the overthrow of the Iraqi monarchy in 1958, six of the eight RIAF Vampire FB.52s were operational, but none of the six Vampire T.55s were available. Fatal accidents included a pilot on his first solo who stalled on approach as he attempted to raise the undercarriage, and a mid-air collision between two aircraft in cloud over Jordan, with the loss of both pilots.

In 1960 Vampire T.55 333 was returned to Chester for overhaul and the fitment of ejector seats; however, as the work proved to be difficult, the fuselage of a Vampire T.11 (XH316) was substituted, to which the wings and booms of 333 were fitted.

During September 1961 Vampires operating from Habbaniya were used in ground operations against Kurdish rebels in Northern Iraq.

IRELAND

The purchase of three Vampire T.55s by the Irish Air Corps in 1956 was the IAC's first association with jet flying; for over ten years they employed their Vampires alongside Hunting Provost T.53s as advanced trainers, with a secondary duty in the ground attack role.

The first aircraft, 185 (c/n 15775) was flown to 1 Squadron at Baldonnell, near Dublin, on 15 May 1956, followed by 186 (c/n 15765) and 187 (c/n 15766) on 20 July.

In 1960 an order was placed for three more T.55s; 191 (c/n 15815) was delivered from Hatfield on 19 January 1961, followed by 192 (c/n 15816) and 193 (c/n 15817) on 16 March. An additional airframe, 198 (an ex-RAF Vampire T.11, XE977) was donated to Baldonnell on 30 August 1963 as a ground instructional airframe.

Following the Irish Air Corps' re-equipment with Fouga CM.170 Magisters in September 1975, the Vampires were withdrawn from service and placed into storage at Casement aerodrome by 1977.

With the exception of 186 (which was sold to a private buyer in the USA for restoration as N4861K) and 193 (which was relegated to the Baldonnell dump) the remainder were donated to museums: 185 was transported to France in February 1978; 192 and the fuselage of 187 are with the Aero Museum, Waterford Airport, Dublin; and 191 was presented to the Irish Air Museum at Castlemote House. Lastly, 198 is displayed outside the Officers' Mess at Baldonnell.

ITALY

Author's Note:
There is some confusion as to the actual number of Vampires built under licence in Italy and the 'MM' serial numbers assigned to these aircraft. To add further to the confusion, the forty-five new aircraft built by Macchi to replace those sold in Arab countries during 1956/57 were assigned vacant serials within the MM serial block. Some serials were allocated twice and the total number of Italian Air Force Vampires appears greater than those quoted by official sources. The figures referred to in the text are taken from the archives of the Stato Maggiore Aeronautica and contemporary sources.

Only after the signing of the Peace Treaty in Paris in February 1947 and the subsequent withdrawal of the Anglo-American forces of occupation, could Italy consider the process of rebuilding its post-war air force, the Aeronautica Militare Italiana (AMI). Equipped with numbers of surplus American fighters, the AMI looked to Britain for licence-building of large numbers of jet-engined day fighters to establish itself as a respected member within the NATO alliance.

Following discussions with various aircraft companies, the Italian Air Attaché in London, Lt. Col. Duilio Fanali decided to opt for the de Havilland Vampire, and on 24 October 1949 the Director General of FIAT signed a licenced-production and development agreement at Hatfield. This agreement included orders for 5 Vampire FB.5s, 51 Vampire FB.52s and 14 Vampire NF.54s to be built in the UK; 120 Vampire FB.52s built in Italy at the Aeronautica Macchi and FIAT factories (which was increased to 150 the following year); together with a quantity of Venom fighter/bombers and Goblin 2 and Ghost engines.

On 11 March 1950 the first five Vampire FB.5s, VZ252 to VZ256 (MM6000 to MM6004), coded S3–151 to S3–155 respectively, were flown from Hatfield to the Jet Flying School at Foggia/Amendola by Italian Air Force pilots, led by Lt. Col. Fanali.

As it would be at least twelve months before Italian production lines could begin delivering substantial quantities of Vampires to the AMI, the order for FB.52As procured from de Havilland's ensured that units could become operational much sooner. The fifty-one aircraft supplied from Chester between July 1950 and December 1951, together with a further ten which were probably dispatched as component sets to FIAT, were serialled

S3–156 to S3–166, S3–171 to S3–210 (within the range MM6005–MM6019 and MM6024–MM6059). The first Vampires were received by the 3 Group Training School at Foggia/Amendola, who converted the pilots for the first operational units – 79 and 81 Squadriglia (Flight) of 6 Gruppo (Squadron), 4 Stormo Caccia (Fighter Wing), which replaced their Mustangs at Napoli/Capodichino in August 1951.

The component units of the 4 Stormo were quick to become operational and in September 1951 sixteen Vampires participated in the joint Western Union exercise 'Cirrus' at Wiesbaden in Germany. Between 1951 and 1952 6 Gruppo also provided the aircraft and pilots for the AMI's official aerobatic team, the Cavallino Rampante.

At this stage, production of the licence-built Vampires in Italy was well under way, with FIAT constructing ninety-three at their Turin plant, and Macchi assembling twenty-seven at Varese, under the designation FB.52A. The serial range for this first block was in the range MM6023 to MM6142; the first Vampire to come off the production lines

No. 3 Group Training School at Foggia/Amendola was responsible for training the first jet pilots for the Italian Air Force using Vampire FB.52As. (Aeronautica Militare)

flew on 18 December 1951 from Venegono near Milan, piloted by Macchi's chief test pilot, Guido Carestiato. It was followed on 22 December by FIAT's first aircraft, test flown by Simeone Marsan at Turin/Caselle.

The second block of thirty licence-built Vampires were serialled MM6155 to MM6184, with Macchi and FIAT producing seventeen and thirteen aircraft respectively. When the British Government placed an embargo on military exports to Egypt, fifty-eight ex-AMI Vampires were rebuilt by Macchi; in March 1956 forty-three of these aircraft were flown via Brindisi–Athens–Cairo, with the remaining fifteen airframes shipped in crates. To replace those dispatched to Egypt, Macchi built a further forty-five new aircraft.

Various British Foreign Office statements report on the purchase of thirteen Italian-built Vampires to Egypt in March 1955, together with a further eighteen during October. This last order was routed via Syria, who retained some aircraft to join the thirteen Vampires originally delivered to them in 1954.

Between October 1951 and June 1956 Vampires also served with 2 Stormo at Bergamo and 4 Stormo at Napoli/Capodichino; the 7 Group Fighter School (which had been renumbered from 3 Group Fighter School in February 1953); 1, 3 and 4 Zona Areas at Milan/Brescia, Rome/Ciampino and Foggia/Amendola, and the Reparto Sperimentale Volo at Rome/Ciampino. By the autumn of 1960 Vampires had been replaced by F-84G Thunderjets and F-86 Sabres, with 4 Zona at Foggia/Amendola becoming the final AMI unit to fly single-seat Vampires when it transferred its aircraft to Macchi for disposal in November.

The Anglo-Italian agreement of October 1949 included fourteen Vampire NF.54s,

Vampire FB52s of No. 4 Stormo at Napoli/Capodichino, 1952. The aircraft wear the 'Prancing Horse' unit marking on the fin. (Stato Maggiore Aeronautica)

ordered as interim night-fighters for the AMI. During the spring of 1951 Lt. Col. Fanali was tasked with the formation of a small nucleus of pilots to be trained in night-fighter techniques, who returned to Foggia/Amendola from Hatfield in May following their conversion.

On 4 June 1951 the first two Hatfield-built Vampire NF.54s, 3–167 (MM6016) and 3–168 (MM6017) were delivered to 3 Group Flight School, based at Foggia/Amendola. Unfortunately, MM6017 was lost on 28 October 1951 when it crashed near Ponte del Cesano on the Adriatic Riviera.

The remainder of the AMI order for Vampire NF.54s was assembled at Chester with deliveries commencing with 3–169 (MM6018) and 3–170 (MM6019) on 22 July 1952. Between October 1952 and March 1953 Italian pilots continued to ferry their NF.54s from Chester, with the last two, 3–219 (MM6151) and 3–220 (MM6152), being delivered on 25 March 1953.

By early 1953 the 3 Group Flight School had become the All-Weather Fighter School – Scuola Caccia Ogni Tempo (SCOT) – and together with their thirteen Vampire NF.54s, possessed a Douglas C.53 (MM61765) fitted

with radar mounted in a 'Pinocchio' nose for the training of radar operators. During 1953/1954 SCOT Vampires made frequent exchange visits with the RAF Meteor NF.11s at Malta, and in May 1954 several of the unit's Vampires were transferred to Squadriglia Volo Senza Visibilta of 4 Stormo at Napoli/Capodichino.

In May 1956 SCOT began to relinquish its Vampires for F-86K Sabres, the last two being transferred to Reparto Sperimentale Volo at Practica di Mare in October 1959.

JAPAN

One Vampire T.55 (c/n 15752) was ordered by the Japanese Air Self-Defence Force (JASDF) for evaluation in 1955, and was given the 'Class B' registration G–5–14 in October of the same year to enable the aircraft to be test flown by the manufacturers. Fitted with ejector seats, the Vampire was delivered to the packers on 19 November 1955 for shipment to the Vampire Unit at Hamamatsu Air Base, Shizuoka Province, in Southern Japan.

During March and April 1956 the trainer (now re-serialled with the JASDF number 63–5571) was demonstrated by George

One Vampire T.55 was ordered by Japan for evaluation in 1956, following which it was preserved at Hamamatsu air base. (Yoshihiro Aoyama)

Errington to air force representatives, including the Station Commander, Gen. Otavi, and the Vampire Unit's chief pilot, Col. Hidaka.

Despite being damaged when it was accidentally dropped from its trestles, the Vampire trainer performed well during the full-scale appraisal at Hamamatsu. However, the JASDF decided against any further orders and the aircraft was retained for comparison trials (together with a North American T-28B) during the flight development of the Japanese-built Fuji T-1 trainer. The Vampire was eventually preserved and displayed at Hamamatsu Air Base.

JORDAN

Originally formed in 1949 as the Arab Legion Air Force, the Royal Jordanian Air Force (RJAF) changed both its name and role at the beginning of 1956. When under RAF supervision, Jordan's air force was primarily a transport force for army support until the arrival of ten ex-RAF Vampire FB.9s, which took over the security of the kingdom following the RAF's final withdrawal from Amman and Mafraq in May 1957. Britain encouraged the development of the RJAF, with whom it had long association, and the

gift of the FB.9s, which were delivered between November 1955 and February 1956, enabled the creation of Jordan's first jet fighter unit, 1 Squadron at Amman.

The ten ex-RAF Vampire FB.9s were WL506, WR190, WR201, WR210, WR248, WR250, WR258, WX202, WX206 and WX208. In service with the RJAF, these Vampires were renumbered F600 to F609, and were augmented in October 1956 by seven Vampire FB.52s, F610 to F616, donated by the Egyptian Air Force. The Jordanian civilians quickly nicknamed the Vampire 'Abu Tiki', which translates as 'Father of the Whistle'.

All flying training in the RJAF was closely supervised by RAF officers, and the further gift of two ex-RAF Vampire T.11s, XD548/T209 and XD552/T210, in July 1955 enabled a programme of *ab initio* training to be developed using Chipmunks, Harvards and Vampire T.11s. In May 1960 a further Vampire T.11, WZ545/T213, was delivered to the RJAF to assist pilots to convert to their newly acquired Hawker Hunters.

During the crisis in the Middle East between July and October 1958 following the assassination of the Iraqi president and the revolt in the Lebanon, both Iraq and Jordan

Ten Vampire FB.9s were delivered to Jordan to equip 1 Squadron at Amman. The aircraft still carry their former RAF serials. (RJAF)

agreed to oppose the newly formed United Arab Republic. But the RJAF was in no position to confront the forces of Egypt and Syria; only six of the fourteen Vampire fighter/bombers were operational, and neither of the remaining Vampire trainers were available for service. Fortunately, the timely intervention of British troops and a squadron of RAF Hunters, in response to King Hussein of Jordan's appeal for assistance, helped to contain the emergency.

In 1958, following the RJAF's re-equipment with Hunter fighters, the Vampires were transferred to 2 Squadron. During 1962 both 1 and 2 Squadrons were combined to form a new 1 Squadron, and during the fighting against Israel in June 1967, two Vampire FB.52s were lost when Amman was attacked.

The six remaining Vampire single-seaters were withdrawn from the RJAF soon after the Six Day War of 1967, but the Vampire trainers were retained until 1972, when they were also retired.

Note: In 1959 squadron markings were introduced, comprising an eagle superimposed on an Arabic numeral 2 within a white disc on each side of the nose, which was flanked by a black/white chequered arrowhead. Black/white chequered rectangles also flanked the tail-boom roundels and were featured on the wingtips.

KATANGA

In September 1961 Katanga received two Vampire trainers (5801 and 5802) from the Portuguese Air Force. Because of their poor condition, neither aircraft was ever used after delivery, nor did they carry Katanganese Air Force markings. Both are believed to have been destroyed at Kolwezi in December 1961 during a strafing attack on the rebel airstrip by a Canberra B(I)58 of 5 Squadron, Indian Air Force.

LEBANON

Founded in June 1949 with the assistance of RAF advisers, the organization and size of the Lebanese Air Force (LAF) was similar to that of its Arab neighbour, Jordan. Equipped with an assortment of aircraft, the LAF's main airfield was at Khaldeh/Beirut International Airport, with Rayak and Tripoli also available for operational flying.

On 24 August 1953 a Christchurch-built Vampire T.55 (L151) was delivered to Rayak for jet conversion training. Two months later the first two (L152 and L153) of the six Vampire FB.52s ordered as fighter/bombers were flown out from Hatfield to form the Pursuit Bomber Squadron at Khaldeh. The balance of the order for single-seaters was eventually completed in April 1955 when four Vampire FB.52s (L155 to L158), together with a further two Vampire T.55s (L154 and L159) arrived at Khaldeh.

During the reorganization of the LAF in 1956, the now operational Vampire Pursuit Bomber Squadron was renamed 1 Squadron, and a fourth Vampire T.55 L160 (ex-demonstrator G–APFV) was added to the strength in November 1957. The squadron's activities included navigation exercises over Jordan and Syria, army support manoeuvres, civil defence duties and air gunnery practice in Cyprus.

The Muslim-led rebellion in 1958 against the Christian pro-NATO President, Camille Chamoun, saw the LAF Vampires carrying out many strikes against tribesmen in the Baalbek area and Druze fighters in the Shouf Mountains. Reconnaissance patrols were also increased over the Bekaa Valley and near the Syrian border following clashes between security forces and armed tribesmen.

Prior to the outbreak of fighting, the LAF Order of Battle in February 1958 showed the disposition of the Vampires as:

Four Vampire T.55s were ordered by Lebanon, the first of which, L151, is shown at Hatfield prior to delivery on 24 August 1953. (Hawker Siddeley via Philip Birtles)

Khaldeh/Rayak:
6 Vampire FB.52 5 operational
Rayak:
4 Vampire T.55 nil operational

The American-funded Middle East military aid package deal, which six months earlier saw the delivery of six ex-RAF Hunter F.6s for 2 Squadron, LAF, in November 1958, also probably included seven refurbished ex-RAF Vampire single-seaters as fighter/bombers and for jet conversion training. The

aircraft (four FB.5s and three FB.9s) were VV694, WA365 and WL497 (delivered 23 May 1958) and VV453, WA128, WG929 and WL586 (delivered 19 June 1958). The aircraft were re-serialled L161 to L167 in LAF service.

Although the LAF had been established at Rayak AFB, it proved unsuitable for jet operations, and technicians and maintenance personnel (called the 'Khaldeh Detachment') were posted to Khaldeh to serve the Vampire squadron. By 1963 Rayak had been

Vampire FB.52 L158 of 1 Squadron, Lebanese Air Force, at Beirut, May 1958. It was originally delivered to the Lebanon in 1953. (via P.R. Keating)

refurbished and was able to receive and operate jet aircraft; accordingly it was made the LAF HQ, with all fixed-wing aircraft transferring there on 2 September.

With further deliveries of Hunter fighter and trainer versions, 1 Squadron was disbanded during 1964 and the Vampires were withdrawn from service and probably scrapped. At least one aircraft (L160) was taken on charge by the Geographical Affairs Directorate for aerial survey work.

The last official Vampire flight by the LAF was undertaken on 20 September 1974 by Lt. Matar and Lt. Faraj, when they made a 55 minute photographic sortie over towns in the west of the Lebanon.

During the mid-1970s, Vampire FB.52 L155 was noted derelict outside the Elias Kordahy barracks at Beirut AFB, but it is unlikely to have survived the intense fighting in the city during later years.

MEXICO

In early 1960 Mexico purchased fifteen Lockheed T-33A jet trainers, plus a further fifteen surplus Vampire F.3s from the RCAF, as the first step towards the modernization of the Fuerza Aerea Mexicana (Mexican Air Force). Deliveries of the refurbished Vampires, which were numbered FAM–1 to FAM–15, commenced almost immediately, but they were still being ferried during February 1962 when FAM–1, FAM–2 and FAM–13 were staging through Love Field, Dallas, Texas. The ex-RCAF serials of the Vampires included 17002, 17012, 17016, 17017, 17019, 17030, 17039, 17040, 17044, 17047, 17065, 17067, 17078 and 17085.

The Vampires were issued to Escuadron Aereo de Palea 200 at Aeropuerto International, Mexico City, but moved during 1961 (following a £2m refurbishment programme) to Base Aerea Militar No. 1 Santa Lucia, Edo de Mexico City. With the acquisition of the Lockheed T-33As for Escuadron 202, both units became the responsibility of No. 7 Air Group.

In service, the Vampires were known as the 'Aguacates' (Avocados) because of their overall olive drab colour scheme with yellow drop-tanks and bands around the wings and tail-booms; they also sported a 'shark's mouth' nose marking and large squadron badge below the cockpit. In later years the Vampires were resprayed silver overall.

During 1962 two late-standard ex-RAF

Mexico purchased fifteen Vampire F.3s from RCAF to equip 200 Squadron at Santa Lucia. The aircraft were originally finished in an olive drab colour scheme. (Santiago A. Flores)

This is one of two ex-RAF Vampire T.11s flown by the Mexican Air Force. It still carries its former serial and the badge of 200 Squadron under the cockpit. (Enrique Velasco)

Vampire T.11s (WZ414 and XD439) were purchased by the Mexican Air Force, via an aviation broker, and delivered to 200 Squadron as operational trainers. Retaining their original silver finish, with cherry-red painted fins and a squadron badge below the cockpit, the trainers carried their RAF serials for some time but were later renumbered 16 and 17.

Mainly because of their high accident rate and lack of ejection seats, the Vampire fighters were withdrawn from service in 1970 and placed into storage at Santa Lucia. Five aircraft had been written off during their service, and some of the survivors were issued to the Air College at Zapopan, Jaliscoa, as instructional airframes. At least one (probably FAM–5) is preserved at the Office of the Secretary of Defence, Mexico City.

Towards the end of their careers, the Vampire T.11s were transferred to the Flying School at Zapopan AFB, where they operated alongside former USAF Fairchild PT-19s, North American AT-6s and T-28 piston-engined trainers. In 1970 the Vampire trainers were retired, but at least one unidentified aircraft is known to have joined FAM–5 on display in Mexico City.

NEW ZEALAND

During 1950/51 the post-war Royal New Zealand Air Force (RNZAF) underwent a major re-equipment programme to replace its large number of wartime aircraft; orders for new aircraft were approved, including eighteen Vampire FB.52s for 14 Squadron at Ohakea. These aircraft, serialled NZ5721 to NZ5738, were delivered from Chester between October 1950 and August 1951; the first arrived at Auckland on board the SS *Rangitikei* on 10 April 1951, and the last two on 15 February 1952. The Vampires were reassembled at Hobsonville, and the first aircraft (NZ5729) was flown on 22 August 1951 when de Havilland (A) test pilot Brian Walker flew it to Whenuapai.

Deliveries to RNZAF Base Ohakea began on 28 August 1951 with NZ5721; a week later (on 3 September 1951), the first unit to fly the type, 14 Squadron, was re-formed under the command of Sqn Ldr R.A. Rayner. The squadron became operational in October; two months later, it participated in exercises against P-51D Mustangs of the Territorial Air Force, when Vampires claimed a 100 per cent 'kill' rate.

Six Christchurch-built Vampire T.55s (NZ5701 to NZ5706), which had been ordered in 1951, were delivered between July and December 1952. They were all built to an early standard with framed canopies and lacking ejector seats. The first two aircraft (NZ5701 and NZ5702) were test flown at Hobsonville on 25 August 1952 by Wg Cdr J.M. Checketts.

In 1952 eight more Vampire fighters were ordered as attrition aircraft to replace the four aircraft lost in flying accidents during the year. These aircraft, serialled NZ5750 to NZ5757, were the first of the refurbished ex-RAF Vampire FB.5s (WA299, VZ843, WG846, WA379, WA249, WA338, WA376 and WA311) for the RNZAF. Deliveries were made between July and September 1953, and some went into storage soon after arrival.

On 7 October 1952 14 Squadron moved to Nicosia as part of the Commonwealth Strategic Reserve. All their Vampire FB.52s were passed to 75 Squadron at Ohakea and the unit was obliged to hire sixteen Vampire FB.9s and a T.11 from the RAF.

During the next two years, 14 Squadron participated in many air exercises, as well as making frequent deployments to the Canal Zone. Between May and June 1953 it flew to East Africa to mark the occasion of the Queen's Coronation; code-named 'Long Trek Two', the squadron's three flights flew to Kenya, Dar-es-Salaam and Entebbe respectively. In April 1955 14 Squadron transferred to Tengah for Operation 'Firedog' and relinquished its Vampires in the November in favour of Venom FB.1s.

Meanwhile, as the RNZAF's only resident jet fighter unit, 75 Squadron assumed the responsibility for the conversion and operational training of all Vampire pilots. The squadron was split into three flights, with 'C' Flight as the operational conversion flight; in 1954 the Fighter Operational Conversion Flight was formed at Ohakea from 'C' Flight to take over the jet training role.

A decision to convert the three Territorial Air Force squadrons from Mustangs to Vampires was abandoned in May 1955. With the premature retirement of the TAF's Mustangs and with the future of the TAF in doubt, it was decided to train TAF pilots at Ohakea during their annual camps. This was achieved by increasing the strength of 75 Squadron and the FOCU with a further order of refurbished single-seat Vampires and with a batch of new T.11s.

Vampire FB.52 NZ5726 shortly after arrival of Ohakea on 23 October 1951 to equip 14 Squadron. The unit moved to Cyprus the following year. (RNZAF)

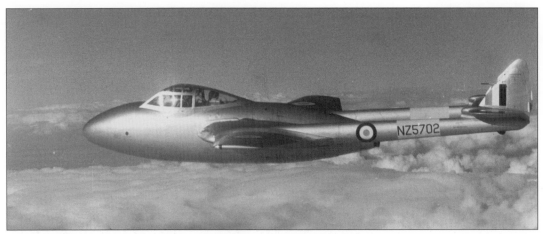

Christchurch-built Vampire T.55 NZ5702 of the RNZAF in 1952. (RNZAF)

Mixed formation of Vampire FB.52s and a T.55 of 75 Squadron over the Wellington area, January 1954. (RNZAF)

Five late-standard Vampire T.11s, NZ5707 to NZ5711 (ex-XH265, XH266, XH271, XH317 and XH366), equipped with ejector seats, were delivered to Auckland between December 1955 and September 1956. One more ex-RAF Vampire FB.5, NZ5758 (ex-VZ838), was received in October 1955, and between January and October 1956 a further twenty FB.5s, NZ5759 to NZ5778 (ex-WA428, WG826, WA317, WA383, WA388, WA342, WA314, VZ841, WA374, VZ852, WA306, WA444, WL493, WA452, WA451, WA411, WA385, WA375, WA392 and WG805 respectively) were accepted. Also obtained were sets of Vampire FB.9 wings (complete with the 8 in increase to the starboard fillet that was characteristic of the installation of refrigeration equipment) which gave rise to rumours that the RNZAF were flying the tropicalized version.

With the disbandment of the TAF in 1957

Vampire T.11 NZ5710 of 14 Squadron was built at Chester and originally serialled XH317. It was delivered to New Zealand in April 1956, and is seen off the Monawatu coast in January 1971. (RNZAF)

and transfer of 75 Squadron to Tengah in March 1958 to fly Canberras, the requirement for large numbers of Vampires ceased and a considerable number were withdrawn from service and placed in storage at Woodbourne. A few remained with the FOCU until June 1958 when it disbanded and re-formed as the Jet Conversion Unit, using Vampires in the advanced training role; in July 1958, 14 Squadron returned from Singapore and continued to operate Vampires until the end of 1959, when they also re-equipped with Canberras.

In early 1960 the Jet Conversion Unit was replaced by the Bomber Operational Conversion Unit, which continued to operate two Vampire FB.5s and six T.11s for jet conversion training and army cooperation exercises.

During March 1962 75 Squadron returned from Tengah and re-formed at Ohakea, taking over the role of the BOCU. On 1 September 1963 75 Squadron reverted to the fighter/ground attack role, with a unit

establishment for eight Vampire FB.5s and four T.11s. These aircraft remained with the squadron until May 1970 when A-4K Sky Hawks were received and the Vampires were passed to 14 Squadron, who had recently given up their Canberras. In 1972 14 Squadron re-equipped with BAC 167 Strikemasters and their Vampires were retired from RNZAF service when the last four aircraft – FB.5s NZ5770 and NZ5774, and T.11s NZ5708 and NZ5711 – were flown to Woodbourne on 15 December.

Twenty-one Vampires had been written off as the result of flying accidents, and a further twenty-three converted to instructional airframes for use at Hobsonville, Wigram and Woodbourne. Four ex-RAF airframes which were bought by the RNZAF in 1955/56 were used for instructional purposes at Hobsonville and Woodbourne until the early 1960s; these were Vampire 1 TG443/INST166, Vampire 3 VT806/INST167, and Vampire 9s WL514/INST169 and WR202/INST171. The remainder were sold as scrap or to private collectors. Four aircraft are preserved at various military establishments: an FB.5, NZ5757, is at the RNZAF Museum at Wigram, together with a privately owned T.11, NZ5707; two further FB.5s are mounted at the main gates at Te Rapa and Ohakea, serialled NZ5765 and NZ5772 respectively.

The New Zealand Warbirds Association at Wanaka, Otaka Province, operate several aircraft on the air show display circuit, including an ex-RAAF Vampire T.35, A79–649 (ex-ZK–VAM and VH–ICP), which was purchased in 1990 and made its public debut in March 1992.

NORWAY

One of the proposals of a Royal Commission appointed by the post-war Norwegian Government to examine the establishment of its air force was the replacement of war-surplus Spitfires by a more modern type of aircraft. In 1948 the Royal Norwegian Air Force (RNoAF) settled on the de Havilland Vampire and placed an order for twenty F.3s and thirty-six FB.52s to equip three day fighter squadrons based at Gardermoen. To speed up deliveries the Vampire F.3s were diverted from the production lines at Preston and dispatched to Norway via Hatfield.

On 7 May 1948 two of the initial batch of

four aircraft (VT832:B–AC, VT833:B–AE, VT834:B–AB and VV188:B–AD) were delivered to Norway for technical evaluation by the newly formed 'C' Flight of 331 Squadron at Gardermoen. All twenty Vampire F.3s had been delivered by October 1949, by which time 'C' Flight had been renumbered 336 Squadron. The serials of the twenty aircraft were VF323:B–AV, VF324:B–AO, VF325:B–AV, VF326:B–AP, VF328:B–AR, VF330:B–AW, VF331:B–AS, VF334:B–AT, VG692:B–AI, VG693:B–AK, VG694:B–AL, VG695:B–AM, VG696:B–AN, VT832:B–AC, VT833:B–AE, VT834:B–AB, VT835:B–AF, VV188:B–AD, VV212:B–AG and VV214:B–AH.

The order for thirty-six Vampire FB.52s was divided between Hatfield (eleven aircraft) and Chester (twenty-five aircraft), with deliveries to Gardermoen between December 1949 and April 1951. The serials were:

Hatfield:
V0047:B–BA, V0062:B–BB, V0074:B–BC, V0076:B–BD, V0098:B–BE, V0252:B–BP, V0258:B–BR, V0264:B–BS, V0270:B–BT, V0307:B–BU and V0330:B–BV.
Chester:
V0108:B–BF, V0126:B–BH, V0135:B–BG, V0184:B–BI, V0195:B–BK, V0209:B–BL, V0222:B–BM, V0238:B–BN, V0245:B–BO,

Three Vampire F.3s being prepared at Hatfield in July 1948 for delivery to the newly formed 'C' Flight of 331 Squadron at Gardermoen. Most of the ferry flights included a stopover at Lubeck in Germany. (de Havilland)

One of the original twenty Vampire F.3s to be delivered to Norway, P42408 'B–AE' (formerly VT833) served with various units between May 1948 and February 1957, when it was placed into storage. (BAe)

V0404:B–CA, V0412:B–CB, V0421:B–CC, V0424:B–CD, V0435:B–CE, V0436:B–CF, V0438:B–CG, V0443:B–CH, V0445:B–CI, V0447:B–CK, V0449:B–CL, V0453:B–CM, V0456:B–CN, V0459:B–CO, V0467:B–CP and V0468:B–CR.

The first Vampire FB.52s were allocated to 336 Squadron, followed by 337 and 339 Squadrons, which comprised the Gardermoen Vampire Wing; the F.3s were transferred to the Jet Training Flight (later renamed 718 Squadron) at Sola AFB, who undertook jet conversion.

In September 1950 twelve Vampires from 336 Squadron were detached to North Weald to participate in the RAF Fighter Command exercise 'Emperor'. One of the Norwegian pilots, Lt. Oskar Harby, acquitted himself well when he attacked four other Vampires who were posing as jet bombers and successfully drove them off.

A further order for six Vampire T.55s was placed in late 1951 and the work was subcontracted to de Havilland's Christchurch factory. The first aircraft was transferred to Hatfield in June 1952 and delivered to Gardermoen AFB on 4 July. Although most of the T.55s were operated by the jet training wing at Sola AFB, two were used for continuation training and instrument ratings by 337 Squadron. The six trainers were delivered between July and November 1952 and allocated the serials 15016 PX–E, 15018 PX–G, 15027 PX–M, 15030 ZK–X, 15033 ZK–Y and 15051 ZK–Z.

Vampire F.3 V0421 was built at Chester and delivered to Norway in December 1950. The aircraft served exclusively with 337 Squadron and is seen at Bardufoss during 1954, before it was placed into storage and eventually scrapped. (Erling Sole)

The T.55s' career with the RNoAF was to be brief, for they were soon replaced by Lockheed T-33s and returned to Britain in three batches between February and December 1955. Following refurbishment at Hullavington the aircraft were reissued to the RAF as XJ771 to XJ775.

Because of the country's commitment as a member of NATO, Norway was constrained to re-equip with more modern aircraft, supplied under the MDAP agreement. 336 Squadron converted to F-84G Thunderjets in February 1953; 339 Squadron received F-86K Sabres in 1955; and 337 Squadron disbanded in late 1955.

On 14 February 1957 the single-seat Vampires (nine F.3s and twenty-five FB.52s) were struck off charge with the RNoAF. Twenty Vampires were written off during the nine years of operational service, and those which escaped the breaker's axe at Vaernes were allocated to various Norwegian military establishments as gate guards or instructional airframes.

One ex-Swiss Vampire FB.6, J–1146, was purchased in 1991 by the Warbirds of Norway, based at Gardermoen. Originally supplied to the Swiss Air Force in March 1952, it became the first fighter aircraft to gain a civil registration in Norway when a special experimental-series LN–17 was allocated, and first flew as such on 14 May 1993. Following the removal of the pointed, Venom-style nose and Swiss markings, the Vampire has been painted to represent ZK–P of 337 Squadron.

Author's Note: Initially, all the Vampires in RNoAF squadron service were coded with the prefix B– in accordance with the then current three-digit practice (Spitfires were prefixed A–, Harvards M–, etc.). In the spring of 1951 the system was changed, giving the squadrons their own individual code identification: 331 Squadron BA; 336 Squadron BA later PX; 337 Squadron BB later ZK; 339 Squadron BB later SI; Jet Training Wing/718 Squadron DP.

Former Norwegian Vampire T.55s at Vaernes in February 1955, prior to being flown back to the UK for eventual issue to the RAF. The aircraft already carry the RAF serials XJ771 to XJ773. (Erling Sole)

PORTUGAL

Following the successful demonstration of a Vampire to the Portuguese Air Force in Lisbon during January 1951, two early-standard Vampire T.55s were ordered for evaluation purposes and delivered to Pora Air Base, to the north-east of Lisbon, in late 1952. The original intention was to use the Vampires for jet conversion and upgrading of Portuguese P-47 Thunderbolt pilots following their training in the USA, prior to receiving F-84G Thunderjets.

The first Vampire trainer (1801) was transferred from Christchurch on 30 October 1952, followed by the second (1802) on 4 December 1952; in service, the aircraft were renumbered 5801 and 5802 respectively.

When Portugal eventually decided to purchase Lockheed T-33A jet trainers for its air force, the Vampires were transferred to the newly formed jet training squadron at BA 1 Sintra in 1953, where they were operated until 1961. Both aircraft were later sold to Katanga and shipped to Johannesburg during September of the same year.

Vampire FB.9 5801 (ex-SAAF 248) is preserved at the Museo Do Ar in Averca.

RHODESIA

In 1953 the Southern Rhodesian Air Force (SRAF) placed an order for sixteen Vampire FB.9s and sixteen Vampire T.11s to replace its ageing Spitfires. It was envisaged that pilots would complete their basic training on Provost T.52s, progressing to Vampire T.11s for jet conversion, before completing their tactical training on Vampire FB.9s. The FB.9s (fitted with Goblin 3 engines) serialled WX212, WX219, WX228, WX231 to WX233, WX235 to WX242, WX256 and WX260, were delivered between December 1953 and August 1954, and in service with the SRAF were renumbered SR100 to SR115. They were followed, between March and October 1955, by Vampire T.11s XE816 to XE819, XE823 to XE826, XE938 to XE941, XH268 to XH270, and XH275, which were also renumbered SR116 to SR131.

In late 1954 political changes within

One of the two Vampire T.55s ordered by Portugal, 5801 is seen at Sintra before its sale to Katanga. (Col. Albano Fernandez)

Vampire FB.9 5801 was originally delivered to the South African Force in 1953 as 248. Following the withdrawal of the type from service it was presented to the Museo Do Ar at Alverca, Portugal. The serial was originally allocated to a Vampire T.55. (via Mike Hooks)

Rhodesia resulted in the air force changing its name to the Rhodesian Air Force; shortly afterwards it changed its name again when the Queen conferred the prefix 'Royal'. The Vampire serials were changed accordingly to RRAF 100 to RRAF 115 for the fighters and RRAF 116 to RRAF 131 for the trainers.

1 (Fighter) Squadron re-formed at New Sarum, Salisbury, with Vampire FB.9s during 1956, and between August and October 1958, was detached to RAF Khormaksar in Aden to support the Venoms of 8 Squadron, RAF, which were engaged on anti-terrorist strikes. The squadron's Vampires were replaced by Hunter FGA.9s in 1963.

Rhodesian Vampires also equipped 2 (F) Squadron, which re-formed at New Sarum during October 1956 to train Short Service Unit students. Disbanded in June 1957, the squadron re-formed again as a training unit at Thornhill in September 1958. In March 1960 2 Squadron assumed the secondary role of ground attack/day fighter duties and, following the Unilateral Declaration of Independence in November 1965, was active in the war against guerrillas operating from Angola, Mozambique and Zambia. The Vampires were finished in matt dark earth

and dark green camouflaged top surfaces with sky undersurfaces, and several aircraft were lost during the air strikes; by 1964 the squadron was also providing advanced flying and operational conversion training courses.

In March 1968 the old serial system was dropped in favour of random serials, prefixed with the letter R; Vampire trainers used serials in the 4000 series, for example R4028 (ex-SR125/RRAF 408) and R4213 (ex-SR130/RRAF 413); whereas the FB.9s used serials in the 1000 and 8000 series, for example R1380 and R8128.

During 1969 additional Vampires and spares were received from the South African Air Force, including 19 T.55s, 13 FB.9s and 4 FB.52s.

Rhodesia was declared a republic in March 1970 and the 'Royal' prefix was dropped; the official title then became the Rhodesian Air Force.

Following retirement, some Vampires were sold to Australia and South Africa. Three Vampires are preserved in a static display at the Zimbabwe Military Museum, Gweru: an all-silver FB.9, RRAF112 (ex-WR199), and the camouflaged FB.52 R1380 (ex-SAAF) form the centrepiece, together with a camouflaged T.55, R4220 (ex-SAAF).

Rhodesia was renamed Zimbabwe in 1979 and continued to use its Vampire FB.9s of 2 Squadron for internal security operations. The camouflage was matt dark earth and dark green, with sky undersides. (via Winston Brent)

Almost devoid of national markings, Vampire T.11 4221 of 2 Squadron of the Zimbabwean Air Force in 1981. (RhAF via Winston Brent)

SAUDI ARABIA

In order to promote friendlier relations following the end of the Suez War, Egypt presented four Vampire FB.52s to Saudi Arabia in July 1957. The gift followed an agreement by King Saud to a joint command between Saudi Arabian and Egyptian armed forces (which never became more than a liaison), and a further fifteen aircraft were acquired from Egypt during late 1957. All the aircraft were operated by 5 Squadron at Jeddah, probably to provide jet experience for pilots destined to fly Lockheed T-33s and F-86 Sabres. Very little is known of their subsequent service histories, except that 501 was originally allocated for ground instruction. The Vampires were withdrawn in 1958 after being declared surplus because of an alleged lack of spares. At least nine (including 506, 507, 511, 518 and 519) were noted derelict at Jeddah as late as 1993. Several of the airframes showed Saudi markings painted directly over Italian or Egyptian Air Force roundels.

One Saudi Vampire, 505, was rebuilt to static display standard during 1993 and is preserved in its original colour scheme at the Base Headquarters, Prince Abdullah Air Base, Jeddah, while 514 is set on concrete blocks at the same location. A further Vampire, 515, is mounted in a flying attitude on a plinth at a roundabout in North Jeddah, alongside Harvard 201.

SOUTH AFRICA

During late 1949 the South African Air Force (SAAF) decided on a replacement aircraft for their Spitfire 9s, opting for the de Havilland Vampire. On 21 January 1950 the first five of an initial batch of ten Preston-built Vampire FB.5s (201 to 210) were delivered by sea to Cape Town, and transferred to No. 11 Air Depot at Brooklyn (renamed Ysterplaat) for reassembly. The first aircraft was flown by de Havilland test pilot R.W. Jamieson on 6 February 1950. The final aircraft of this order was delivered the following June.

A further ten Vampire FB.52s (211 to 220)

Immaculately preserved former Saudi Arabian Air Force Vampire FB.52 514 at the Base Headquarters, Prince Abdullah Air Base, Jeddah. (RSAF)

Following retirement, many of the Saudi Vampire FB.52s languished on the dump at Jeddah, typified by 507 photographed in January 1976. (via P.R. Keating)

Vampire FB.5s 203 and 205 of the South African Air Force flying past Table Mountain, soon after delivery in January 1950. (Hawker Siddeley via Philip Birtles)

were delivered to South Africa in early 1951. The twenty aircraft were allocated to 1 (City of Pretoria) Squadron at Waterkloof (which later moved to Swartkop) and featured the unit's code letters on the nose, e.g. AX–A 210, AX–G 206 and AX–K 207.

To provide jet conversion and advanced pilot training, South Africa placed another order for six early-standard Vampire T.55s (221 to 226); the first was delivered to Ysterplaat for reassembly in May 1952. Following a decision to concentrate all jet

conversion training at the Air Operational School (AOS), Langebaanweg, the majority of 1 Squadron's Vampires were transferred there by mid-1952, where they were later joined by the Vampire trainers.

With the return of 2 (Cheetah) Squadron from Korea to Waterkloof during 1953, it was decided to equip it with Vampire FB.9s purchased from de Havilland's, Chester. The delivery of these aircraft (227 to 256) began in June 1953, and while in service with 2 Squadron they were distinguishable by red

Delivered in 1953, Vampire FB.9 235 of 2 Squadron at Waterkloof was eventually preserved as a gate guardian at Langebaanweg. The red nose trim applied to the Vampires of 2 Squadron is seen to advantage. (via Mike Hooks)

South African Air Force Vampire T.55 276 was built at Chester and is seen with the Test Flight and Development Centre, Waterkloof, in May 1976. (via P.R. Keating)

trim on their noses, wingtips and tail bullets.

The final SAAF order for Vampires was for twenty-one late-standard T.55s (257 to 277), which were delivered from Chester between February 1954 and June 1955.

When 1 and 2 Squadrons re-equipped with Canadair Sabre 6s in September 1956, some single-seat Vampires were transferred to the AOS at Langebaanweg as operational fighter trainers. The majority were placed in storage at No. 15 Air Depot (Snake Valley), Pretoria, and were scrapped in December 1967. Some were sold to the Rhodesian Air Force,

including four FB.52s (211, 213, 215 and 216) and thirteen FB.9s (228, 232, 234, 238, 240, 245, 249–252 and 254–256).

Vampire trainers continued to serve with the AOS, which moved to Pietersburg in 1966 and was renamed the Advanced Flying School; they were replaced by licence-built Impalas (Macchi 326Ms) in 1967. Following their withdrawal, nineteen T.55s were sold to Rhodesia: 221, 223, 224, 226, 258–268, 270, 271 and 275–277.

Quite a number of Vampires are stored at various locations in South Africa on behalf of the SAAF Museum: single-seat examples are

208 and 241 with the SAAF Museum, Ysterplaat, while the largest quantity are found at Swartkop with FB.52s 219 and 254, T.55s 221, 222 and 271, and the ex-Zimbabwe T.11 R4032. At Port Elizabeth FB.5 205 arrived in March 1991 for restoration, whereas FB.52 229 has been with Atlas Aircraft, Bonaero Park, since 1974 for airframe apprentice training.

Two Vampire T.55s remained with the Test Flight and Development Centre at Waterkloof as electronic equipment test bed aircraft until 12 February 1985, when they were finally withdrawn. They were both delivered in flying condition to the Historic Flight at Lanseria, where they are held on behalf of the SAAF Museum, joining another T.55, 277.

SWEDEN

The Royal Swedish Air Force (RSwedAF) was eager to obtain jet experience as soon as possible, in order to remain effective in post-war Europe. In September 1945 Lt. Gen. Bengt Nordenskiold, the C-in-C of the RSwedAF, visited Hatfield for discussions with the de Havilland Aircraft Co. On 9 February 1946 the Swedish Government placed the first large contract for the British aircraft industry when they negotiated with de Havilland to supply seventy Vampire J28As (F.1s) serialled 28001 to 28070, sufficient to equip one Wing; the contract also included a quantity of Goblin 2 engines and the licensed production of Goblin 3 engines at Svenska Flygmotor, Trollhatten.

The first Vampires were completed at Preston in May 1946, and flown to Hatfield on the 22nd, where they were handed over to representatives of the RSwedAF. On 4 June 1946 five J28As (28001–28005) were delivered to F13 Wing at Norrkoping by a group of Swedish pilots, accompanied by John Cunningham. The flight was made direct from Hatfield and showed a marginal fuel reserve.

A second batch of J28As (28007, 28009 and 28011) was delivered to Norrkoping on 17 October 1946, led by Roland Beamont. The flight, via Eindhoven and Lubeck, was made without any navigational aids and lasted three hours.

The order was completed in August 1947, by which time the Vampires had replaced the J.22 fighters of the F13 Wing. Between 1950 and 1953 a number of J28As were operated by the F3 Wing at Malmslatt, while the F20 Wing (the equivalent of the RAF Staff College) flew the type at Uppsala as advanced trainers until 1956. Sweden had used its J28As to develop jet fighter tactics and, although valuable experience was obtained, their usefulness had been restricted by the fuel limitations of the early Vampires.

In 1948 a quantity of J28Bs (Vampire FB.50s) were purchased as a stop-gap replacement until SAAB J29 jet fighters could be delivered to the RSwedAF. The order for 310 aircraft (serialled 28101 to 28410) was placed at Chester, with the exception of thirteen airframes which were subcontracted to Hatfield. The first J28Bs (28101 and 28102) were delivered on 27 May 1949 to F8 Wing at Barkarby, with further deliveries going to F9 Wing at Gothenburg during the following month. In the summer of 1952 the F4 Wing at Froson became the last to equip with J28Bs when it eventually relinquished its J26 Mustangs.

During 1953 the F14 Wing at Halmstad began to replace its SAAB B18 bombers with ground attack Vampires, fitted with rockets; the aircraft's designation was changed from J28B to A28B (J = Fighter; A = Attack). By 1955 the A28Bs had become obsolete and were withdrawn. But designated Sk28B, many remained in use as training aircraft at the Central Flying School at F5 Lungbyhed from 1956 to 1967.

To provide advanced training for Swedish pilots destined to fly their new SAAB J29 jet fighters, twenty early-standard Vampire T.55s

J28A Vampire 28055 of the F13 Wing, Norrkoping. The aircraft served with the Swedish Air Force from May 1947 until November 1955, when it was sold to the Dominican Republic. (via Leif Hellstrom)

Seen with the F18 Wing, Tullinge, J28B Vampire 28179 was built at Chester and delivered to Sweden in August 1950. (via Leif Hellstrom)

(designated J28Cs by the RSwedAF) were received from Hatfield between February and July 1953. The aircraft (28411 to 28430) were mainly operated by the CFS at Lungbyhed and provided 100 hours of advanced training to pilots who had previously completed their basic flying training on SAAB Safirs. The first course commenced during March 1954, although training was initially carried out at F14 Halmstad because of the lack of hard surface runways.

In 1955 a further batch of fifteen Vampire trainers (28441 to 28455) were delivered to Sweden; they were late-standard aircraft fitted with ejector seats and modified canopies, and were designated Sk28C–2s. At the same time the earlier J28C Vampire trainers were redesignated Sk28C–1s.

In late 1956 the Swedish Government authorized the conversion of twenty J28Bs to Vampire T.55 standard, with ejector seats and modified canopies. A total of twelve airframes were converted with the new front fuselages supplied by de Havilland's at Chester. The airframes converted were 28249, 28251,

28256, 28265, 28266, 28273, 28278, 28287, 28293, 28297, 28299, 282303, 282315 and 282331 (note: fourteen airframes are listed; two were probably supplied as components). Designated Sk28C–3s by the RSwedAF and T.55A by de Havilland's, the aircraft were re-serialled 28456 to 28467.

Vampire trainers were also used by the RSwedAF as continuation trainers by the various operational Wings, but in 1968 the last Sk28Cs were replaced by the Sk60 (SAAB 105). All remaining aircraft were either scrapped, or in a few cases preserved at various museums in Sweden.

Eleven J28As, 83 J28Bs and 3 Sk28Cs were lost during nine years of service – the most tragic being four J28Bs of F14 that crashed into the side of a hill in north-west Sweden in poor visibility during March 1956.

Wing	Type	Years	Base	Role
F3	J28A	1950–53	Malmslatt	Fighter
F4	J28B	1952–57	Froson	Fighter
F5	Sk28B	1956–67	Lungbyhed	Trainer
	Sk28C	1953–68		

Sk28C–1 Vampire 28423 with the CFS of the F5 Wing, Ljungbyhed. Built at Christchurch and delivered to Sweden in May 1953, it was eventually scrapped in 1967. (via L. Berns)

Wing	Type	Years	Base	Role
F8	J28B	1949–53	Barkarby	Fighter
	J28B	1954–65		RSwedAF HQ Sqn
F9	J28B	1949–52	Gothenburg	Fighter
F10	J28B	1951–53	Angelholm	Fighter
F11	J28B	1953–55	Nykoping	Recce
F13	J28A	1946–52	Norrkoping	Fighter
F14	A28B	1953–57	Halmstad	Strike
F15	J28B	1952–56	Soderhamn	Fighter
F18	J28B	1950–57	Tullinge	Fighter
F20	J28A	1953–56	Uppsala	Trainer
F21	J28B	1954–55	Lulea	Recce

SWITZERLAND

Few people would have believed that when the Swiss Air Force (or Flugwaffe) received their first three Vampires for evaluation in July 1946, it would be another forty-five years before the aircraft were finally retired from active service. The use of the Vampire by several generations of Swiss pilots, first as an interceptor, then as a ground attack fighter, and later as a trainer and as a target aircraft for anti-aircraft defence, proved its versatility; its durability was enhanced by careful conservation of airframe hours and a comprehensive maintenance and modification programme.

Switzerland had traditionally bought its military equipment from France and Germany, but at the end of the Second World War it turned to the British aircraft industry as market leaders in the development of jet technology. During October 1945 a Swiss Technical Commission visited England to examine and test contemporary fighter aircraft, and although several types were evaluated, a preference for the de Havilland Vampire was soon determined. Between March and April 1946 a team of Swiss pilots, including Maj. Willi Frei, Maj. Laderach and Lt. Col. Primault, together with civil and embassy staff members again visited England to make a final selection of the aircraft to be

ordered. On 26 March they were given the opportunity to test fly a Vampire at Hatfield and came to the conclusion that the aircraft would fulfil the requirements of the Flugwaffe.

Shortly after their return the Swiss Army High Command obtained the Federal Council's approval to purchase three Vampire F.1s for further evaluation. The first of these (J–1001) was delivered to Geneva Airport on 29 July 1946 by John Cunningham, accompanied by Geoffrey de Havilland Jnr in J–1002. J–1001 was never officially accepted by the Swiss Air Force and was used by the Swiss procurement agency, Kriegstechnische Abteilung (KTA) for pilot training; its career was cut short when it crashed after take-off at Dubendorf on 2 August 1946.

A replacement aircraft, J–1004, was used for the Service clearance trials of the Mk.8 Type 14 RP installation at the A&AEE Boscombe Down between October 1946 and July 1947. Much of the test flying was undertaken by Flt Lt. A.E. Gunn at Lyme Bay and Imber ranges; he also flew the aircraft to Geneva to demonstrate the installation on the Payerne ranges. The aircraft was handed over to the Swiss Air Force in August 1947.

All three of the surviving Swiss Vampire F.1s were withdrawn from service on 10 April 1961.

Despite arguments put forward by some air force personnel that the piston-engined Hawker Sea Fury was more suited to the ground attack role, the Federal Council procured a substantial order for Vampires during the summer of 1947. The order, worth 64.5 million SFr for seventy-five Vampire FB.6s (J–1005 to J–1079), plus ammunition and spares, to replace the air force's Messerschmitt Bf 109Es, was eventually placed at the end of 1948.

On 1 April 1949 the first of these Hatfield-built Vampire FB.6s, J–1005 was flown to Emmen by the KTA's chief test pilot, Ernst Wyss, and delivered to the Flugwaffe the

The first two Vampire F.1s, J1001 and J1002, being prepared at Hatfield for their delivery flight to Switzerland, 27 July 1946. The first Vampire was flown by John Cunningham, the second by Geoffrey de Havilland. (de Havilland via John Wilson)

following month. As soon as sufficient aircraft had become available, a training course for potential flying instructors, drawn from experienced pilots of the Surveillance Wing, was held during the summer of 1949. In April 1950 the first fifty militia pilots underwent their conversion training at Kloten/Zurich Airport; by May three squadrons had converted from the D–3801 and D–3802 single-seat fighters and were declared operational: Fliegerstaffeln (Fl.St.) 7 at Interlaken, and Fl.St.8 and Fl.St.9 at Meiringen.

The last two Vampire FB.6s to be delivered (J–1078 and J–1079) were ferried from Hatfield in May 1950 and accepted by the Flugwaffe on 13 February 1951.

In the spring of 1949 the Federal Council authorized the further order for 100 Vampire FB.6s (J–1101 to J–1200) to replace the Flugwaffe's C–3603 fighter/bombers. This batch of Vampires was to be built under licence by the Federal Aircraft Works (F+W) at Emmen at a cost of 108 million SFr; their Goblin engines were to be supplied by the de Havilland Engine Co. at Leavesden and transported to Emmen by Swiss Air Force Ju.52s. To secure the future of the Swiss aviation industry, the construction of the Vampires would be subcontracted to the firms of Pilatus Stans (fuselage) and the Aircraft Factory Altenrhein (wings, engine nacelles and fuel tanks), with the final assembly at Emmen. Deliveries took place between March 1951 (J–1102) and November 1952 (J–1200).

To assist in the development of aircraft radar technology and techniques, a Vampire NF.10, J–1301 (ex-company prototype, G–5–2), was ordered and delivered to the KTA at Emmen on 17 January 1951. Trials were disappointing and the aircraft was later used to test navigation and electronic equipment, and also radio equipment for the Swiss-built Venoms. In August 1958 the aircraft was handed over to the Flugwaffe for ECM trials and renumbered U–1301. The aircraft fell foul of the 1960 safety regulations which required it to be fitted with ejector seats and it was returned to the KTA in December 1961. It was eventually withdrawn from service to be used as an instructional airframe at Payerne.

The introduction of jet aircraft was to cause many problems for Swiss pilots, as handling techniques differed greatly from those of their previous piston-engined (and tail-wheeled) aircraft. When trials involving WLM gliders for initial familiarization proved unsatisfactory, the Flugwaffe again turned to de Havilland's for the Vampire trainer as the logical answer to their pilot training problems. In 1953 three early-standard Vampire T.11s (U–1001 to U–1003) were ordered for evaluation and supplied as kits, with final assembly at F+W Emmen; deliveries were made between September 1953 and January 1954.

Following evaluation at Dubendorf, which included spinning trials and an assessment of the engine performance, seven further trainers (fitted with Martin Baker 3B ejector seats) were ordered. The construction of the trainers would be shared between de Havilland's and F+W Emmen, the former being responsible for the supply of the wooden fuselage and Goblin 35 engines, while the licence-built final construction, together with the supply of metal components, was undertaken at Emmen. These Vampires (U–1104 to U–1010) were delivered to the Flugwaffe between January and June 1956 for service with Pilotenschule (Pilot School) 1 at Sion/Emmen.

The final batch of licence-built Vampire T.55s (U–1011 to U–1030) was delivered between July 1958 and June 1959. Their delivery followed an instruction given on 1 June 1957 to reserial the Flugwaffe's Vampire trainers: U–1001 to U–1030 became U–1201 to U–1230.

An opportunity to purchase a further nine ex-RAF Vampire T.11s from de Havilland's was realized in the summer of 1967: the aircraft were transported by road from Chester to Altenrhein for a complete overhaul and upgrading to T.55 standard. Delivered to the Flugwaffe between February 1968 and November 1969 as U–1231 to U–1239, the original airframes and delivery dates to the FFA were XD608 (27 October 1967), XH301

(20 October 1967), XK636 (16 November 1967), XH308 (27 October 1967), XD594 (18 September 1967), WZ570 (28 September 1967), XJ773 (6 July 1967), XD440 (17 August 1968) and XD544 (24 August 1967).

In addition to pilot training, Vampire T.55s were employed in testing weapons, photo-reconnaissance and electronic equipment; U–1201 and U–1202 were converted in 1968 to carry AS-11 missiles and provide simulation training for Mirage pilots; U–1203 was operated in the ECM role between 1966 and 1979; and U–1211 and U–1218 were modified to carry cameras in the nose for the production of a series of public relations films for the Swiss Air Force and a television company.

With the delivery of licence-built Venoms to the Flugwaffe in 1954, Vampires were switched from the fighter role to that of ground attack, and were equipped with sixteen unguided 3 cm RPs and a variety of bomb loads. This role was retained until 1968 when the first Hunter Mk. 58 fighter/ground attack aircraft were supplied, followed by Dassault Mirage fighters; Vampires were then relegated to the training role.

The first seventy-five hours of the student's syllabus was spent flying the Pilatus P-3 (which was later replaced by the P-7) at Locarno/Magadino. This was followed by a further 100 hours with Pilotenschule 1 at Emmen and Sion, with the first five weeks devoted to conversion to the Vampire T.55 with formation and instrument training, and some ground and air combat training prior to going solo on the Vampire FB.6. The students then went to Dubendorf for their advanced operational and conversion training.

During 1960 the single-seat Vampires (and the three T.11s) were subject to new safety regulations which involved the installation of Martin Baker Mk.2F/V ejector seats, a pressurized cockpit and a reinforced single-skin canopy. A further three Vampire FB.6s, serialled J–1080 to J–1082, were assembled

Swiss-built Vampire FB.6 J–1105 served for thirty-nine years, until struck off charge and sold in December 1990. (Bundesamt fur Militarflugplatze)

during 1960 from available spares held by F+W Emmen; these aircraft were issued on 1 July, 20 July and 16 August respectively.

Following trials with J–1191, a further fifty-five single-seaters were modified during 1971 (with another four aircraft in 1974) with improved avionics for instrument flying training. During the late 1970s these aircraft were fitted with new UHF radio equipment, which was housed in a pointed nose similar to that of the Venom.

In 1978 twelve Vampire FB.6s were allotted to Zielfliegerkorps 5 (Aerial Target Corps) at Sion as target presentation aircraft; they were painted in a striking red and black striped scheme and fitted with Venom underwing fuel tanks. Until replaced by Pilatus PC-9s in 1990, the Vampires were used as target markers for instructional and refresher courses for military personnel assigned to anti-aircraft artillery units.

With the delivery of the first BAe Hawk T.66s in January 1990, flying training on Vampires was gradually reduced. On 12 June 1990 a small ceremony was held at Emmen to mark the final withdrawal of the aircraft from

service with the Flugwaffe; some fifty-nine fighter and thirty trainers were then on strength.

Due to their excellent condition and low airframe hours (which averaged

With its distinctive markings and Venom-style IFR nose, this is Vampire FB.6 of ZFK 5 at Sion, October 1987. The aircraft behind are Pilatus PC–7s. (Gordon Bain)

approximately 2,000 hours for each aircraft), the remaining single-seat Vampires that had not been presented to museums were auctioned at Dubendorf, and the trainers were offered in a single auction at Sion in March 1991. Many of the Vampires were sold to various enthusiasts around the world, including J–1102 and U–1234 to Kermit Weeks in the USA, and J–1184, U–1221 and U–1236 to the Scandinavian Historic Flight as SE–DXY, SE–DXV and SE–DXX. Several were sold to buyers in the UK: Lindsay Wood Promotions at Andover bought three aircraft in September 1991, including U–1212, U–1214 and U–1215 as G–DHWW, G–DHVV and G–DHZZ; Sandy Topen brought J–1167 to Cranfield in August 1991 and repainted it in the shark's mouth markings of 112 Squadron as VZ304. In addition to these, Vampire FB.6 J–1172 had been earlier flown to Colerne in July 1974 for presentation to the Manchester Air and Space Museum; the following month Hatfield-built Vampire FB.6 J–1108 was flown from Dubendorf for presentation to the Mosquito Aircraft Museum at Salisbury Hall.

Finally Vampire T.55 U–1216 (c/n 976) was flown to Boscombe Down on 7 June 1990 for the RAF Benevolent Fund.

Originally built by F+W at Emmen, it was delivered to the Flugwaffe in March 1959; before presentation to the RAFBF it was allocated the RAF serial ZH563 – some thirty-four years after the last RAF Vampire serial had been officially issued!

SYRIA

There is uncertainty as to the exact number of Vampire fighters delivered to Syria. A Foreign Office report dated 15 October 1955 stated that eighteen ex-Italian Vampires had been sold to Egypt, with deliveries through Syria; it was suspected that not all the Vampires had reached Egypt, and the following month the Italian Government officially confirmed the sale of thirteen aircraft to Syria the previous year. More ex-Italian Vampire FB.52s were delivered in October 1956 after reconditioning at the Macchi factory in Milan, and photographic evidence confirms the serials MDN–1 to MDN–10.

In July 1956 two late-standard Vampire T.55s ordered by Syria, 493 (c/n 15768) and 494 (c/n 15769), were delivered from Chester to Hatfield. The aircraft became part of the British Government's arms embargo at the time of the Suez crisis and were stored at

Eleven Vampire FB.52s, destined for Syria, lined-up at the Macchi factory, Milan. (AMI)

The order for two Vampire T.55s for Syria fell foul of the government's 1956 arms embargo and they were placed into storage at Hatfield, where they are seen in April 1960. (de Havilland via Philip Birtles)

Hatfield; they were not delivered and were scrapped during the early 1960s.

VENEZUELA

Venezuela ordered twenty-four Vampire FB.5s for the Fuerza Aerea Venezolana (FAV) in 1949 to replace its P-47 Thunderbolts. The aircraft were assigned to Escuadron de Caza 36 at Boca de Rio, Aragua (later renamed Marshal Sucre Air Base), and the first two aircraft were shipped out to Maracay in December 1949.

Under the supervision of a de Havilland support team, the aircraft were reassembled at Maiquetia and transferred to Boca de Rio where de Havilland test pilot John Wilson was stationed to carry out the flight testing and provide training for FAV pilot Lt. Alberto Vivas Serrano. As both Vampires, 1/A/36 and

Vampire FB.5 SA-35 of 'A' Flight, Escuadron de Caza 35, Venezuelan Air Force. (via Philip Birtles)

This Vampire T.55, 2–E–35 of Escuadron de Caza, was renumbered 0053 in 1961, and made the last flight of the type in Venezuela in 1970. It was subsequently presented to the Israeli Air Force Museum at Hatzerim and restored to represent an aircraft from the Egyptian Air Force. (MAP)

2/A/36 (first flown on 23 January and 2 February 1950 respectively) were single-seaters, very little training could be achieved. However, despite the briefest of instruction, Lt. Serrano converted the remaining squadron pilots without incident. The final aircraft of the order was delivered to Venezuela by 1952.

Following their training, the pilots and aircraft were transferred to Escuadron de Caza 35, which had formed at Boca de Rio on 10 December 1952 under the command of Capt. Nestor Porfirio Rodriguez. Once operational, the squadron was split into three flights, with eight aircraft each.

In 1952 a Vampire T.55 was ordered for evaluation purposes and on 16 September 1952 the aircraft, 23/A/36 (c/n 15060), was transferred from Christchurch for packing and shipment to Maiquetia. A successful evaluation resulted in a further order for five T.55s, 2/E/35

to 6/E/35 (c/ns 15809 to 15813), to provide jet conversion and weapons training with the training flight at Mariscal Air Base. The five trainers were shipped from Liverpool Docks in May 1958 to join the original Vampire T.55, which was re-serialled 1/E/35.

The Vampire fighters saw action in January 1958 when 200 army paratroopers revolted and seized two bases near Maracay, following the arrest of the army commander for allegedly plotting to overthrow the government. In a show of force, the Vampires attacked the Presidential Palace and the Ministry of Defence building, with the loss of one aircraft which was hit by anti-aircraft fire. The Vampires went into action again during June when they strafed the naval buildings at Puerto Cabello.

In December 1960 Escuadron de Caza 35 was transferred to El Liberator Air Base in

Palo Negro, Aragua, under the command of Capt. Carlos Paiva Paiva.

On 12 July 1961 Grupo Aereo de Caza 12 (No. 12 Fighter Group) was re-formed, and comprised Escuadron de Caza 34 with Venoms, Escuadron de Caza 35 with Vampires and Escuadron de Caza 36 with F-86F Sabres. The former identification letters (i.e., 2B–34; 4C–35; 1C–36) were changed to four-digit serials; consequently the Vampire trainers became 0023 (ex-1E–35), 0053 (ex-2E–35), 0055 (ex-3E–35), 7029 (ex-4E–35) and 7060 (ex-5E–35).

With the arrival of the first Canadian CF-5s in early 1972, the Vampires were gradually withdrawn from service. The last training missions were flown by Capt. Jose Borges Blasco in FB.5 3C–35, and Lt. Col. Justo E. Saavedra and Lt. Ramon Pinedo Castillo in T.55 0053. In mid-1972 the last Vampire trainer was ferried from Lt. Vincente Landaeta Gil Air Base to El Libertador Air Base by Lt. Col. Saavedra and Lt. Perez.

Following retirement, several aircraft were still to be found as late as 1990 at various locations in Venezuela: at the Museo de la FAV, Maracay, were Vampires FB.5 (6035) and T.55 (7029), together with an unidentified Vampire FB.5; another anonymous Vampire is preserved at Mariscal Sucre. Finally, an ex-FAV Vampire T.55, 0053, was donated to the Israeli Air Force Museum at Hatzerim AFB in the Negev Desert.

FROM THE COCKPIT

Sqn Ldr Bill Shrubsole first flew the Vampire in 1946. Between that date and his last flight in a Vampire T.11 in 1959, he flew operationally with 54, 247 and 93 Squadrons. He also spent a tour as an instructor with No. 229 OCU, of which he was a founder member.

I joined 54 Squadron at Odiham in July 1946 and flew the Tempest II. The squadron was the second unit to receive the Vampire (after 247 Squadron), followed by 130 Squadron. The need for three new Tempest squadrons in the Middle East saw 54 Squadron tasked with converting selected pilots to the Tempest at the beginning of September 1946. After carrying out a very rapid course on how to fly the Tempest, the original 54 Squadron pilots, with the exception of myself who had only been back in the UK a few weeks and another pilot due to leave the RAF, were shipped to the Middle East to become 249 Squadron.

In October 1946 54 Squadron was back in business when Sqn Ldr Lyne arrived at Odiham and informed me that we constituted the new 54 Squadron to be equipped with Vampires. From that moment events moved at a fast pace and on 1st November, I flew a Vampire (TG302) for the first time.

Conversion to the Vampire presented no real problems. In fact compared to the more complex and powerful piston-driven fighters of the day, the Vampire was an easy aeroplane to fly. Without the long nose in front that we were accustomed to, we all, without fail, experienced a minor difficulty with attitude flying for the first few trips. What we felt was a reasonable straight and level attitude invariably proved to be a fairly rapid climbing attitude. It was also necessary to come to terms with the sluggish response of the jet engine to the throttle, but it was something we adapted to quite quickly.

Conversion completed, Sqn Ldr Lyne set about forming the first post-war formation aerobatic team. A little later, 54 Squadron performed another first – the first jet crossing of the Atlantic. By then, and because of the crossing, the squadron was re-equipped with the Vampire F.3 – I flew my first F.3 (VT823) on 20th July 1948 whilst on attachment to 247 Squadron. The squadron eventually traded the Mk. 3s for the Mk. 5 version, and I first flew the Vampire 5 on 17th October 1949 when I collected VV526 from the MU at Shawbury.

All aircraft have their idiosyncrasies and the Vampire I was no exception. Perhaps the most noteworthy was the lack of feel regarding elevator control, which was minimal at low altitude and virtually nil at high altitude. In handling terms it meant that it was very easy to induce an unintentional high-speed stall. The problem was compounded by the Vampire's tendency (and that applied to all Vampires), to flick, often quite viciously, during a high-speed stall. Crude but effective modification to the elevator control introduced a reasonably satisfactory form of proportional feel to the elevator control of later marks of the Vampire.

Master Pilot Bill Sykens joined 608 (North Riding) Squadron RAuxAF in December 1946 and flew Mosquitos and Spitfires before converting to Vampires in May 1950. Until the auxiliary squadrons disbanded in March 1957, Bill flew a succession of Vampire F.1s, F.3s and FB.5s.

During the war I flew Blenheims and Dakotas, and my rank was the cause of great satisfaction to me. At the time it was unique; not only was I the only Master Pilot in the RAuxAF, it automatically made me the most senior of the non-commissioned aircrew – as well as the highest paid NCO!

The Vampire was certainly not over-endowed with room; adequate, but no more. All marks were beautiful to fly except when fitted with overload tanks, when it turned into a positive bitch and had to be treated with the utmost respect. We suffered three fatalities, all attributed to the same cause – stalling on take-off with overload tanks fitted. A strong venturi effect formed between the fuselage and the undercarriage, and the technique to overcome this problem was to climb away virtually on the point of the stall and lift the undercarriage before the aircraft was airborne. I had the undercarriage stay down a few times, when my action was to simply climb to 5,000 ft and try again. At this height the stall was so gentle it was easily coped with.

All marks of the Vampire were underpowered and the short range of the Mk. I was really ridiculous. I personally could see no advantage in their speed and manoeuvrability over the Spitfire which they replaced. However, the greatly improved view, especially when taking off because of its tricycle undercarriage was greatly appreciated.

Stan Burge flew Spitfire F.22s with 73 Squadron in Malta as the unit began re-equipping with the Vampire F.3. In June 1949 he joined No. 1 Ferry Unit at Manston and was responsible for ferrying Vampires to the Middle East.

I joined 73 Squadron in February 1948. At the time the squadron was flying the Spitfire F.22, with a few Mk. IXs still on strength which were quickly phased out. Our first Vampire F.3 was delivered in July 1948 and I first flew one on 5th August. For about three months we were flying both the Vampire and the Spitfire and I often flew both types on the same day, which made one think as the techniques were quite different.

I much preferred the Vampire, which was much smoother and easier to fly. One could sit in the cockpit and see the runway just in front of the nose. Take-off was incredibly simple, with no swing and amazing visibility. Trim changes were limited to elevator only, and we flew the Vampire in very much the same way as we flew the Spitfire, even down to the curved approach on landing.

The limitation of the Vampire initially was its short endurance at low altitude due to the high fuel consumption. At high altitude it improved considerably. Our practice gunnery scores improved immensely over those obtained in the Spitfire as it was a better gun platform, without the constant trim changes, and the fact that the four cannons were packed closely together under the fuselage, giving a very concentrated fire.

One problem we did have was the occasional loss of the canopy. I lost one during an air-to-air firing sortie off Cyprus. It blew off as I opened fire and struck the tailplane, making a large dent, and also shredded the fin and rudder. I flew on quite well and landed without a deal of trouble. Modifications were made by de Havilland's and we did not have any further problems.

Despite its part-wooden construction, the Vampire's airframe could survive the most dramatic of accidents, as these four pictures show. Remarkably, the pilots were all able to walk away from these aircraft.

On 18 September 1950 the throttle jammed on this 54 Squadron Vampire FB.5 VZ828, during formation aerobatics. The pilot, FLt Lt Paddy Minnis, escaped serious injury when it crashed short of the runway at Odiham. (Paddy Minnis)

The engine failed on Pt Off. Michael Allaby's Vampire (WA277) soon after take-off from Pembrey, 4 January 1954. He was able to force-land safely in a marshy field close to the airfield. (Michael Allaby)

Many Vampire accidents were attributed to engine failure, and Pt Off. Pete Jarvis was fortunate to put his aircraft down at Faldingworth airfield when the engine cut during a loop on 20 October 1955. The Vampire was from No. 8 FTS at Swinderby. (Pete Jarvis)

This aircraft (WG847) was the last Vampire FB.5 to be built, and was delivered to 14 Squadron at Fassberg in November 1953. Five months later, on 22 April 1954, the engine cut during the climb-out and Fg Off. 'Mo' Stilwell was forced to bellyland 1 mile east of the airfield. (Brian Pettit)

Sqn Ldr John Harvey joined 71 (Eagle) Squadron at Wildenrath as a Pt Off., and between September 1952 and March 1955 flew a total of 400 hours on Vampires.

71 Squadron was a mixed role, day fighter/ground attack unit. We flew both in the high-level interception role, for which one flight was on Battle Flight with aircraft at different states of readiness on the dispersal pans. The other half of our time was spent on low-level flying, navigation, air-to-ground gunnery and rocket firing. Our ranges were at Nordhorn, away to the north east and a fair distance from base.

Early in my tour with 71 Squadron, while I was still eager to impress, we were looking for a convoy of army lorries along a certain stretch of road to the north of our area. The section leader asked me to 'assess' or 'get' the number of vehicles in the trees. I made a couple of passes and after the third pass I gave him the first part of the registration number of one of the trucks and apologized that I couldn't get close enough to read it all. He gave me a monster 'rocket' and later explained that he wanted to know how many vehicles there were in the convoy – not their registration numbers!

W.R. Burrows trained at Nos 8 AFTS and 203 AFS before flying Vampires at No. 229 OCU, Chivenor, and 4 Squadron at Jever.

RAF Chivenor was an Operational Conversion Unit. After a check flight in a Meteor 7, I climbed into a Vampire 5 (no Vampire trainers then) with the Pilot's Notes behind the reflector of the gyro gun sight. The Vampire, whilst not as fast as the Meteor, was more pleasant to fly; more manoeuvrable, a better gun platform, and at altitude it could turn inside almost anything then flying. I understand a Vampire would glide 80 miles for 40,000 ft. It took time to

climb so high but on several occasions I took a standard armed Vampire 5 to 45,000 ft without any problems. The Meteor wallowed above 37,000 ft.

The Vampire (and Meteor) was not meant to be spun. Pulling too hard on the top of a loop could put you in a spin which rotated so quickly that it was difficult to tell the direction and whether the aircraft was in an inverted spin. This was unpleasant and I had, on occasion, released my harness and prepared to climb out before the aircraft came out of the spin of its own accord. The loss of height was alarming.

Another peculiar thing about some of the earlier Vampires was the fuel gauging. There were five separate fuel gauges, one for each tank. To be asked for your fuel state during formation flying required adding five figures (all different) and responding quickly. Mental arithmetic while flying seems to suffer in comparison with the classroom! Later Vampires had a single integrating fuel gauge.

Brakes on the Vampire and Meteor were effective but could easily burn out. They consisted of a 450 lb psi air bag similar to a car tyre inner tube. When inflated it pressed the brake pads against the hub of the wheel. Brake failures on landing required override of the micro switch and retraction of the undercarriage. Pilots without the courage to do this usually went a greater distance than the airfield boundary!

Between January 1949 and January 1950 Lt. Cdr Roy Kilburn flew Sea Vampires on acceptance test flights as a Maintenance Test Pilot at the Receipt and Despatch Unit, RNAS Culham.

I found the Vampire an easy and forgiving aircraft to fly compared to the other types with their piston power-torque effects. One usually carried out some aerobatics on completion of routine air tests – partly to apply negative 'g' and find out what fell out of the bilges. On one occasion, while trying to push it beyond one-and-a-half vertical rolls, the aircraft fell out at the top into an inverted spin. There was nothing vicious about it, and I recall diagnosing the situation and applying rear stick (rather than forward for conventional spin recovery) and necessary rudder. We recovered level flight with the loss of about 6,000 ft.

I recall hearing the story of the Vampire returning from Lee-on-Solent from a series of 'rubber deck' landings with a carrier off-shore when the pilot, who was so accustomed to having the undercarriage up, forgot to lower it on approach to the airfield and completed a belly landing on the runway. Asked afterwards whether he had heard the Tower on the radio exhorting him to lower the undercarriage, he replied that their transmissions were drowned out by the noise of some warning horn blowing in his ears!

AVM Charles Maughan flew Vampires with 98 Squadron at Fassberg between 1951 and 1953.

For my part, I had previously flown Meteors with 263 Squadron at Wattisham. When posted to 98 Squadron, my first flight on Vampires was as a participant for the AOC's inspection, and I recall thinking what a pleasant and undemanding aircraft it was to fly. It was also eminently reliable, comparatively simple to service, and could sustain a fair amount of damage from bird strikes. As a high proportion of our sorties were at low level or in army support, this was just as well.

The Vampire's engine was extremely reliable; engine fires were virtually unknown and bird ingestion caused only minor damage. Only when the engine was

uprated did flame cans tend to split with consequent fires. Although there was a modification programme to improve the cans, it seemed to us that there was an unwillingness to reduce the front-line strength too drastically so that it was undertaken on a progressive basis.

Once or twice a year the squadrons rotated through Sylt for air-to-air firing camps. It was during one of these detachments that Command changed the fuel from AVTAG to AVTUR (or maybe the other way round). All went well for some days but then came incidents in the air of pilots being unable to increase engine power, irrespective of throttle movement. Aircraft were grounded for a while and the immediate solution offered was a piece of string in the cockpit which, when given a sharp tug, activated a hammer which struck the cylinder housing the fuel piston, thus releasing the piston and permitting power to be increased. In due course, oil was added to the fuel and all was well.

Between December 1956 and October 1966 Lt Cdr Jim Purvis flew Sea Hawk fighters with 802 Squadron, and also carried out further flying appointments with the RN College, Dartmouth and 728 FRU Squadron in Malta. He also completed several tours flying Scimitars with 736 and 803 Squadrons, and it was as Senior Pilot with the latter squadron, while operating from HMS *Victorious* in December 1960, that he was forced to eject when a catapult launch went wrong. However, four years earlier, as a young student pilot with No. 56 Course, No. 7 FTS at Valley, Jim Purvis became the third (and last) pilot to ditch a Vampire – and survive!

In May 1956 we moved from Provosts at RAF Syerston to Vampires at RAF Valley. After 11 hours flying Vampire T.11s, which included two solo flights, I took off on Saturday 23rd June 1956 for my first solo flight in a Vampire FB.5 (WA285).

Climbing out from the airfield I heard a bang and saw that my speed was falling off. Looking in my mirror it appeared to me – incorrectly – that part of the fuselage had blown outwards. Later I found that the tailplane of the Mk. 5 looked quite different from the T.11 from the cockpit and this had given me a false impression.

I realized that I had lost power but I can only recall looking at the airspeed; I settled into a glide at quite low airspeed. By this time I had no prospect of turning back and gliding to the field and realized that I either had to ditch or bale out.

Neither of these alternatives seemed attractive, and the description in the Pilot's Notes was discouraging. I had to put out a distress call, omitting my position as I felt that it was obvious since I had just taken off. I was instructed to call on the distress frequency, and hoping for helpful advice I asked with some urgency whether I should ditch or bale out.

I decided to ditch for several reasons: one, it gave me more time; two, I had seen more than one successful ditch from the carrier *Ocean*, when badly damaged aircraft returned from operations in Korea; three, the process of rolling over and dropping out by bunting had always struck me as difficult in the extreme.

I flattened out over the sea, jettisoned the canopy which was immediately followed by my 'bone dome', and held off as long as possible until the aircraft touched the sea. The Notes had not

informed me what to expect: firstly, the aircraft bounced, and secondly I was blinded from then on by sea spray. On second impact the nose went under and the aircraft sank at once. I unstrapped and tried to scramble out under water only to find that my dinghy had snagged, so I let it go and escaped. I then swam to the surface – about ten strokes – and only then remembered to inflate my Mae West. My experience of swimming under water certainly helped me at this point.

Almost before I had really absorbed what was happening, I was on the surface with a few pieces of broken wooden fuselage around me and quite a lot of oil. I had no dinghy but was unhurt apart from a gash on the leg and a small cut on the head. I was seen after about half an hour by a friend, 'Fred' Labilliere, who was in one of the Vampires searching for me, and was then rescued by helicopter.

The aftermath of this adventure was surprising; the publicity officer notified the press and all the Sunday newspapers reported the story. Like everything else in the papers the story was 'improved': I was a hero who saved Holyhead by staying with my aircraft to avoid loss of life and it was the first successful 'ditch' of a Vampire. [The first was achieved by Pt Off. Peter Dimock in July 1951 while, coincidentally, flying from RAF Valley; the other was by a Norwegian pilot, who put his aircraft down in the Trondheim fjord in December 1953.] The nicest touch was a telegram from my friends on the Observer course: 'Well done: but stick to single seats!' I did

APPENDICES

1. Vampire Performance Details

	Engine	Span (ft)	Length (ft in)	Height (ft in)	Wing Area (sq ft)	Weight (lb)	AVW (lb)	Max Speed (mph)	Ceiling (ft)	Range (ms)
Vampire (proto)	Goblin 1	40	30 9	9 0	266	5,898	8,000	490	–	580
Vampire F.1	Goblin 2	40	30 9	8 10	266	6,372	10,298	540	40,000	730
Vampire F.2 & IV	Nene 1	40	30 9	8 10	266	7,762	13,448	575	49,000	1,118
Vampire F.3	Goblin 2	40	30 9	8 10	266	7,134	11,970	531	43,500	1,050
Vampire FB.5	Goblin 2	38	30 9	8 10	262	7,253	12,360	535	40,000	1,145
Vampire FB.6	Goblin 3	38	30 9	8 10	262	7,283	12,390	548	42,800	1,220
Vampire FB.9	Goblin 2	38	30 9	8 10	262	7,283	12,390	548	42,800	1,220
Vampire NF.10	Goblin 3	38	34 7	6 7	262	6,984	11,350	538	40,000	1,220
Vampire T.11	Goblin 3	38	34 7	6 7	262	7,380	11,150	538	40,000	840
Vampire F.20	Goblin 2	38	30 9	8 10	262	7,263	12,660	526	43,500	1,145
Vampire FB.30	Nene 2-VH	38	30 9	8 10	262	7,600	11,000	570	49,000	1,220
Vampire T.35	Goblin 35	38	30 9	6 7	262	7,380	11,680	538	40,000	787
Vampire FB.52	Goblin 3	38	30 9	8 10	262	7,283	12,360	548	42,800	1,220
Vampire FB.53	Nene 102B	38	30 9	8 10	262	7,656	12,628	568	44,000	1,220
Vampire T.55	Goblin 35	38	30 9	6 7	262	7,380	11,680	538	40,000	787

Note:

Still air ranges at 30,000 ft.

Max speed (clean) at sea-level.

Engine thrust ratings:

de Havilland Goblin 1 (prototype):	2,700 lb s.t.
de Havilland Goblin 1:	3,100 lb s.t.
de Havilland Goblin 2:	3,100 lb s.t.
de Havilland Goblin 3:	3,350 lb s.t.
de Havilland Goblin 35:	3,500 lb s.t.
Rolls-Royce Nene 1:	4,500 lb s.t.
Commonwealth Aircraft Corp. Nene 2-VH:	5,000 lb s.t.
Hispano-Suiza Nene 102B:	5,000 lb s.t.

2. MANUFACTURERS

de Havilland Aircraft Co. Ltd, Hatfield, Herts.
de Havilland Aircraft Co. Ltd, Hawarden, Chester
de Havilland Aircraft Co. Ltd, Christchurch, Hants.
English Electric Co., Preston, Lancs.
Fairey Aviation Co., Ringway, Manchester
Marshall of Cambridge (Engineering) Ltd
de Havilland Aircraft Pty, Ltd, Bankstown, Sydney, New South Wales, Australia
Hindustan Aircraft Ltd, Bangalore, India
Societe Nationale de Constructions Aeronautiques de Sud-Est, Marignane, Marseilles, France
Societa per Azioni Fiat, Turin, Italy
Aeronautica Macchi S.A., Varese, Italy
A combine formed by the Swiss Federal Aircraft Plant, Emmen; Flug und Fahrzeugwerke A.G., Altenrhein; and Pilatus Flugzeugwerke A.G., Stans, Switzerland

de Havilland Aircraft Co., Hatfield, Herts.

3 Prototypes
LZ548/G First flew 20 September 1943
LZ551/G First flew 17 March 1944. Converted to Sea Vampire F.10 September 1945
MP838/G First flew 21 January 1944

3 DH 108
TG283 Completed April 1946. Fuselage ex-Preston. First flew 15 May 1946
TG306 Completed August 1946. Fuselage ex-Preston. First flew 23 August 1946
VW120 Completed July 1947. First flew 24 July 1947

32 Vampire FB.5 (Delivered between 1 July 1949 and 29 March 1951)
VZ808–838, VZ840

3 Vampire NF.10 (Private venture)
G–5–2 First flew 28 August 1949. To Switzerland as J-1301 1.51
G–5–5 To RAF as WP256 9.51
G–5–9 To RAF as WP232 3.51

19 Vampire NF.10 (Delivered between 30 March 1951 and 23 August 1951)
WM659, WP232–WP249

114 Vampire T.11 (Delivered between 29 January 1953 and 30 August 1955)
WZ453, WZ460, WZ464–466, WZ496, WZ472–474, WZ478, WZ496, WZ503–505, WZ571, WZ573–575
XD453, XD458–459, XD509, XD531–532, XD541, XD550–551, XD595–603, XD627
XE820, XE822, XE830, XE848–862, XE868–871, XE885–889, XE893–897, XE919–921, XE928–937, XE942–961, XE991–998
XH271–274

SWITZERLAND 75 Vampire FB.6 (Delivered between 1 April 1949 and 28 April 1950)
J-1005–J-1079

NORWAY 5 Vampire FB.52 (Delivered between 10 December 1949 and 16 May 1950)
V0047 B–BG, V0062 B–BB, V0074 B–BC, V0076 B–BD, V0098 B–BE

VENEZUELA 4 Vampire FB.5 (Delivered in 1949/50)
1/A/36–4/A/36 ?

EGYPT 28 Vampire FB.52 (Delivered between March 1950 and March 1955)
1500–1527

SWEDEN 22 Vampire J28B (Delivered between May 1950 and March 1951)
(C = finished at Chester)
28148 C, 28203 C, 28213 C, 28217, 28218, 28227, 28237, 28238 C, 28247 C, 28248 C, 28252, 28253 C, 28254, 28255, 28256, 28257, 28259 C, 28261, 28262, 28265, 28266, 28271 C

INDIA 39 Vampire FB.52 (Delivered between September 1950 and March 1951)
HB732–HB770

ITALY 10 Vampire FB.52 (Delivered as sets of components for FIAT in November 1950)

Vampires on the assembly line in 1949 awaiting their Goblin engines. These airframes, including 28109 and 28110, are J.28Bs destined for Sweden. (Darryl Cott)

ITALY 2 Vampire NF.54 (Delivered 4 June 1951)
S3-167–S3-168

IRAQ 9 Vampire FB.52 (Deliveries between May 1953 and November 1955)
336–341, 389–391

de Havilland Aircraft Co., Hawarden, Chester

67 Vampire FB.5 (Delivered between 30 Match 1951 and 12 November 1951)
VZ839, VZ841–852, VZ860–877
WG793–807, WG826–837, WG840–847
WL493

225 Vampire FB.9 (Delivered between 2 November 1951 and 13 March 1952)
WL493–518, WL547–587, WL602–616
WP990–999
WR102–158, WR171–180, WR182–186, WR189–204, WR207–211, WR213–231, WR233–236, WR238–242, WR244–249, WR253–255, WR259–266
WX208–212, WX214, WX215, WX222, WX223, WX242
(The last five aircraft (WR265, WR268, WX212, WX215 and WX223) were dispatched to Marshalls on 12/13 March 1953 to be completed.)

55 Vampire NF.10 (Delivered between 27 November 1951 and 13 June 1952)
WM660–677, WM703–733
WP250–252
WV689–691

257 Vampire T.11 (Delivered between 26 November 1952 and 27 November 1956)
WZ454, WZ457–459, WZ461–463, WZ467–471, WZ475–477, WZ495, WZ497–498, WZ500–502, WZ510–521, WZ550–570, WZ576–593, WZ607–620
XD376–377, XD379, XD388–392, XD425, XD430, XD434, XD437, XD439–441, XD452, XD455–457, XD463, XD506–508, XD526, XD528–530, XD534–540, XD542–549, XD552–554, XD588–593
XE821, XE827–829, XE832–833, XE885, XE890–892, XE922–927, XE938–941, XE976–990
XH264–270, XH275–278, XH292–330, XH357–368
XK582–590, XK623–637

3 Vampire T.55 (Private venture)
G–ANVF (15485) C/n issued 4 October 1956; cnx 16 May 1957. To Finland as VT–1
G–AOXH (15798) C/n issued 23 September 1954; cnx 18 April 1955. To Chile as J–04
G–APFV (15802) C/n reserved August 1957; ntu. To Lebanon as L–160 2 November 1957

SWEDEN 288 Vampire J.28B (Delivered between 27 May 1949 and 23 May 1952)
28101–28410 (less 28217, 28218, 28227, 28228, 28237, 28252, 28254, 28255, 28256, 28257, 28261, 28262, 28265, 28266)

9 Vampire J.28B (finished at Chester). (Delivered between 10 May 1950 and 16 March 1951)
28148, 28203, 28213, 28238, 28247, 28248, 28253, 28259, 28271

NORWAY 25 Vampire FB.52 (Delivered between 12 May 1950 and 15 March 1951)
B-BF–B-BO, B-CA–B-CR

ITALY 51 Vampire FB.52A (Delivered between 27 July 1950 and 6 December 1951)
S3-156–S3-166
S3-171–S3-210

SOUTH AFRICA 10 Vampire FB.52 (Delivered from April 1951)
211–220

RNZAF 18 Vampire FB.52 (Delivered between 10 April 1951 and 15 February 1952)
NZ5721–NZ5738

INDIA 43 Vampire T.55 (Delivered between 12 May 1953 and 14 April 1954)
IY467–470, IY514–552

ITALY 12 Vampire NF.54 (Delivered between 22 July 1952 and 25 March 1953)
S3-169–S3-170
S3-211–S3-220

VENEZUELA 20 Vampire FB.5 (Delivered 1952)
S3-156–S3-166
S3-171–S3-210

FINLAND 6 Vampire FB.52 (Deliveries from 16 January 1953)
VA-1–VA-6

SOUTH AFRICA 30 Vampire FB.9 (Deliveries from April 1953)
227–256

SWEDEN 10 Vampire T.55 (Delivered between August 1953 and November 1953)
28431–28440

LEBANON 4 Vampire T.55 (Delivered between 24 August 1953 and 2 November 1957)
L151, L154, L159, L160 (ex-G-APFV)

SWITZERLAND 3 Vampire T.11 (Delivered between 15 September 1953 and 14 January 1954)
U1001–U1003; later renumbered, U-1201–U-1203 and converted to T.55 standard in 1960

LEBANON 4 Vampire FB.52 (Delivered between October 1953 and March 1955)
L152, L153, L155, L156 (ex-CF511), L158

IRAQ 5 Vampire T.55 (Delivered between December 1953 and 20 September 1955)
334–335, 386–388

CHILE 5 Vampire T.55 (Delivered between 29 December 1953 and 1 June 1954)
J.01–J.05
Also 15798/G–5–11/G-AOXH (became J.04); delivered 20 October 1956 (ex-demonstrator for South American tour)

SOUTH AFRICA 21 Vampire T.55 (Delivered between February 1954 and 17 June 1955)
257–277

CEYLON 5 Vampire T.55 (Delivered to packers between 25 June 1954 and July 1954)
CF501–CF505
Delivered by sea but the contract was cancelled and the airframes returned to Chester without being unpacked from their crates. CF501–CF503 were eventually resold to Finland as VT-4, VT-3 and VT-2 respectively.

BURMA 8 Vampire T.55 (Delivered between 30 November 1954 and 22 February 1955)
UB501–UB508

EGYPT 12 Vampire T.55 (Delivered between 28 June 1955 and February 1956)
1570–1581

FINLAND 9 Vampire T.55 (Delivered between July 1955 and March 1956)
VT-1–VT-9
(**Note:** VT-1, ex-15485/G-ANVF; VT-2, ex-CF-503; VT-3, ex-CF-502; VT-4, ex-CF-501)

INDONESIA 8 Vampire T.55 (Delivered between 21 September 1955 and 28 October 1955)
J-701–J-708

SWEDEN 15 Vampire T.55a (Delivered between 25 October 1955 and February 1956; renamed SK.28C-2 in Swedish service)
28441–28455

JAPAN 1 Vampire T.55 (Delivered 19 November 1955)
15752/G–5–14/63-5571

SWITZERLAND 7 Vampire T.55 (Delivered between 13 January 1956 and 26 June 1956)
U–1004 to U–1010; later renumbered, U-1204 to U-1210

EIRE 6 Vampire T.55 (Delivered between 5 May 1956 and 16 March 1961)
185–187, 191–193

SYRIA 2 Vampire T.55 (Delivered to Hatfield 24 July 1956. Order embargoed and not delivered. Scrapped at Hatfield)
493, 494

AUSTRIA 5 Vampire T.55 (Delivered between 26 March 1957 and 25 May 1961)
5C-YA–5C-YC, 5C-YR–5C-YS

INDIA 13 Vampire T.55 (Delivered between 5 October 1957 and 6 February 1958)
BY377–386 (BY996–998 assembled later from components)

VENEZUELA 5 Vampire T.55 (Delivered from 30 May 1958)
2E-35–6E-35

Refurbished Aircraft

INDIA 5 Vampire T.55 (Delivered October 1954)
XE983/BY1005, WZ498/BY1006, XD532/BY1007, XE945/BY1008, WZ417/BY1009

30 Vampire NF.10 (resold to India as NF.54)
First batch bought from July 1953 to January 1954: 18 aircraft delivered between April and October 1954
WM659, WM660, WM661, WM662, WM664, WM665, WM666, WM667, WM675, WM710, WM715, WM719, WM720, WM721, WM724, WM728, WV689, WV690
Second batch bought from February to March 1957: 12 aircraft delivered between August 1957 and March 1958
WM676, WM707, WM708, WM709, WM717, WM723, WM725, WM731, WM732, WP246, WP249, WV691

AUSTRIA 3 Vampire T.55 (Delivered July 1964)
WZ618/5C-VD, XK634/5C-VE, XH320/5C-VF

SWITZERLAND 9 Vampire T.11 (Delivered from ex-RAF stock between 6 July 1967 and 17 August 1968)
U-1231–U-1239
XD440/U-1238, XD544/U-1239, XD594/U-1235, XD608/U-1231, XH301/U-1232, XH308/U-1234, XJ773/U-1237, XK636/U-1233, WZ570/U-1236

IRAQ
'333' returned to Chester inside an Antonov AN.12 in early 1960 to be modified to take ejector seats. The job proved too large for HSA so they substituted the fuselage of XH316 (the booms and wings coming from the original '333'). The aircraft was repainted to old original drawings with Iraqi markings, i.e. four-band fin flash, and flown to Hatfield for acceptance by the Iraqi Air Attaché.

67 Vampire T.11 resold to HSA/de Havilland

WZ416 Nov. 1967	WZ425 Nov. 1967	WZ450 Jan. 1969	WZ464 Oct. 1967
WZ471 July 1963	WZ476 Dec. 1968	WZ498 July 1963	WZ505 Oct. 1967
WZ514 Jan. 1969	WZ515 Dec. 1968	WZ518 Dec. 1968	WZ553 Nov. 1967
WZ557 Nov. 1967	WZ570 Dec. 1964	WZ589 Oct. 1967	WZ590 Dec. 1968
WZ608 Nov. 1967	WZ618 Feb. 1963		
XD365 Dec. 1968	XD403 Dec. 1968	XD405 Oct. 1967	XD425 Nov. 1967
XD434 Nov. 1967	XD435 Nov. 1967	XD440 Dec. 1964	XD445 Dec. 1967
XD447 Dec. 1967	XD527 Nov. 1967	XD532 July 1963	XD534 Oct. 1967
XD535 Oct. 1967	XD540 Oct. 1967	XD544 Dec. 1964	XD593 Dec. 1968
XD594 Dec. 1964	XD595 Nov. 1967	XD598 Dec. 1964	XD608 Dec. 1964
XD610 Dec. 1968	XD616 Nov. 1967		
XE852 Oct. 1967	XE855 Oct. 1967	XE856 Oct. 1967	XE864 Dec. 1968
XE872 Nov. 1967	XE874 Oct. 1967	XE935 Nov. 1967	XE945 June 1963
XE979 Dec. 1968	XE983 June 1963	XE985 Nov. 1967	XE995 Dec. 1968
XE998 Dec. 1967			
XH292 Jan. 1969	XH301 Dec. 1964	XH308 Dec. 1964	XH312 Nov. 1967
XH316 Dec. 1963	XH320 Feb. 1964	XH330 Feb. 1964	
XJ773 Dec. 1964			
XK623 Dec. 1968	XK625 Dec. 1968	XK627 Dec. 1968	XK634 Feb. 1964
XK636 Dec. 1964	XK637 Nov. 1967		

de Havilland Aircraft Co., Christchurch, Hants.

1 prototype Vampire T.11
G–5–7 c/n 15000. First flew 15 November 1950, later WW456

2 pre-production Vampire T.11
WW458 – Vampire T.11 delivered to the Royal Navy 21 January 1952
WW461 – Vampire T.11 delivered to the Royal Navy 22 May 1952 and evaluated as T.Mk.22

123 Vampire T.11 (Delivered between 1 March 1952 and 11 March 1955)
WZ414–430, WZ446–456, WZ493, WZ494, WZ499, WZ506–509, WZ544–549
XD375–387, XD395–404, XD424, XD426–428, XD431, XD432, XD442, XD443, XD449–451,
XD454, XD460–462, XD510–525, XD527 (Chester-built; received for finishing 1 June 1954) XD533,
XD606–607, XD625, XD626
XE816–819, XE823–826, XE831, XE863–867, XE872–883
To Flt Refuelling, Tarrant Rushton for refin, etc.
XD605, 606, 607, 626
XE817, 819, 823, 831, 864, 865, 876, 877, 878, 879, 880

73 Sea Vampire T.22 (Delivered between 26 May 1952 and 25 May 1955)
XA100–131, XA152–172
XG742–748, XG765–777
To Flt Refuelling, Tarrant Rushton for refin, etc.
XA126–130, XA152–168, XA171–172
XG742–743, XG746, XG766, XG769, XG771–774

43 Vampire T.55

NZ5701–NZ5706	RNZAF	29 Apr. 1952 – 15 Dec. 1952
221–226	SAAF	26 May 1952 – 29 Sept. 1952
PX-E, PX-G, PX-M	RNoAF	25 June 1952 – 10 Nov. 1952
ZK-X, ZK-Y, ZK-Z		
2A-36	Venezuelan AF	16 Sept. 1952
5801–5802	Portugal	30 Oct. 1952 – 4 Dec. 1952
333	Iraq AF	25 Mar. 1953
28411–28430	RSwAF	7 Feb. 1953 – 2 July 1953
L151	Lebanon	26 May 1953

English Electric Co., Preston, Lancs.

154 Vampire F.1 (Delivered between 23 April 1945 and 3 December 1946)
TG274–315, TG328–355, TG370–389, TG419–448
VF265–283, VF300–314
(To France: TG284, 288, 294, 296, 310, 311, 331, 332, 333, 335, 339, 340, 341, 342, 343, 344, 347,
350, 353, 354, 355, 378, 379, 383, 422, 423, 425, 428, 430, 433. Delivered between Dec. 1948 and Aug.
1949; TG275 to Hatfield for F.3 conversion to Sea Vampire: TG285, 286, 314, 328, 421, 426, VF268,
269; TG283/306 to Hatfield for DH 108 conversion.)

1 Vampire F.11 (Delivered 21 May 1947; to Australia June 1948)
TX807
(TX808 fuselage not completed)

138 Vampire F.3 (Delivered between 22 April 1947 and 7 May 1948)

VF315–348	(VF362–392 re-serialled VG692–732)
VG692–703	(VV209–211 to India; VV212–214 to R)
VT793–835, VT854–874	No. AF; converted to Sea Vampire – VF317
VV187–214	VF315 (F.20), VG701, VT795, VT802–805 (F.21s)

788 Vampire FB.5 (Delivered between 24 May 1948 and 23 October 1951)
VV215–232, VV443–490, VV525–569, VV600–640, VV655–700, VV717–736
VX461–464, VX471–476, VX950–990
VZ105–155, VZ161–197, VZ206–241, VZ251–290, VZ300–359
WA101–150, WA159–208, WA215–264, WA271–320, WA329–348, WA355–404, WA411–460
WE830–849
WF578, WF579, WF584–586
To France: VV568, 718, 720–723, 725–736, VX950–952, 954–972, VZ120, 129, 130, 132–141, 144, 152, 153, 154, 161–169, 172, 176, 191, 196, 197, 207, 208, 209, 211, 215, 217–221, 223, 226, 257, 258, 270, 282, 284, 285. Delivered between May 1949 and March 1950. To Italy: VZ252–VZ256. Delivered 11 March 1950: Sea Vampire conversions – VV215, 548, 631, 635, VX973, VZ142, 143, 145, 146, 148, 823

18 Vampire FB.5 (Delivered to Hatfield for Sea Vampire F.20 conversion between June and November 1948)
VV136–153

42 Vampire FB.9 (Delivered between 19 November 1951 and 19 February 1952)
WG848–851, WG865–892, WG922–931 (To Lebanon: WG929)

SWEDEN 70 Vampire F.1 designated J28A (Delivered between 4 June 1946 and 18 August 1947)
28001–28070

SWITZERLAND 4 Vampire F.1 (Delivered between 29 July 1946 and 25 July 1947)
J1001–J1004

CANADA 86 Vampire F.3 (Delivered between 30 September 1947 and 13 February 1948)

17001–17042	**Note:** 17043 w/o 3 November 1947. Airframes serialled VP674–698
17044–17086	VP715–753
	VP766–787.

SOUTH AFRICA 10 Vampire FB.5 (Delivered between January and March 1950)
201–210

Fairey Aviation Co., Ringway, Manchester

51 Vampire FB.9 (Delivered between 13 May 1952 and 30 November 1953)
WR181, 187–188, 205–206, 212, 232, 237, 243, 250–252, 256–257, 267–269
WX201–207, 213, 216–221, 224–241, 259–260, 339–342
(WR187 renumbered from WX340; WR188 renumbered from WX341)
(WX261–308, 327–376, 403–435, 459–487 all cancelled)
To SAAF: WX219, WX228, WX231, WX233, WX235–WX242, WX260
(**Note:** WR181–WX235 were fitted with Goblin 2 engines; WX236–WX260 with Goblin 3 engines)

30 Vampire T.11 (Delivered between 5 July 1954 and 11 October 1955)
XD393–394, 403, 435–436, 444, 448, 594, 604, 608–624

16 Vampire FB.52 (Delivered between 29 May 1953 and 11 January 1955)

V0700	256	SAAF	Delivered to Chester 29 May 1953
V1050	342	Iraq	Delivered to Hatfield 25 August 1953
V1052	343	Iraq	Delivered to Hatfield 25 August 1953
V1055	344	Iraq	Delivered to Hatfield 26 August 1953
V0799	L152	Lebanon	
V1010	L153	Lebanon	

A poor but interesting photograph of Vampire T.11 XD436 during final assembly at Ringway in August 1954. The trainer wears its construction number on the tail-booms in place of a serial number. (Clarke via Scholefield)

V0781	CF510	Ceylon	To Chester 1 December 1954 (to Egypt as 1533)
V0788	CF511	Ceylon	To Chester 20 May 1954 (to Lebanon as L156)
V0792	G–5–16		To Chester 7 September 1954 (to Egypt as 1531)
V0796	CF510	Ceylon	To Chester 12 July 1954
V0795	G–5–17		To Chester 7 September 1954 (to Egypt as 1530)
V1053	G–5–15		To Chester 17 September 1954 (to Egypt as 1532)
V1058	G–5–12		To Chester 17 September 1954 (to Lebanon as L155)
V1047	G–5–12		To Chester 10 November 1954 (to Egypt as 1524)
V0800			To Chester 17 December 1954 (to Egypt as 1534)
V1064			To Chester 11 January 1955 (probably to Egypt as 1535)

(**Note:** in addition, a large number of fuselages were also built at Ringway and taken by road to Chester for completion. Examples noted in June 1953 included V0689, V0721, V0736, V0743.)

Marshall of Cambridge (Engineering) Ltd

2 Vampire T.11 (Delivered 30 March 1954 and 26 March 1954 respectively)
XD429 (c/n 15297)
XD438 (c/n 15262)

3. RAF Vampire Serial Applications

LZ548/G	E.6/41	SB/24539/C.23(a)	de Hav., Hatfield
LZ551/G	E.6/41	SB/24539/C.23(a)	de Hav., Hatfield
MP838/G	E.6/41	SB/24539/C.23(a)	de Hav., Hatfield

TG274–315, TG328–355, TG370–389, TG419–448   **Vampire F.1**
120 aircraft built to Con. No. 6/ACFT/4182/C.4(b) dated 13 May 1944 at English Electric Co., Preston. Pressure cabin and teardrop canopy fitted from 51st aircraft; Goblin 2 engine fitted from 41st aircraft. TG274 delivered 23.4.45; TG448 delivered 4.8.48. TG276/280 converted to Mk.II; TG283/306 off-set for DH 108; TG284/288/294/296/310/311/331/332/333/335/340/341/342/343/344/347/350/353/354/355/378/379/383/422/423/425/428/430/433 for Armée de l'Air.

TX807–846, TX953–970   **Vampire II/IV**
58 Mk.IIs ordered 23.2.45 to Con. No. 6/ACFT/4182/C.4(b) at English Electric Co., Preston. Later reduced to 40 aircraft and then altered to 2 Mk.II and 38 Mk.IV. Mk.IV. Contract cancelled 25.9.45 allowing TX807/808 to emerge as Mk.II; TX808 fuselage not completed, but used for repair of TG280.

VF265–283, VF300–348, VF330–350, VF362–392   **Vampire F.1/F.3**
120 aircraft built to Con. No. 6/ACFT/5421/C.20(a) dated 7.5.45 at English Electric Co., Preston. Blocks VF330–350, VF362–392 deleted 10.5.45 and allotted serials VG692–732, VG750–760; **VF265–314 built to F.1, VF315–348 built to F.3.** VF315 diverted to Con. No. 6/ACFT/1791 for conversion to F.20 prototype for Royal Navy. VF265 delivered 1.8.46; VF348 delivered 6.8.47.

VG692–732, VG750–760   **Vampire F.3**

52 aircraft built to Con. No. 6/ACFT/5421/C.4(a) dated 10.5.45 at English Electric Co., Preston. Re-allocated block VG704–732, VG750–760 cancelled 25.9.45; only 12 aircraft built, VG692–703. VG692 delivered 6.8.47; VG703 delivered 2.9.47. VG701 to Royal Navy as F.21; to Norway (ex-RAF stock) VG692–696.

VL140–168, VL193–223   **Vampire F.1**

60 aircraft ordered to Con. No. 6/ACFT/5421/C.20(a) dated 7.8.45. Order cancelled 25.9.45.

VN856, VN860   **E.18/45**

Two DH 108 aircraft to be built to Con. No. SB.66562 dated 13.12.45 at de Havilland, Hatfield. Serials cancelled 8.2.46 following decision to off-set TG283 and TG306 from English Electric production lines and complete as DH 108s at Hatfield.

VP674–698, VP715–753, VP766–792, VP811–853, VP864–874   **Vampire F.3**

MoS serials for 150 aircraft to be built to Con. No. 6/ACFT/218/CB.7(a) dated 11.5.46 by English Electric Co., Preston for the RCAF. Serial allocation cancelled and 85 built, VP864–907 as 17001–17085; 17043/VP732 crashed 3.11.47 and was replaced by 17086/VP787. 17001 delivered 30.9.47; 17086 delivered 13.2.48.

VT793–836, VT854–874   **Vampire F.3**

64 aircraft built to Con. No. 6/ACFT/936/CB.7(a) dated 6.12.46 by English Electric Co., Preston; VT836 cancelled 24.2.48. VT795, VT802–805 to Sea Vampire F.21; VT832–836 to Norway. VT793 delivered 2.9.47; VT874 delivered 23.3.48.

VV136–165   **Sea Vampire F.20**

30 aircraft ordered to Spec. 45/46P against Con. No. 6/ACFT/1048/CB.7(a) dated 21.3.47 at English Electric Co., Preston. VV154–165 cancelled 14.1.48; **VV136–153 built as FB.5**, probably to Con. No. 6/ACFT/2677/CB.7(a) and flown to Hatfield for conversion to F.20. VV136 delivered 6.10.48; VV153 delivered 2.5.49.

VV187–232   **Vampire F.3/FB.5**

46 aircraft built to Con. No. 6/ACFT/1053/CB.7(a) dated 9.4.47 at English Electric Co., Preston. **VV187–214 built as F.3; VV215–232 built as FB.5.** VV187 delivered 2.4.48; VV232 delivered 28.9.48. To India VV209–211; to Norway VV188/212–214.

VV443–490, VV525–569, VV600–640, VV655–700, VV717–736   **Vampire FB.5**

200 aircraft ordered as F.3, but built as FB.5 to Con. No. 6/ACFT/1387/CB.7(a) dated 9.7.47 at English Electric Co., Preston. VV443 delivered 28.9.48; VV736 delivered 17.6.49. VV612/613 to Venom prototype at Hatfield; **VV675 converted to FB.9**. To France: VV568 (as Mk. 51)/718/720–723/725–736; to Royal Navy VV548/631/635; to RAAF VV465 as Mk. 31 prototype; to Lebanon (ex-RAF stock) VV453/694.

VW120   **DH 108**

Third prototype aircraft built to Spec. E.18/45 against Con. No. 6/ACFT/1067/CB.7(a) dated 10.7.47 at de Havilland, Hatfield utilizing a Vampire fuselage.

VX461–464   **Vampire FB.5**

4 aircraft built to Con. No. 6/ACFT/936/CB.7(a) dated 8.6.48 at English Electric Co., Preston, as

replacement aircraft against overseas diversions, i.e., VT832–835. VX461 delivered 17.11.48; VX464 delivered 17.11.48.

VX471–477   Vampire FB.5

7 aircraft built to Con. No. 6/ACFT/1053/CB.7(a) dated 8.6.48 at English Electric Co., Preston. Ordered as replacement aircraft against overseas diversions, i.e., VV188 and VV209–214. VX471 delivered 17.11.48; VX476 delivered 23.12.48. **Note:** no record of VX477 being built or delivered.

VX950–990, VZ105–155, VZ161–197   Vampire FB.5

129 aircraft built to Con. No. 6/ACFT/2467/CB.7(a) dated 7.8.48 at English Electric Co., Preston. VX950 delivered 20.6.49; VZ197 delivered 2.12.49. To Royal Navy VX973/VZ142/143/145/146/148; to France VX950–952/954–972/VZ120/129/130/132–141/144/152–154/161–169/172/176/191/196/197.

VZ206–241, VZ251–290, VZ300–359   Vampire FB.5

136 aircraft built to Con. No. 6/ACFT/2467/CB.7(a) dated 11.8.48 at English Electric Co., Preston. VZ206 delivered 2.12.49; VZ359 delivered 19.5.50. VZ252–256 diverted to Italy and replaced on this contract by WF578/579/584–586; to France VZ207–209/211/215/217–221/223–226/257/258/270/282/284/285.

VZ808–852, VZ860–904, VZ909–952   Vampire FB.5

134 aircraft built to Con. No. 6/ACFT/2961/CB.7(a) dated 21.10.48. **VZ808–838, VZ840 built at Hatfield; VZ839, VZ841–852, VZ860–877 built at Preston.** VZ808 delivered 1.7.49; VZ877 delivered 28.8.51. VZ810/814–815/817–818/820–822 to France under Con. No. 6/ACFT/3858/CB.7(a); VZ823 to Royal Navy; VZ824–827/878–904/909–952 direct to overseas customers; to RNZAF (ex-RAF stock) VZ838/841/843/852; to Lebanon (ex-RAF stock) VZ873. **VZ878–904, VZ909–952** not delivered to RAF; probably diverted to overseas order.

WA101–150, WA159–208, WA215–264, WA271–320, WA329–348,   Vampire FB.5
WA355–404, WA411–460

320 aircraft built to Con. No. 6/ACFT/2981/CB.7(a) dated 28.10.48 at English Electric Co., Preston (VHF fitted from WA237). WA101 delivered 15.5.50; WA460 delivered 4.9.51. To RNZAF (ex-RAF stock) WA249/299/306/311/314/317/338/342/374–376/379/383/385/388/392/411/428/444/451/452; to Lebanon (ex-RAF stock) WA128/365.

WE830–849   Vampire FB.5

20 aircraft built to Con. No. 6/ACFT/3974/CB.7(a) dated 15.8.49 at English Electric Co., Preston. WE830 delivered 4.9.51; WE849 delivered 22.10.51.

WF578–579, WF584–586   Vampire FB.5

5 aircraft built to Con. No. 6/ACFT/2467/CB.7(a) dated 23.2.50 at English Electric Co., Preston, as replacements for VZ252–256 diverted to Italy. WF578 delivered 2.2.51; WF586 delivered 9.2.51.

WG793–807, WG826–837   Vampire FB.5

27 aircraft built to Con. No. 6/ACFT/5614/CB.7(a) dated 5.8.50 at de Havilland, Chester. WG793 delivered 29.8.51; WG837 delivered 12.11.51. To RNZAF (ex-RAF stock) WG805, 826.

WG840–851, WG865–892, WG922–931   Vampire FB.5/FB.9

50 aircraft built to Con. No. 6/ACFT/5613/CB.7(a) dated 5.8.50 at Chester and Preston. WG840–847

built as FB.5s at Chester; WG848 onwards built as FB.9s. WG840 delivered 22.10.51; WG931 delivered 19.2.52. To RNZAF (ex-RAF stock) WG846; to Lebanon (ex-RAF stock) WG929.

WL493–518, WL547–587, WL602–616   **Vampire FB.9**
82 aircraft built to Con. No. 6/ACFT/6093/CB.7(a) dated 8.12.50 at Chester and Preston. Contract amended 29.10.51 to allow **WL493** to emerge as FB.5. WL493 delivered 2.11.51; WL616 delivered 14.3.52. To RNZAF (ex-RAF stock) WL493/514; to Jordan (ex-RAF stock) WL506; to Lebanon (ex-RAF stock) WL497/586.

WM408–429, WM441–468   **Vampire FB.9**
50 aircraft ordered against Con. No. 6/ACFT/6093/CB.7(a) dated 22.12.50 by de Havilland Aircraft Co. Block cancelled 4.1.51.

WM659–677, WM703–733   **Vampire NF.10**
50 aircraft built to Con. No. 6/ACFT/6214/CB.7(a) dated 10.1.51 by de Havilland, Chester. WM659 delivered 12.12.51; WM733 delivered 21.5.52. To Indian AF (ex-RAF stock), WM659/660–662/664–667/675–676/707–710/715/717/719–721/723–725/728/731–732.

WP232–256   **Vampire NF.10**
25 aircraft built to Con. No. 6/ACFT/6441/CB.7(a) dated 13.2.51 at Chester and Hatfield. (**WP232–249 built at Hatfield**). WP232 delivered 30.3.51; WP256 delivered 11.9.51. To Indian AF (ex-RAF stock) WP246/249.

WP990–999, WR102–111, WR114–158, WR171–215, WR230–269   **Vampire FB.9**
150 aircraft built to Con. No. 6/ACFT/6402/CB.7(a) dated 28.2.51 at de Havilland, Chester, with subcontracts to Fairey Aviation, Ringway. WP990 delivered 14.3.52; WR269 delivered 23.12.52. To Jordan (ex-RAF stock) WR190/201/210/248/250/258; to RNZAF (ex-RAF stock) WR202 as GI; to SRAF WR199.

WV689–691   **Vampire NF.10**
3 aircraft built to Con. No. 6/ACFT/6214/CB.7(a) dated 16.5.51 at Chester. WV689 delivered 11.6.52; WV691 delivered 18.6.52. All three aircraft were later delivered to the Indian AF.

WW456   **Vampire T.11**
Prototype aircraft built by de Havilland, Christchurch, as private venture, G–5–7. Serial allocated for evaluation with RAF.

WW458–WW461   **Vampire T.11**
2 pre-production aircraft built to Spec T.111 against Con. No. 6/ACFT/7075/CB.7(a) dated 5.7.51 at de Havilland, Christchurch. WW458 delivered 21.1.52; WW461 delivered 22.5.52. WW461 later evaluated by Royal Navy as T.22.

WX201–241, WX259–308, WX327–376, WX403–435, WX459–487   **Vampire FB.9**
203 aircraft to be built to Con. No. 6/ACFT/7150/CB.7(a) dated 12.7.51 at Chester, with subcontracts to Fairey Aviation, Ringway. **WX261 *et seq*., cancelled 15.11.53 resulting in only 42 aircraft being built; WX339 renumbered WR181, WX340 to WR187, WX341 to WR188, WX342 to WR205.** WX201 delivered 12.12.52, WX260 delivered 22.11.53. To SRAF WX212/219/228/231–233/235–242/259/260; to Jordan WX202/206/208.

WZ414–430, WZ446–478   **Vampire T.11**
50 aircraft built to Con. No. 6/ACFT/7381/CB.7(a) dated 3.10.51 at Christchurch, Chester and Hatfield.

WZ414 delivered 1.3.52; WZ478 delivered 14.4.53. To Indian AF (ex-RAF stock) WZ467/471; to Mexico (ex-RAF stock) WZ414.

WZ493–521, WZ544–593, WZ607–620   Vampire T.11
93 aircraft built to Con. No. 6/ACFT/7382/CB.7(a) dated 3.10.51 at Christchurch, Chester and Hatfield. WZ493 delivered 11.2.53; WZ620 delivered 14.9.53. To Indian AF (ex-RAF stock) WZ498; to Chile (ex-RAF stock) WZ512; to Jordan (ex-RAF stock) WZ545; to Swiss AF (ex-RAF stock) WZ570; to Austria (ex-RAF stock) WZ618.

XA100–131, XA152–172   Sea Vampire T.22
53 aircraft built to Con. No. 6/ACFT/7704/CB.7(a) dated 8.2.52 at de Havilland, Christchurch. XA100 delivered 19.5.53, XA172 delivered 25.10.54. To Chile (ex-RN stock) XA107/128/166; to RAN (ex-RN stock) XA101/167.

XD375–405, XD424–463, XD506–554, XD588–627   Vampire T.11
160 aircraft built to Con. No. 6/ACFT/8981/CB.7(a) dated 12.2.53 at Christchurch, Chester, Hatfield and Ringway. XD375 delivered 29.9.53; XD627 delivered 23.8.54. To Mexico (ex-RAF stock) XD439; to Swiss AF (ex-RAF stock) XD440/544/594/608; to India (ex-RAF stock) XD532; to Jordan (ex-RAF stock) XD548/552; to Chile (ex-RAF stock) XD614; to Austria (ex-RAF stock) XD598.

XE816–833, XE848–897, XE919–961, XE975–998   Vampire T.11
135 aircraft built to Con. No. 6/ACFT/9751/CB.7(a) dated 29.7.53 at Christchurch, Chester and Hatfield. XE816 delivered 19.8.54; XE998 delivered 25.7.55. To SRAF (ex-RAF stock) XE816–819/823–826/938–941; to Chile (ex-RAF stock) XE857; to India (ex-RAF stock) XE945/983; to Irish AF (ex-RAF stock) XE977 as GI.

XG742–748, XG765–777   Sea Vampire T.11
20 aircraft built to Con. No. 6/ACFT/10521/CB.7(a) dated 24.6.54 at Christchurch. XG742 delivered 3.11.54; XG777 delivered 25.5.55. To Chile (ex-RN stock) XG769/772/777; to RAN (ex-RN stock) XG766/770.

XH264–278, XH292–330, XH357–368   Vampire T.11
66 aircraft built to Con. No. 6/ACFT/11204/CB.7(a) dated 17.8.54 at Hatfield and Chester. XH264 delivered 28.7.55; XH368 delivered 9.5.56. To RNZAF (ex-RAF stock) XH265/266/271/317/366; to SRAF (ex-RAF stock) XH268–270/275; to Swiss AF (ex-RAF stock) XH301/308; to Austria (ex-RAF stock) XH320.

XJ771–776   Vampire T.11
6 aircraft issued from Royal Norwegian AF as free gift. Serials allocated 9.2.55. XJ771 delivered 28.2.55; XJ776 delivered 23.11.55. To Swiss AF (ex-RAF stock) XJ772; to Chile (ex-RAF stock) XJ774.

XK582–590, XK623–637   Vampire T.11
24 aircraft built to Con. No. 6/ACFT/12203/CB.5(b) dated 30.6.55 at de Havilland, Chester. XK582 delivered 2.5.56; XK637 delivered 27.11.56. To Austria (ex-RAF stock) XK634; to Swiss AF (ex-RAF stock) XK636.

ZH563   Vampire T.55
1 aircraft supplied from Swiss AF (ex-U–1216) for RAF Benevolent Fund; delivered to Boscombe Down 7.6.90. Re-registered G–BVLM on 6.4.94 for Royal Jordanian Historic Flight.

4. MAINTENANCE AIRFRAMES

Following the end of their operational careers, a large number of Vampire airframes were relegated for ground training purposes with various RAF Technical Training Schools and Air Training Corps squadrons; many were later displayed at Service establishments as gate guardians or employed for fire, crash and rescue training duties. From June 1947 some 152 Vampires destined for use as maintenance airframes were renumbered in a numerical series suffixed by 'M', although not all of the allocations were taken up and were subsequently cancelled. A further five Vampire airframes used by the Royal Navy were prefixed with 'A' sequence serials.

The following list shows the instructional airframe serials and their previous identities:

6355M TG281	6528M TG282	6613M TG291	6695M VT827	6717M VV191	6797M TG280	6950M VZ265
6951M VF318	6851M TG278	6860M VF306	6869M VF336	7004M TG277	7006M TG299	7045M VF274
7046M VF307	7047M TG382	7048M TG429	7049M TG437	7050M TG440	7051M TG447	7052M TG289
7053M TG300	7054M TG304	7055M TG336	7056M TG371	7057M TG381	7058M TG389	7059M TG445
7060M VF301	7061M VF311	7062M VF272	7063M TG308	7064M TG309	7065M TG312	7066M TG337
7067M TG373	7068M TG376	7069M TG385	7070M TG387	7071M TG420	7072M TG432	7073M TG442
7074M VF304	7075M VV205	7076M VF316	7077M VF319	7078M VT801	7079M VT871	7080M VT854
7081M VT859	7082M VT810	7083M VF321	7084M VF335	7085M VF342	7086M VG697	7087M VT796
7088M VT800	7089M VF332	7132M VZ117	7176M VZ216	7197M VV199	7198M VT871	7199M VT856
7200M VT812	7201M VT861	7202M VF344	7203M TG349	7235M TG329	7296M XE989	7323M VV217
7356M VV695	7357M VX953	7365M WG849	7368M WZ575	7370M WA275	7371M VV480	7372M VZ335
7373M WL498	7409M VZ851	7419M WP244	7420M WZ419	7423M XD457	7446M XE923	7450M XD430
7461M XE828	7472M XE926	7473M XE946	7553M XK629	7557M WZ423	7560M XK630	7564M XE982
7575M WL607	7577M VV542	7585M XE822	7588M VZ183	7598M WA215	7604M XD542	7629M XD386
7630M VZ304	7634M WA450	7646M VX461	7651M XD519	7652M WZ544	7660M WA236	7705M WL505
7727M WZ494	7728M WZ458	7732M XD393	7734M XD536	7736M WZ559	7737M XD602	7760M XH298
7761M XH318	7763M XH358	7814M XD511	7815M XD617	7824M XE887	7830M XH273	7866M XH278
7871M XE890	7878M XD601	7880M WZ502	7882M XD525	7887M XD375	7889M WZ557	7890M XD453
7893M WZ562	7902M WZ550	7918M XD444	7928M XE849	7934M XE932	7939M XD596	7951M XD538
7990M XD452	7998M XD515	8023M XD463	8033M XD382	8118M WZ549	8122M XD613	8123M XJ774
8124M XD614	8125M XE857	8148M XA165	8159M XD528	8160M XD622	8161M XE993	8174M WZ576
8175M XE950	8203M XD377	8487M J1172	8582M XE874	8595M XH278		

A2249 VF269	A2320 VF317	A2346 VV215	A2369 WW458	A2370 WW461

5. VAMPIRE SQUADRONS RAF

3 Squadron 'J5':'A'

Re-equipped from Tempest V at Wunstorf. To Gutersloh 25.6.48; to Wildenrath 31.3.52. Sabre delivered 5.53. Vampire F.1 4.48–9.49. Vampire FB.5 5.49–7.53. Vampire T.11 8.54–3.56.

4 Squadron 'UP':'B'
Re-equipped from Mosquito FB.6 at Wunstorf; to Jever 1.3.52. Sabres delivered 10.53.
Vampire FB.5 5.50–3.54. Vampire FB.9 2.53–5.54. Vampire T.11 9.54–5.59.

5 Squadron
AAC
Renumbered from 595 Squadron at Pembrey 11.2.49; to Chivenor 25.10.49; to Llandow 13.3.51.
Disbanded 25.9.51.
Vampire F.3 2.49–9.51.
2 TAF ('B')
Re-formed at Wunstorf 1.3.52. Venom FB.1 delivered 12.53.
Vampire FB.5 3.52–7.54. Vampire FB.9 6.52–9.54. Vampire T.11 8.53–10.59.

6 Squadron
Re-equipped from Tempest F.6 at Deversoir. To Habbaniya 6.1.50; Deversoir 8.2.50; Mafraq 31.3.50; Deversoir 29.6.50; Habbaniya 22.11.50; Shaibah 18.6.51; Habbaniya 19.9.51; Abu Sueir 13.11.51; Habbaniya 27.11.51; Abu Sueir 28.1.52; Nicosia 31.5.52; Abu Sueir 28.7.52; Sharjah 17.9.52; Amman 20.1.54. Venom FB.1 delivered 2.54.
Vampire FB.5 9.49–4.52. Vampire FB.9 2.52–5.54. Vampire T.11 8.53–9.57.

8 Squadron
Re-equipped from Brigand B.1 at Khormaksar. Venom FB.1 delivered 3.55.
Vampire FB.9 12.52–12.55. Vampire T.11 9.53–1.60.

11 Squadron 'EX':'L'
Re-equipped from Mosquito FB.6 at Wunstorf. Venom FB.1 delivered 8.52.
Vampire FB.5 8.50–7.54. Vampire FB.9 3.54–8.54. Vampire T.11 10.53–12.57.

14 Squadron 'B'
Re-equipped from Mosquito B.35 at Fassberg. Venom FB.1 delivered 5.53.
Vampire FB.5 3.51–6.54. Vampire T.11 9.53–5.59.

Vampire FB.5s of 11 Squadron lined up for the AOC's Inspection at Wunstorf, 1952. The nearest is the 'personal' aircraft of Fg Off. J.W. Price. (AVM John Price)

16 Squadron 'EG':'L'

Re-equipped from Tempest F.6 at Gutersloh; to Celle 3.11.50. Venom FB.1 delivered 1.54.
Vampire FB.5 12.48–6.54. Vampire T.11 9.53–6.57.

20 Squadron

AAC ('TH')
Renumbered from 631 Squadron at Llanbedr 11.2.49; to Valley 19.7.49. Disbanded 16.10.51.
Vampire F.1 2.49–2.51. Vampire F.3 11.49–10.51.
2 TAF ('L')
Re-formed at Jever 1.7.52; to Oldenburg 28.7.52. Sabre delivered 10.53.
Vampire FB.5 2.53–1.54. Vampire FB.9 6.52–7.54. Vampire T.11 7.54–5.59.

23 Squadron

Re-equipped from Mosquito NF.36 at Coltishall. Venom NF.2 delivered 11.53.
Vampire NF.10 9.51–8.54. Vampire FB.5 5.51–2.52. Vampire T.11 5.54–6.58.

25 Squadron

Re-equipped from Mosquito NF.36 at West Malling. Meteor NF.12 delivered 11.53.
Vampire NF.10 7.51–3.54. Vampire F.3 (2) 5.51–7.51. Vampire FB.5 (4) 1.51–10.51. Vampire T.11
6.53–3.54.

26 Squadron 'XC':'T'

Re-equipped from Tempest F.2 at Gutersloh; to Wunstorf 7.1.50; Oldenburg 13.8.52. Sabre delivered
11.53.
Vampire FB.5 4.49–2.54. Vampire FB.9 6.52–6.54. Vampire T.11 9.54–7.59.

28 Squadron

Re-equipped from Spitfire FR.18 at Kai Tak; to Sek Kong 30.3.51. Venom FB.1 delivered 2.56.
Vampire FB.5 1.51–2.52. Vampire FB.9 2.52–8.56. Vampire T.11 12.53–6.62.

32 Squadron 'GZ'

Re-equipped from Spitfire FR.18 at Nicosia; to Shallufa 4.1.51; Deversoir 27.1.52; Kabrit 15.9.54;
Shaibah 14.1.55. Venom FB.1 delivered 9.54.
Vampire F.3 7.48–6.50. Vampire FB.5 3.50–8.52. Vampire FB.9 4.52–1.55. Vampire T.11 8.53–1.57.

45 Squadron

Re-equipped from Hornet F.3 at Butterworth. Venom FB.1 delivered 12.55.
Vampire FB.9 5.55–5.56. Vampire T.11 1.54–11.57.

54 Squadron

Re-equipped from Tempest F.2 at Odiham. Meteor F.8 delivered 4.52.
Vampire F.1 10.46–10.48. Vampire F.3 4.48–9.50. Vampire FB.5 10.49–6.52. Vampire T.11 11.54–1.59.

60 Squadron

Re-equipped from Spitfire F.18 at Tengah. Venom FB.1 delivered 4.55.
Vampire FB.5 12.50–5.52. Vampire FB.9 2.52–8.55. Vampire T.11 12.53–11.59.

67 Squadron 'B'

Re-formed at Gutersloh 1.9.50; to Wildenrath 5.5.52. Sabre delivered 5.53.
Vampire FB.5 9.50–9.53. Vampire T.11 6.54–5.57.

Line-up of Vampire FB.9s of 28 Squadron at Sek Kong, 1954. The scar on the hillside is the military road from Tsun Wan to Sek Kong, known locally as the 'TWISK'. (AVM Brian Huxley)

Vampire T.11 XH359 of 45 Squadron, Butterworth, 1957. The trainer wears the markings normally applied to the squadron's Venoms. (No. 45 Sqn Assce)

Wearing standard Fighter Command camouflage, Vampire F.1 TG/287 served with 54 Squadron between November 1946 and July 1948. (MAP)

71 Squadron 'L'
Re-formed at Gutersloh 16.10.50; to Wildenrath 11.3.52. Sabre delivered 10.53.
Vampire FB.5 9.50–11.53. Vampire T.11 6.54–5.57.

72 Squadron 'FG'
Renumbered from 130 Squadron at Odiham 1.2.47; to North Weald 22.3.50. Meteor F.8 delivered 4.52.
Vampire F.1 2.47–10.48. Vampire F.3 6.48–2.50. Vampire FB.5 10.49–9.52.

73 Squadron
Re-equipped from Spitfire F.22 at Ta Kali; to Habbaniya 4.5.53. Venom FB.1 delivered 11.54.
Vampire F.3 7.48–6.50. Vampire FB.5 4.50–7.52. Vampire FB.9 11.51–10.54. Vampire T.11 1.54–6.57.

72 Squadron at Odiham, 1947. The CO was Sqn Ldr R.N.H Courtney DFC & Bar; his Vampire is on the left and still wears its former 130 Squadron markings. (via Brian Courtney)

Vampire FB.5s of 73 Squadron at Istres, 4 October 1950. The aircraft were en route Malta–Odiham for the Fighter Command exercise, 'Emperor'. (Peter Strugnell)

Refuelling from a German bowser while visiting Fassberg, a Vampire of 112 Squadron (VX462) is seen wearing the 'Sharkmouth' markings, which were resurrected in February 1952 and perpetuated on the unit's Sabres and Hunters. (A.J. Berry)

93 Squadron 'T'

Re-formed at Celle 15.11.50. Sabre delivered 4.54.
Vampire FB.5 10.50–5.54. Vampire FB.9 11.53–5.54. Vampire T.11 7.54–4.60.

94 Squadron 'A'

Re-formed at Celle 15.12.50. Venom FB.1 delivered 1.54.
Vampire FB.5 10.50–6.54. Vampire T.11 9.53–9.57.

98 Squadron 'L'

Re-equipped from Mosquito B.35 at Fassberg. Venom FB.1 delivered 8.53.
Vampire FB.5 3.51–11.53. Vampire T.11 11.53–7.57.
(A few Vampires were retained until 9.55 due to technical problems with Venoms.)

112 Squadron 'T':'A'

Re-formed at Fassberg 12.5.51; to Jever 7.3.52; Bruggen 6.7.53. Sabre delivered 1.54.
Vampire FB.5 4.51–4.54. Vampire T.11 6.55–3.57.

118 Squadron 'A'

Re-formed at Fassberg 15.5.51. Venom FB.1 delivered 11.53.
Vampire FB.5 4.51–6.54. Vampire T.11 10.53–8.57.

130 Squadron

Fighter Command ('AP')
Re-equipped from Spitfire LF.IX at Odiham. Renumbered 72 Squadron 1.2.47.
Vampire F.1 10.46–2.47.
Re-formed at Bruggen 1.8.53. Sabre delivered 1.54.
Vampire FB.5 8.53–4.54.

The black nose flash and fin bullets signify that this Vampire FB.5, WA382, belongs to 118 Squadron at Fassberg. Seen during June 1952, it is fitted with the metal bar above the air intake to prevent the access panel becoming detached in flight. (G.P. Aird via Andy Thomas)

Liberally daubed with yellow distemper for exercise 'Coronet' in 1953, this is Vampire VX474 of 118 Squadron. (Butcher via R.L. Ward)

145 Squadron 'B'
Re-formed at Celle 1.3.52. Venom FB.1 delivered 4.54.
Vampire FB.5 3.52–9.54. Vampire T.11 12.53–4.56.

151 Squadron
Re-formed at Leuchars 15.9.51. Meteor NF.11 delivered 4.53.
Vampire NF.10 2.52–10.53. Vampire FB.5 12.51–7.53. Vampire T.11 6.55–10.57.

Lined up at Celle in 1952, Vampire FB.5s of 'A' Flight, 145 Squadron. (Sqn Ldr Bob Newall)

185 Squadron

Re-formed at Hal Far 15.9.51; to Luqa 23.7.52; Idris 14.8.52; Nicosia (APC) 15.9.52; Habbaniya 13.10.52. Disbanded 1.5.53.
Vampire FB.5 9.51–5.53. Vampire FB.9 5.52–5.53.

213 Squadron

Re-equipped from Tempest F.6 at Deversoir (temporary move to Shallufa 12.8.53–30.10.53). Disbanded 30.9.54.
Vampire FB.5 11.49–6.52. Vampire FB.9 4.52–10.54. Vampire T.11 9.53–10.54.

234 Squadron 'A'

Re-formed at Oldenburg 1.8.52. Sabre delivered 1.54.
Vampire FB.5 9.52–3.54. Vampire FB.9 8.52–1.54. Vampire T.11 7.54–3.56.

247 Squadron 'ZY'

Re-equipped from Tempest II at Chilbolton; to Odiham 27.6.46. Meteor F.8 delivered 4.52.
Vampire F.1 3.46–5.49. Vampire F.3 7.48–12.49. Vampire FB.5 11.49–8.52. Vampire T.11 12.54–1.58.

249 Squadron

Re-equipped from Tempest F.6 at Deversoir; to Shaibah 14.7.51; Deversoir 23.10.51; Amman 1.6.54. Venom FB.1 delivered 4.54.
Vampire FB.5 1.50–6.52. Vampire FB.9 5.52–3.55. Vampire T.11 11.54–10.57.

266 Squadron 'A'

Re-formed at Fassberg 14.7.52. Venom FB.1 delivered 4.53.
Vampire FB.5 7.52–6.53. Vampire T.11 10.53–11.57.

595 Squadron '7B'

Equipped at Pembrey. Renumbered 5 Squadron 11.2.49.
Vampire F1 10.46–9.48.

Vampire FB.9s of 213 Squadron, c. 1952. (via Andy Thomas)

Parked in the snow at Geilenkirchen in January 1956, a Vampire trainer of 234 Squadron is seen with the unit's Sabre fighters. (Robin Brown)

A Vampire F.1 of 247 Squadron makes a low pass over two of its companions at Odiham in April 1948. Three months later the squadron converted to the Vampire F.3. (via Brian Courtney)

631 Squadron '6D'

Equipped at Llanbedr. Renumbered 20 Squadron 7.2.49.
Vampire F1 9.48–2.49.

Commonwealth Squadrons

14 Squadron RNZAF

Formed at Ohakea 3.9.51 with Vampire FB.52; transferred to Nicosia 7.10.52. Equipped at Nicosia 10.52; transferred to Tengah 1.4.55. Venom FB.1 delivered 4.55.
Vampire FB.9 10.52–11.55. Vampire T.11 10.53–5.58.

631 Squadron flew Vampires in the anti-cooperation role at Llanbedr from September 1948 to February 1949. Depicted is one of the unit's Vampire F.1s, TG444. (Gp Capt. K.W.T. Pugh)

421 (Red Indian) Squadron RCAF

Formed at Chatham, New Brunswick 15.9.49. Transferred to Odiham 15.1.51. Disbanded 2.12.51.
Vampire FB.5 1.51–1.52.

78 Wing RAAF

Formed Williamstown, NSW 5.52. To Hal Far 28.7.52; Nicosia 1.1.53; Hal Far 9.2.53; Horsham St Faith 18.5.53; Ta Kali 9.6.53; Wahn 26.7.53; Ta Kali 3.8.53; Idris 12.10.53; Ta Kali 31.10.53; Nicosia 31.5.54; Ta Kali 5.7.54. Returned to Australia 24.1.55 and de-activated.
Vampire FB.9 7.52–12.54. Vampire T.11 9.53–12.54.

Ferry Squadrons

No. 1689 Flight

Formed at Aston Down 6.3.46 under the control of No. 20 MU, for the training of ferry pilots. Moved to Benson and renamed Ferry Training Unit 9.4.53.
Vampire F.1 11.47–1.49. Vampire FB.5 5.49–8.51.

Ferry Training Unit

Re-formed from No. 1689 Flight at Benson 9.4.53, and became the central unit within Ferry Wing for standardization and examination.
Vampire FB.5 2.54–7.54. Vampire T.11 5.55–1.58.

No. 1 Overseas Ferry Unit

To Manston (from Pershore) 17.5.48; to Chivenor 17.7.50; to Abingdon 19.3.51. Renumbered 147 Squadron 1.2.53.
Vampire F.3 7.50–5.51. Vampire FB.5 5.51–11.51.

147 Squadron

Re-formed from No. 1 (Long Range) Ferry Unit at Abingdon 1.2.53. To Benson 16.4.53. Merged with 167 Squadron 15.9.58 to form Ferry Squadron.

167 Squadron

Re-formed from No. 3 (Long Range) Ferry Unit at Abingdon 1.2.53. To Benson 16.4.53. Merged with 147 Squadron 15.9.58 to form Ferry Squadron.

173 Squadron

Re-formed from No. 4 (Home) Ferry Unit at Hawarden 1.2.53. Disbanded 1.9.57.

187 Squadron

Re-formed from No. 2 (Home) Ferry Unit (which had itself formed out of No. 2 Ferry Pool 6.46) at Aston Down 1.2.53. Disbanded 2.9.57.

RAuxAF

501 (County of Gloucester) Squadron 'RAB':'SD'

Re-equipped from Spitfire LF.16e at Filton. Disbanded 10.3.57.
Vampire F.1 1.49–6.51. Vampire FB.5 3.51–3.57. Vampire FB.9 2.55–3.57.

502 (Ulster) Squadron 'V9'

Re-equipped from Spitfire F.22 at Aldergrove. Disbanded 10.3.57. Vampire FB.5 3.51–3.57. Vampire FB.9 7.54–3.57. Vampire T.11 11.55–3.57.

A section of Vampire F.1s of 501 Squadron, RAuxAF from Filton, 5 February 1950. (Geoff Kidd)

600 (City of London) Squadron

One aircraft delivered for jet conversion pending re-equipment from Spitfires at Biggin Hill. In February 1950 it was officially announced that 600 Squadron would convert to Meteors (first delivery 3.50). Vampire F.1 10.49–4.50.

601 (County of London) Squadron 'HT'

Re-equipped from Spitfire LF.16e at North Weald. Meteor F.8 delivered 8.52. Vampire F.3 11.49–9.52.

602 (City of Glasgow) Squadron 'LO'

Re-equipped from Spitfire F.22 at Abbotsinch. Disbanded 10.3.57. Vampire F.3 2.52–11.53. Vampire FB.5 1.51–3.57. Vampire FB.9 11.54–3.57. Vampire T.11 12.56–2.57.

603 (City of Edinburgh) Squadron

Re-equipped from Spitfire F.22 at Turnhouse. Disbanded 10.3.57. Vampire FB.5 5.51–3.57. Vampire FB.9 8.55–3.57. Vampire T.11 12.56–1.57.

604 (County of Middlesex) Squadron 'NG'

Re-equipped from Spitfire LF.16e at North Weald. Meteor F.8 delivered 8.52. Vampire F.3 11.49–10.52.

605 (County of Warwick) Squadron 'RAL':'NR'

Re-equipped from Mosquito NF.30 at Honiley. Disbanded 10.3.57. Vampire F.1 7.48–11.51. Vampire FB.5 3.51–3.57.

607 (County of Durham) Squadron

Re-equipped from Spitfire F.22 at Ouston. Disbanded 10.3.57. Vampire FB.5 6.51–2.57. Vampire FB.9 4.56–3.57.

608 (North Riding) Squadron

Re-equipped from Spitfire F.22 at Thornaby. Disbanded 10.3.57. Vampire F.1 4.51–6.51. Vampire F.3 5.50–3.54. Vampire FB.9 4.52–3.57. Vampire T.11 4.56–3.57.

Two Vampire F.3s of 601 Squadron, RAuxAF, get airborne from Ta Kali during their summer camp in June 1952. (via John Rawlings)

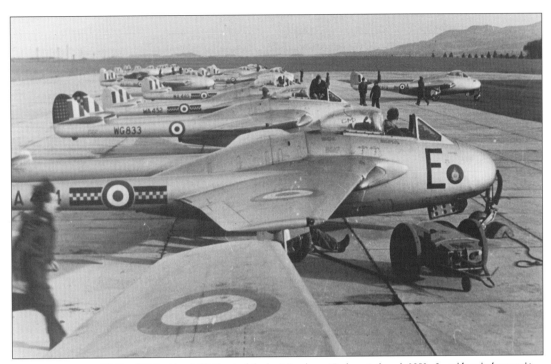

A 'Wing-Ding' comprising 603 (City of Edinburgh) and 612 (County of Aberdeen) Squadrons at Turnhouse in the early 1950s. Second from the foreground is the 'personal' aircraft of the Scottish Wing Leader, Wg Cdr E.G.L. Millington CBE, DFC, which bears the fin markings of the squadrons under his command. (Flt Lt Duncan McIntosh)

Vampire FB.5 VZ336 'L' of 605 (County of Warwick) Sqn RAuxAF at Honiley, 1956. The squadron markings comprised a light blue nose flash and bars flanking the roundel, all edged in red. (M.P. Marsh)

609 (West Riding) Squadron

Re-equipped from Spitfire LF.16e at Church Fenton (with a planned UE of ten Vampires and two Meteor T.7s). A high-level decision in January 1951 to re-equip with Meteors instead saw the Vampires withdrawn.
Vampire FB.5 11.50–2.51.

612 (County of Aberdeen) Squadron '8W'

Re-equipped from Spitfire LF.16e at Dyce. To Leuchars 7.51; Edzell 10.51; Dyce 11.52. Disbanded 10.3.57.
Vampire FB.5 5.51–3.57.

613 (City of Manchester) Squadron 'Q3'

Re-equipped from Spitfire F.22 at Ringway. Disbanded 10.3.57.
Vampire F.1 (2) 9.49–6.50. Vampire F.3 (1) 9.52–2.53. Vampire FB.5 2.51–3.57. Vampire FB.9 6.54–3.57. Vampire T.11 8.56–3.57.

614 (County of Glamorgan) Squadron

Re-equipped from Spitfire F.22 at Llandow. Disbanded 10.3.57.
Vampire F.3 7.50–9.52. Vampire FB.5 9.51–3.57. Vampire FB.9 12.54–3.57.

Flying Training Units

No. 202 AFS 'N':'O':'P'

Formed at Valley 12.3.51 and began course training 4.51. Flying task completed 31.5.54 and unit renumbered No. 7 FTS 1.6.54.
Vampire F.1 5.51–7.53. Vampire FB.5 3.51–6.54. Vampire T.11 9.52–6.54.

No. 203 AFS 'FMI'

Formed at Driffield 26.8.49 for the training of jet fighter pilots. With the opening of No. 202 AFS at

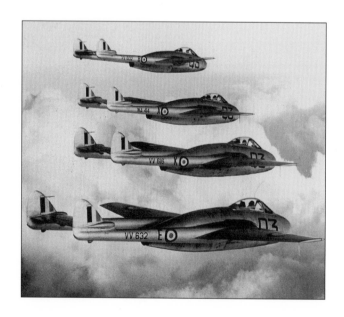

613 (City of Manchester) Squadron received Vampire FB.5s in February 1951. Four of them are seen here in their original markings. (R.A. Scholefield)

With 'The Rock' as a back drop, the Vampires of 614 Squadron put on a show of formation flying as part of their two-week detachment in August 1955. (via John Rawlings)

Valley, to where all Vampire training had been transferred, No. 203 AFS reduced its commitment and all Vampire aircraft were ferried out by 9.51. The unit continued to train Meteor pilots until disbandment in 6.54.
Vampire F.1 5.49–9.51. Vampire FB.5 7.49–8.53. Vampire FB.9 1.53–9.53.

No. 206 AFS
Formed from the nucleus of No. 102 FRS at Oakington 7.11.51 and began course training 5.12.51. First Provost/Vampire course commenced 21.4.54. Renumbered No. 5 FTS 1.6.54.
Vampire FB.5 2.54–6.54. Vampire T.11 12.53–6.54.

No. 208 AFS
Formed at Merryfield 19.11.51 for the training of day fighter pilots; no. 1 Course commenced training 25.2.52. Renumbered No. 10 FTS 1.6.54.
Vampire F.1 12.51–11.52. Vampire FB.5 8.52–6.54. Vampire FB.9 10.52–6.54. Vampire T.11 1.53–6.54.

No. 210 AFS
Formed at Tarrant Rushton 4.11.52 to provide refresher courses for Vampire and Meteor pilots under the aegis of Flight Refuelling Ltd – the only civilian-manned AFS in the RAF. All flying ceased 12.3.54 and aircraft transferred to No. 206 AFS.
Vampire FB.5 10.52–5.54.

No. 226 OCU 'BB':'HX':'KR':'UU'
Moved to Bentwaters from Molesworth 10.10.46 (unit originally formed from No. 1335 CU 15.8.46). To

Vampire T.11 XD428 of No. 206 AFS, Oakington. The unit only existed for a few months before being renumbered No. 5 FTS on 1 June 1954. (Sqn Ldr Maurice Biggs)

Driffield 26.8.49 and renumbered No. 203 AFS. On 1.9.49 the former 203 AFS at Stradishall was renumbered No. 226 OCU. In December 1950 the Vampire Flight was detached to Leuchars to form No. 229 OCU. No. 226 OCU disbanded at Stradishall 3.6.55.
Vampire F.1 9.46–12.49. Vampire FB.5 9.49–2.51. Vampire FB.9 9.49–12.50. Vampire T.11 5.53–6.55.

No. 229 OCU 'ES':'RS'
Formed at Leuchars as lodger unit 15.12.50 and began course training 8.1.51. To Chivenor 28.3.51.
Vampire FB.5 12.50–7.57. Vampire T.11 1.53–11.58.

No. 233 OCU
Formed at Pembrey 23.11.52 to augment the work of No. 229 OCU in training the large number of pilots required for Vampire squadrons. Disbanded 1.9.57.
Vampire FB.5 10.52–6.57. Vampire FB.9 1.55–6.57. Vampire T.11 2.53–7.57.

No. 1 FTS
Renumbered from No. 22 FTS at Syerston 1.5.55 for the training of Royal Navy pilots; unit transferred to Linton on Ouse 28.10.57. Vampire Flight formed 1.10.65 as a lodger unit for the training of foreign national students; unit moved to No. 7 FTS Church Fenton 4.1.66.
Vampire FB.5 1.58–5.59. Vampire FB.9 1.58–6.59. Vampire T.11 1.58–1.66.

No. 3 FTS
Renumbered from No. 7 FTS at Leeming 4.11.66; Vampire Flight transferred from No. 7 FTS 1.11.66 as a lodger unit and retained for the advanced training of foreign national students. A farewell fly-past on 29.11.67 marked the withdrawal of the Vampire from RAF service. Flight disbanded 4.1.68.
Vampire T.11 11.66–1.68.

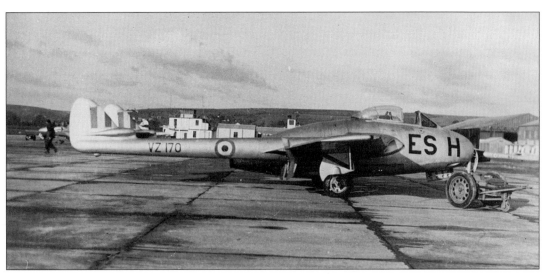

Following service with 54 Squadron, VZ170 was transferred to No. 229 OCU, and is depicted on the flight-line at Chivenor in 1953. (Colin Sloan)

No. 4 FTS
Renumbered from No. 205 AFS at Middleton St George 1.6.54; transferred to Worksop 9.6.56. Disbanded 9.6.58. Reformed at Valley (ex-No. 7 FTS) 15.8.60.
Vampire FB.5 10.54–6.58. Vampire FB.9 9.56–6.58. Vampire T.11 10.54–9.63.

No. 5 FTS ('A–' on some T.11s)
Renumbered from No. 206 AFS at Oakington 1.6.54; first Provost/Vampire course graduated 22.12.54 (unit temporarily detached to Graveley from 1.7.57 to 31.8.57).
Vampire FB.5 6.54–10.59. Vampire FB.9 9.56–6.59. Vampire T.11 6.54–9.63.

No. 7 FTS
Renumbered from No. 202 AFS at Valley 1.6.54. Redesignated No. 4 FTS 14.8.60. Reformed at Church Fenton 23.3.62; disbanded 30.11.66. Vampire Flight transferred from Linton on Ouse on 4.1.66 as lodger unit for the training of foreign national students; unit moved to No. 3 FTS Leeming on 1.11.66.
Vampire FB.5 6.54–10.59. Vampire FB.9 1.57–10.59. Vampire T.11 6.54–8.60; 3.62–11.66.

No. 8 FTS
Renumbered from No. 203 AFS at Driffield 1.6.54; transferred to Swinderby 22.8.55. The first course of RAF pilots to be trained on Provost/Vampire scheme at unit commenced 24.8.55. Unit disbanded 19.3.64.
Vampire FB.5 7.55–6.59. Vampire FB.9 10.55–4.59. Vampire T.11 7.55–3.64.

No. 9 FTS
Renumbered from No. 10 FTS at Merryfield 1.7.54. Disbanded 16.2.55.
Vampire FB.5 7.54–2.55. Vampire T.11 7.54–2.55.

No. 10 FTS
Renumbered from No. 208 AFS at Merryfield 1.6.54. Renumbered No. 9 FTS 1.7.54.
Vampire FB.5 6.54–7.54. Vampire T.11 6.54–7.54.

No. 11 FTS

Equipped at Swinderby 6.55; absorbed into No. 8 FTS the same month.
Vampire T.11 6.55.

No. 102 Flying Refresher School

Formed at North Luffenham 16.4.51 to provide refresher training for Class 'G' Reservists. With the completion of the last flying course on 2.11.51, the main body was transferred to Oakington on 7.11.51 to form nucleus of No. 206 AFS.
Vampire F.1 4.51–11.51. Vampire FB.5 4.51–12.51.

No. 103 FRS

Formed at Full Sutton 10.4.51. Unit renumbered No. 207 AFS 21.11.51.
Vampire F.1 4.51–11.51. Vampire FB.5 4.51–12.51.

Central Flying School 'FDJ':'I':'N':'O':'V'

Single-seaters used by CFS(A) at Little Rissington to train flying instructors. From 1.7.54, CFS organization changed to accommodate the new all-through Provost/Vampire training scheme; the first course commenced 25.8.54. Vampire T.11s also operated by Standards Flight and 'Vintage Pair'. CFS transferred to Cranwell 12.4.76; Leeming 5.9.77; Scampton 19.9.84.
Vampire F.1 7.47–6.48. Vampire F.3 2.48–12.49. Vampire FB.5 1.52–9.55. Vampire T.11 2.53–6.63 ('Vintage Pair' until 5.86).

A mixed formation of Vampire FB.5s and T.11s from No. 8 FTS, Swinderby, led by Sqn Ldr Pete Eddlestone, over-fly Lincoln Cathedral, 10 October 1955. (via Pete Jarvis)

Royal Air Force College

Equipped at Cranwell for advanced flying training of officer cadets. Last Vampire T.11 (WZ548) disposed of on 14.3.62.
Vampire F.1 5.48–6.49. Vampire FB.9 9.55–10.59. Vampire T.11 10.54–3.62.

Central Navigation Control School/Central Air Traffic Control School

Initial Vampire T.11s delivered to Shawbury to equip 'A' Flight (also equipped with Vampire NF.10s). In 1957 Vampire NF.10s were replaced by further Vampire T.11s. CNCS renamed CATCS 11.2.63. Vampires replaced by Jet Provosts in 1970.
Vampire NF.10 5.54–9.59. Vampire T.11 3.57–11.70.

Central Gunnery School/Fighter Weapons School 'FJW'

Unit operated Pilot Attack Instructor and Short Pilot Attack courses (sic) at Leconfield. Renamed FWS on 1.1.55; disbanded and absorbed into Fighter Weapons School at West Raynham on 15.3.58.
Vampire FB.5 7.49–12.54. Vampire T.11 9.52–4.58.

Central Fighter Establishment (AFDS/DFLS)

Equipped at West Raynham and used in tactical evaluation and service trials.
Vampire F.1 3.46–11.48. Vampire FB.5 11.48–6.53. Vampire T.11 4.58–1.59.

Fighter Combat School

Vampire T.11 3.58–3.59.

Empire Test Pilots School

Equipped at Cranfield for the jet training of test pilots. Unit moved to Farnborough 24.8.47.
Vampire F.1 4.46–7.51. Vampire FB.5 2.49–9.56. Vampire T.11 12.52–9.63.

Armament Practice Station, Acklington 'WH'

Formed 1.5.46 (ex-2 Armament Practice School) to provide armament training detachments for RAF fighter squadrons. Disbanded 25.7.56.
Vampire F.1 8.49–3.50. Vampire F.3 12.49–4.50. Vampire FB.5 4.50–8.52. Vampire T.11 9.52–8.56.

Armament Practice Station Sylt

Station re-opened 1.6.49 following extensive rebuilding programme and hosted detachments of 2 TAF fighter squadrons (plus some RAF squadrons and, later, units of Belgian AF) for periods of armament training. Station/unit disbanded 16.10.61.
Vampire FB.5 6.49–9.54. Vampire T.11 11.52–12.61.

No. 26 APC Nicosia

Formed 15.4.48 to host regular detachments of MEAF fighter squadrons for periods of armament training. Merged with TT Flight at Shallufa 1.1.50 to form TT Unit at Shallufa. Reduced to a number-plate basis on 19.2.51.

No. 27 APC Butterworth

Formed 1.1.49. On 1.4.55, APC became individual unit, but disbanded 1.5.56.
Vampire FB.9 3.55–5.56. Vampire T.11 3.55–5.56.

APC (MEAF)

Formed at Nicosia 1.4.55; to Ta Kali 2.56. Disbanded 1.1.57.
Vampire T.11 10.56–12.56.

APC Habbaniya
Little known of unit. Operated Vampire T.11s XE889 and XE946 from 8.56–3.57.

Far East Examining Squadron/Far East Training Squadron
Equipped at Seletar for local jet conversion of FEAF pilots; disbanded 1.6.51 and reformed as FETS. To Butterworth 13.8.54. Disbanded 31.3.55.
Vampire FB.9 5.52–3.55. Vampire T.11 11.53–3.55.

No. 2 Civilian Anti-Aircraft Co-operation Unit
Formed at Little Snoring 20.7.51; moved to Langham 23.3.58 and disbanded 1.11.58. Unit operated by Marshall Flying Services.
Vampire FB.5 4.54–12.54. Vampire FB.9 4.58–11.58. Vampire T.11 4.58–12.58.

No. 3 – 3/4 CAACU
Formed at Exeter 18.3.51. Renamed 3/4 CAACU 1.6.57. Disbanded 31.12.71.
Vampire FB.5 4.54–8.60. Vampire T.11 4.58–12.71.

No. 4 CAACU
Formed at Llandow 24.9.51. Disbanded 8.54. Operated by Short Bros.
Vampire F.3 9.51–7.54.

No. 5 CAACU
Formed at Llanbedr 16.9.51. To Woodvale 1.1.58. Disbanded 30.7.51.
Vampire F.3 9.51–9.54. Vampire FB.5 6.54–10.56.

No. 228 OCU: Leeming: Vampire T.11
No. 236 OCU: Kinloss: Vampire FB.5
No. 238 OCU: North Luffenham: Vampire T.11
ATDU/AMSDU: Vampire F.3/FB.5
ECFS: Hullavington: Vampire F.1
CCGS: Leconfield: Vampire FB.5
FCCS: Bovingdon: Vampire F.1/FB.5
Handling Squadron: Manby: Vampire FB.5/FB.9
IAM: Farnborough: Vampire FB.5
NGTE: Bitteswell (to Farnborough 15.7.52): Vampire F.1
RAFFC: Manby: Vampire FB.5
Sabre Conv. Unit: Wildenrath: Vampire T.11
SLAW: Old Sarum: Vampire FB.5/T.11
TFU/TRE: Defford: Vampire F.3/FB.5

Royal Navy

700 Squadron
Re-formed 18.8.55 at Ford as the Trials and Requirements Unit; transferred to Yeovilton 9.58.
Sea Vampire F.20 8.55–11.56. Sea Vampire T.22 7.57–10.57.

700X Squadron
Formed 27.8.57 at Ford as Intensive Flying Trials Unit for the Scimitar F.1. Disbanded 29.5.58.
Sea Vampire T.22 11.57–5.58.

702 Squadron

Re-formed 4.4.49 at Culdrose as Naval Jet Evaluation & Training Unit; became 738 Squadron on 26.8.52. Reformed 30.9.57 at Lee-on-Solent; moved to Ford 17.10.57. Disbanded 11.8.58.
Vampire FB.5 5.51–5.52. Sea Vampire F.20 4.49–8.52. Sea Vampire T.22 10.57–8.58.

703 Squadron

Equipped Naval Flight of the Air/Sea Warfare Development Unit at Thorney Island; moved to Lee-on-Solent 25.5.48 for service trials; to Ford 19.4.50. Amalgamated into 700 Squadron on 18.8.55.
Vampire F.1 9.47–10.47. Vampire FB.5 7.50–6.52. Sea Vampire F.20 10.48–8.55.

718 Squadron

Re-formed 25.4.55 at Stretton for the jet conversion of piston-engined pilots; to Honiley 4.7.55.
Disbanded 31.12.55.
Sea Vampire T.22 4.55–12.55.

727 Squadron

Re-formed at Brawdy 16.1.56 as 'Dartmouth Cadet Air Training Squadron'. Disbanded 16.12.60.
Sea Vampire T.22 1.56–12.60.

728 Squadron

Equipped at Hal Far as a Fleet Requirements Unit.
Sea Vampire F.20 7.51–3.55.

736 Squadron

Equipped at Lossiemouth as Advanced Jet Flying School; became part of Naval Air Fighter School in 3.55.
Sea Vampire T.22 11.53–7.54; 10.54–11.58.

Sea Vampire T.22 XA129 was operated by 736 Squadron between March 1955 and June 1956. It is currently stored at Wroughton on behalf of the Fleet Air Arm Museum. (Alan Roach)

738 Squadron

Equipped at Lossiemouth as Naval Air Fighter School; later renamed Naval Air Fighter & Strike School: Vampires used for refresher training.
Sea Vampire T.22 5.54–3.55; 12.58–9.62.

750 Squadron

Equipped at Hal Far as Observer School.
Sea Vampire T.22 1.62–5.65.

759 Squadron

Operated jet conversion courses at Culdrose; transferred to Lossiemouth 28.11.53. Absorbed into 736 Squadron on 12.10.54.
Sea Vampire F.20 10.52–3.54. Sea Vampire T.22 11.53–10.54.

764 Squadron

Re-formed 1.2.55 at Ford as Jet Fighter Pilot Pool; unit moved to Lossiemouth on 21.6.57.
Sea Vampire F.20 6.55–2.56. Sea Vampire T.22 1.55–6.57.
\

766 Squadron

Equipped at Yeovilton as All Weather Fighter Pool.
Sea Vampire T.22 1.56–7.56.

771 Squadron

Equipped at Lee-on-Solent for fleet requirement duties; transferred to Ford 1.9.52. Combined with 703 Squadron to form 700 Squadron on 17.8.55.
Sea Vampire F.20 3.52–8.55. Sea Vampire F.21 1.51–9.51.

Sea Vampire T.22 XG747 was operated by 764 Squadron at RNAS Ford between February 1955 and September 1956. (John Rawlings)

778 Squadron
Equipped at Ford as the Service Trials and Carrier Trials Unit; transferred to Tangmere 7.47.
Sea Vampire F.10 5.46–11.46. Vampire F.1 9.47–4.48.

781 Squadron
Equipped at Lee-on-Solent as a JOAC Flight.
Sea Vampire T.22 10.53–12.64.

787 Squadron
Equipped at West Raynham as part of the Naval Air Fighting Development Unit for trials purposes.
Vampire F.1 9.47–2.50. Vampire FB.5 9.49–8.53. Sea Vampire F.20 2.49–4.51.

802 Squadron
Operated at Lossiemouth during squadron's disembarkation period.
Sea Vampire T.22 12.58–1.59.

804 Squadron
One Sea Vampire T.22, XA112 '924', temporarily attached to squadron between May and September 1958.

806 Squadron
Sea Vampire F.20 VF315 attached to squadron for demonstration tour of Canada and USA between May 1948 and February 1949. Equipped at Lossiemouth for training purposes during Sea Hawk period.
Sea Vampire T.22 4.58–9.59.

808 Squadron
Re-formed 10.8.55 at Yeovilton from 891X Squadron as Sea Venom unit prior to embarkation to Australia.
Sea Vampire T.22 8.55–2.56.

809 Squadron
Equipped at Yeovilton as a Sea Venom unit.
Sea Vampire T.22 6.54–10.54.

831 Squadron
Equipped at Culdrose as Electronic Warfare Squadron; to Watton 26.7.63.
Sea Vampire T.22 11.58–5.64.

890 Squadron
At Yeovilton, equipped with Sea Venoms and prior to embarking HMS *Albion* 19.7.55.
Sea Vampire T.22 8.54–5.55.

891 Squadron
Re-formed 8.11.54 at Yeovilton as an all-weather unit equipped with Sea Venoms.
Sea Vampire T.22 11.54–1.55.

891X Squadron
Formed 1.3.55 at Yeovilton to train Royal Australian Navy pilots pending the formation of 808 Squadron with Sea Venoms.
Vampire FB.5 3.55–5.55.

892 Squadron
Operated at Yeovilton during squadron disembarkation.
Sea Vampire T.22 9.55–2.56.

893 Squadron
Re-formed 6.2.56 at Yeovilton as a Sea Venom unit.
Sea Vampire T.22 2.56–7.57.

898 Squadron
Operated Sea Vampire T.22 XA169 at Brawdy during squadron's disembarkation.

1831 Squadron RNVR
At Stretton as an Attacker FB.2 unit. Disbanded 10.3.57.
Sea Vampire T.22 5.55–3.57.

1832 Squadron RNVR
At Benson as an Attacker FB.2 unit (re-equipped with Sea Hawk F.1s 11.56). Disbanded 10.3.57.
Sea Vampire T.22 7.55–3.57.

1833 Squadron RNVR
At Bramcote and Honiley as an Attacker FB.2 unit.
Sea Vampire T.22.

1836 Squadron RNVR
As per 1832 Squadron.

Other Units

Air Direction Training Unit
Operated jet conversion courses with Airwork-run unit at Brawdy; moved to Yeovilton 1.61.
Sea Vampire T.22 3.58–7.70.

300 Squadron, Indian Navy
Operated Sea Vampire T.22 XA102 '070' while squadron working-up with Sea Hawks at Brawdy during 1960/61.

A&AEE Boscombe Down; RAE and NGTE Farnborough

Station Flights
Abbotsinch 11.59–7.62; Brawdy 8.55–6.70; Culdrose 6.62–9.62; Ford 5.54–1.57; Hal Far 3.59–4.60; Lee-on-Solent ?.57–11.62; Lossiemouth 9.59–1.69; Stretton 10.54–10.56; Yeovilton 8.56–9.67.

INDEX